THE TRANSFORMATION OF
A RELIGIOUS LANDSCAPE

A VOLUME IN THE SERIES

Conjunctions of Religion and Power in the Medieval Past

EDITED BY BARBARA H. ROSENWEIN

A list of titles in the series is available at www.cornellpress.cornell.edu.

The Transformation of a Religious Landscape

Medieval Southern Italy
850–1150

Valerie Ramseyer

CORNELL UNIVERSITY PRESS

ITHACA AND LONDON

Publication of this book has been aided by a grant from the
Medieval Academy of America.

First published 2006 by Cornell University Press

Library of Congress Cataloging-in-Publication Data

Ramseyer, Valerie.
    The transformation of a religious landscape : medieval
southern Italy, 850-1150 / Valerie Ramseyer.
        p. cm. — (Conjunctions of religion and power in the
medieval past)
    Includes bibliographical references and index.
    ISBN-13: 978-0-8014-4403-6 (cloth : alk. paper)
    ISBN-10: 0-8014-4403-9 (cloth : alk. paper)
    1. Salerno (Italy : Province)—Church history.   2. Catholic
Church—Italy—Salerno (Province)—History.   3. Abbazia
della Trinità della Cava (Cava de' Tirreni, Italy)—History.
4. Italy, Southern—History—535-1268.   I. Title.
II. Conjunctions of religion & power in the medieval past.
    BX1546.S26R36 2006
    274.5′7403—dc22
                                                    2005037248

Printed in the United States of America

Cornell University Press strives to use environmentally responsible suppliers and materials to the fullest extent possible in
the publishing of its books. Such materials include vegetable-
based, low-VOC inks and acid-free papers that are recycled,
totally chlorine-free, or partly composed of nonwood fibers.
For further information, visit our website at www.cornellpress.
cornell.edu.

Cloth printing   10 9 8 7 6 5 4 3 2 1

Contents

Maps

GENEALOGIES

Abbreviations

Amatus	Amatus of Montecassino, "Ystoire de li Normani"
Chron. Sal.	Chronicon Salernitanum
API	*Archivio Paleografico Italiano*
Balducci	Balducci, *L'Archivio Diocesano di Salerno*
CDC	*Codex Diplomaticus Cavensis*
Cherubini	Cherubini, *Le Pergamene di S. Nicola di Gallucanta (secc. IX–XII)*
Chron. Cas.	*Chronica Monasterii Casinensis*
Di Meo	Di Meo, *Annali critico-diplomatici del Regno di Napoli della mezzana età*
Guillaume	Guillaume, *Essai historique sur l'abbaye de Cava*
Heinemann	Heinemann, *Normannische Herzogs- und Königsurkunden*
IP	Kehr, *Italia pontificia*, I–VIII
Malaterra	Geoffrey Malaterra, *De Rebus Gestis Rogerii Calabriae et Siciliae Comitis et Roberti Guiscardi Ducis fratris eius*
Ménager	Ménager, *Recueil des actes des ducs normands d'Italie (1046–1127)*
MGH	*Monumenta Germaniae Historica*
Muratori	Muratori, *Antiquitates Italicae Medii Aevi*
Paesano	Paesano, *Memorie per servire alla storia della chiesa salernitana*
Pflugk-Harttung	Pflugk-Harttung, *Acta Pontificium Romanorum Inedita*

PL	*Patrologia Latina*
RIS	*Rerum Italicarum Scriptores*
RNAM	*Regii Neapolitani Archivi Monumenta*
Ughelli	Ughelli, *Italia Sacra*
VQPA	*Vitae Quatuor Priorum Abbatum Cavensium*
William of Apulia	William of Apulia, *La Geste de Robert Guiscard*

The Archives of the Abbey
of the Holy Trinity of Cava

The parchments at Cava are separated into two categories, "armarii" and "arcae." Charters from the "armarii magni" are identified by a capital letter, followed by an Arabic numeral, with approximately 40–50 documents per letter. These include charters that the monastic archivists considered to be the more important ones. Charters in the "arcae" are identified by a Roman numeral followed by an Arabic one, with 120 documents per "arca." Undated charters are found in "arca" CXVI. Paper charters and Greek documents (including bi-lingual ones) are in separate sections. Bi-lingual ones are identified by two small letters, followed by a Roman numeral. In this book, charters not found in the *Codex Diplomaticus Cavensis* will be identified first by their archival identification, followed by editions in parenthesis when available.

ACKNOWLEDGMENTS

Above all, I thank Barbara Rosenwein, who has been part of this project since the beginning, when I first began my research in southern Italy as a graduate student, and now as my editor. She has put an incredible amount of time into the manuscript and has provided valuable comments, insights, and encouragement along the way. Next I thank Graham Loud, whose knowledge of southern Italian archives has been immensely helpful to me, and whose many books and articles were fundamental to the completion of this book. I also give many thanks to the staff at the Biblioteca dell'Abbazia della SS. Trinità di Cava dei Tirreni, in particular, Vincenzo Cioffi. Other scholars who provided assistance in Italy include Errico Cuozzo, Giovanni Vitolo, Hubert Houben, Vera von Falkenhausen, and, finally, Maria Galante, whose paleography course at the University of Salerno immensely improved my reading and understanding of the charters at Cava.

I also thank the scholars who read early chapters of my book: Chris Wickham, Maureen Miller, John Howe, H. E. J. Cowdrey, Brigitte Bedos-Rezak, and Constance Bouchard. A special thanks goes out to the anonymous reader of my manuscript and to my editor at Cornell University Press, John Ackerman. Finally, I am grateful to a host of other scholars, colleagues, and friends who have helped me along the way: Walter Kaegi, Robert Bartlett, and Julius Kirshner at the University of Chicago; R. I. Moore, who was perhaps my greatest inspiration as a graduate student; the various members and participants of the Haskins Society, whose conference has provided me with a forum over the years to discuss my research; Tom Head; Thierry Stasser; Steven Lane; Louis Hamilton; William North; Joanna Drell; Deborah Blumenthal; Fiona Griffiths; Lauren Leve; and, most especially, Pamela Renswick.

Financial support for this project came from a variety of sources: the University of Chicago, a Jacob K. Javits fellowship, the Mellon Foundation, Wellesley College, and the Medieval Academy of America. I am also grateful to Wellesley College for providing me with the time to finish the project, and to my research assistant at Wellesley, Cara Majeski.

V. R.

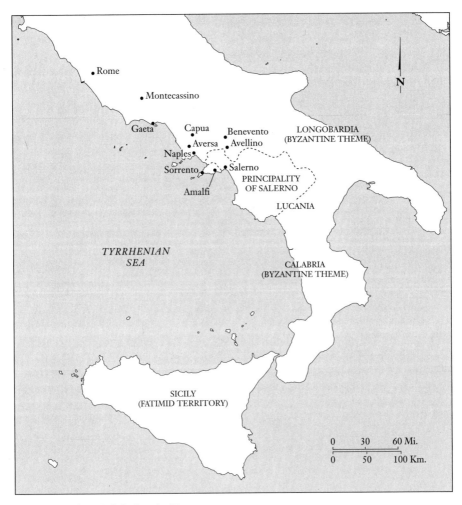

Rome

Montecassino

Gaeta

Capua

Benevento

LONGOBARDIA
(BYZANTINE THEME)

Aversa

Avellino

Naples

Sorrento

Salerno

PRINCIPALITY
OF SALERNO

Amalfi

LUCANIA

N

TYRRHENIAN
SEA

CALABRIA
(BYZANTINE THEME)

SICILY
(FATIMID TERRITORY)

0	30	60 Mi.
0	50	100 Km.

Map 1. Southern Italy before the Normans

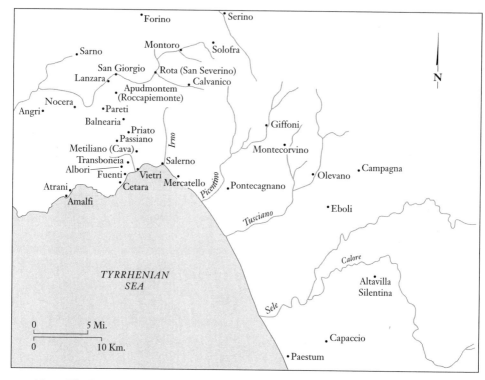

Map 2. The Principality of Salerno (Northern Regions)

Map 3. The Principality of Salerno (Southern Regions)

Introduction

This book is a study of religious life in the Principality of Salerno in the ninth and tenth centuries and of the dramatic changes that occurred in the eleventh and early twelfth centuries as a result of the Norman conquest of southern Italy and the reform program carried out by the archbishop of Salerno and the abbey of the Holy Trinity of Cava. Chronologically it covers the period from c. 849, the date the Principality broke away from Benevento and became an autonomous kingdom, to c. 1130, when King Roger II unified southern Italy and Sicily under a single ruler. Geographically it concentrates on the core regions of the Principality, meaning the modern-day province of Salerno that stretches south to include both Cilento and the Valley of Diano.

The religious landscape of medieval Salerno differed noticeably from the traditions found in Carolingian territories and the ideals of eleventh-century reformers. It had no centralized hierarchy, little standardization of religious practices, a tradition of married clerics, and an overlap in forms of religious life. It also relied heavily upon lay participation and private ecclesiastical foundations. In the eleventh century, the Norman conquest of Salerno and the papal reform program opened the region up to more direct interchange with areas of the former Carolingian empire, and ecclesiastical organization was transformed by local prelates who were influenced by models from centers such as Cluny and Rome. The Benedictine abbey of the Holy Trinity of Cava, founded in the early eleventh century by a local churchman who had taken the monastic habit at Cluny, and the newly bolstered cathedral church of Salerno, transformed by the archbishop Alfanus I who befriended a number of Roman reformers during his initiation into the monastic life at Montecassino, both created ecclesiastical hierarchies dependent on Rome. However, even then the local reformers did not follow to the letter the reforms promoted by the papacy, and practices divergent from Roman traditions continued unabated in the region.

Few studies have looked in depth at religious life in medieval southern Italy. Although numerous articles and conference papers dealing with certain aspects of the topic have been published over the last century, most of these have been highly regionalized, focusing on a specific city or region. They have rarely examined southern Italy as a whole or southern Italy in relationship to other places. In addition, studies have tended to focus on a few specific themes that have dominated the historiography over the last fifty years. The disappearance of bishoprics and the proliferation of private religious foundations in late antiquity, the immigration of Greek monks into the region and the spread of Greek practices and foundations in the early Middle Ages, and the reconstruction of episcopal networks and the spread of large Benedictine abbeys in the High Middle Ages have been the main issues discussed.[1]

This book aims to place the experience of the Principality of Salerno not only into a larger southern Italian framework but also in relationship to the Carolingian and Byzantine empires. Since the region remained effectively outside the Frankish empire during the early Middle Ages, Christian practice and organization remained more closely connected to older Mediterranean traditions and to the Byzantine world. Only with the Norman conquest would the area become more directly linked to northern Europe and the papacy. This book also tries as much as possible to study the earlier period without reference to later developments, since historians have often viewed the early Middle Ages as merely a precursor for later developments. In some cases they have even judged it to be a time of decadence or chaos, because religious life and organization was so radically different from the later period. Religious reform was neither inevitable nor ineluctable, and

---

[1] Jean-Marie Martin's article on southern Italy for the *Storia dell'Italia Religiosa* series reflects well the preoccupations of historians studying the region: the first section examines bishoprics in the Late Roman period and the end to Paleochristian church organization. The second looks at the "eastern presence" and the Greek church. Next he turns to a brief examination of monasteries and bishoprics in the early medieval period, as well as the phenomenon of private churches, followed by lengthy discussions of the reconstruction of episcopal networks and the monastic reform movement in the late tenth through twelfth centuries. Jean-Marie Martin, "L'ambiente longobardo, greco, islamico, e normanno nel Mezzogiorno," in *Storia dell'Italia Religiosa*, ed. Gabriele De Rosa, Tullio Grogy, and André Vauchez (Rome/Bari: Laterza, 1993), 1:193–242.

the accusations of eleventh-century reformers such as Gregory VII, who condemned contemporary practices such as simony, clerical marriage, and lay interference in ecclesiastical matters as iniquitous innovations, must be viewed in their historical context. Many of the practices and traditions that the reformers found abhorrent were widely accepted and represented neither novelties nor signs of decadence. The early medieval system, although radically different from the post-reform Church, had its own logic and served the needs of the Christian population well. Finally, this book argues that diversity in religious life was the norm in the early Middle Ages. All over Latin Christendom and the Byzantine world early medieval church life was marked by regional differences; even the reform movement of the High Middle Ages manifested considerable variety. As a result, it is my hope that the historical processes described in this book will be seen not as the idiosyncrasies of a peripheral and somewhat exceptional region but as an example of the widespread diversity of religious life and religious reform characteristic of medieval Christendom.

The first part of the book discusses the decentralized ecclesiastical system in the Lombard Principality of Salerno up through the mid-eleventh century. Unlike Carolingian regions of western Europe, it had no single political or religious leader claiming authority over churches or religious life. Instead community houses, built by individuals, families, or groups of citizens from small villages, dominated the ecclesiastical landscape. These religious houses served the needs of the local community, and neither the prince nor the bishop of Salerno took much interest in the foundation, administration, or supervision of these churches.

Not surprisingly the de-centralized ecclesiastical system of Salerno produced diverse religious practices. Documents specifically stated that priests and abbots were to officiate in houses according to local custom, and religious practices differed not only from one town to another but also from church to church within the same town or region. Clerical lifestyles and duties also differed from one place to another, and clerics often combined the functions of monk, priest, and deacon. As in other areas of southern Italy and Sicily, the Principality of Salerno had both Latin and Greek foundations as well as religious houses that combined the two traditions. Even the line between the clergy and laity was often blurred.

In the book's second part I discuss how two ecclesiastical powers, the archbishop of Salerno and the abbey of Cava, transformed the ecclesiastical system of the Principality of Salerno in the eleventh century through the creation of ecclesiastical hierarchies. Both the archbishops and abbots built and took over many of the region's religious houses, placing the foundations and their clergy under their direct authority. The duties of clerics became better defined and clerical orders more differentiated. Although private religious foundations continued to provide pastoral care in both city and countryside, by the twelfth century the majority of important churches and monasteries in the province of Salerno belonged to either the cathedral church or the abbey of Cava.

The archbishops and abbots all espoused ideas that mirrored the doctrines of papal reformers in Rome. The province of Salerno clearly participated in the European-wide reform movement, often referred to as the Gregorian Reform, that radically transformed the Catholic Church beginning in the second half of the eleventh century. Nonetheless, the main force behind ecclesiastical reorganization came from local prelates and clerics, with the popes serving more to legitimize and uphold privileges than to create them. Moreover, the archbishops and abbots had to face local realities that came into direct conflict with reformist ideals, in particular, a long tradition of clerical marriage and a vast number of lay-owned houses. In the end, many of the goals of papal reform did not take hold in Salerno. Laypeople continued to build and administer churches and to participate in ecclesiastical appointments, clerics continued to follow local traditions, and priests continued to marry and have families. In addition, Greek clerics and Greek religious practices endured well beyond the medieval period. Thus church reformers in Salerno both followed the larger trends of the Gregorian movement while at the same time maintaining the region's unique traditions and customs.

The ability to research in detail the religious life and ecclesiastical structures of Salerno in the late Lombard and early Norman period is due above all to the rich archives of the abbey of the Holy Trinity of Cava, located about ten kilometers from Salerno. The library at Cava is a largely unexplored repository of charters and manuscripts that stretch back to the late eighth century, and the majority of evidence for this book comes from the charters preserved here. These parchments record a wide variety of legal acts, although the vast majority of them are land transactions, either sales, leases, divisions, exchanges, disputes, or pious donations. For the period of this book, c. 849–1130, over two thousand five hundred charters survive. Logically, most of the charters relate to property owned by Cava. However, the archives also contain many charters that pre-date the abbey's eleventh-century foundation, because after the monks at Cava absorbed numerous churches and monasteries in the province of Salerno and southern Italy during the medieval period, they eventually transferred the archives of these ecclesiastical foundations to the mother house. In addition, the archives of some other religious foundations in the area were given to Cava in the modern period, in particular, during the period of monastic suppression in the nineteenth century.[2] Thus, even though the archives mostly reflect the history of the abbey of Cava itself, religious houses from the Lombard period are amply documented as well, allowing the historian to study in depth religious life and organization in the early medieval period.

[2] The period of monastic suppression brought to the abbey of Cava archives from the certosa of San Lorenzo in Padula, the convent of San Francesco of Eboli, and of the Celestini of Novi Velia. In addition, the commune of Nocera in 1924 gave the archives at Cava charters from the basilica of Santa Maria de Materdomini, while the Baron Fernando De Caro bequeathed charters from Roccagloriosa and Vincenzo Rubini ones from Capaccio. For more information, see Giovanni Vitolo, "L'Archivio della Badia della SS. Trinità di Cava," in *Guida alla storia di Salerno e della sua provincia*, ed. Alfonso Leone and Giovanni Vitolo (Salerno: P. Laveglia, 1982), 894–899 and Leone Mattei Cerasoli, *Guida storica e bibliografica degli archivi e delle biblioteche d'Italia. IV. Badia della SS. Trinità di Cava* (Rome: Istituto Storico Italiano per il Medio Evo, 1937).

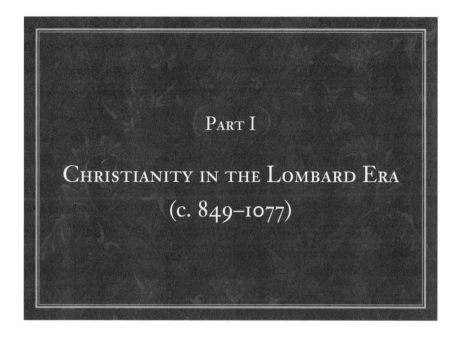

PART I

CHRISTIANITY IN THE LOMBARD ERA

(c. 849–1077)

The Christian landscape of western Europe and the Mediterranean in the period before 1000 was extremely regionalized, prompting historians to utilize terms such as "micro-Christendoms" and "Christianities" when describing it.[1] It was made up of various communities, in contact with one other and sharing certain core beliefs, but also displaying a high degree of variety in terms of practices, organization, and clerical lifestyle. Christians and local churches needed only to adhere to the creeds promulgated by ecumenical councils in order to be considered "catholic," which meant that as a whole they were free to follow their own local customs.[2] Moreover, in some places, such as southern Italy, where Christians lived side-by-side with Jews and Muslims, the line separating the three monotheistic religions was much less impermeable than would be true of a later time.[3] Although Chris-

---

[1] See, for example, Peter Brown, part 2 in *The Rise of Western Christendom: Triumph and Diversity* AD: 200–1000 (Oxford: Blackwell, 1996); Cristina La Rocca, "Cristianesimi," in *Storia Medievale* (Rome: Conzelli, 1998), 113–39; and Claudio Azzara, "Ecclesiastical Institutions," in *Italy in the Early Middle Ages, 476–1000*, ed. Cristina La Rocca (Oxford: Oxford University Press, 2002), 85–101.

[2] Girolamo Arnaldi, "Profilo di storia della Chiesa e del papato fra tarda antichità e alto medioevo," *La Cultura* 35/1 (1997): 8.

[3] Giovanni Vitolo, "Vescovi e Diocesi," in *Storia del Mezzogiorno*, ed. Giuseppe Galasso (Naples: Edizione del Sole, 1990), 3: 99–101.

tianity certainly served as an important form of identity in the early Middle Ages, especially for the clerical elite, whose writings represent the majority of information we have for the period, no idea of Christendom as a well-defined institutional entity with precise boundaries and the ability to extend into all areas of life had yet emerged.[4] People in the early Middle Ages did not belong to a religion as much as they practiced one.

The ecclesiastical system of early medieval Salerno depicts well the regionalism and diversity characteristic of Christianity in the early medieval period. It differed greatly from both the Carolingian Church that engulfed most of western Europe and the Catholic Church that would emerge in the eleventh century. For one thing, it had a decentralized ecclesiastical system, with no single political or religious leader overseeing church life or religious organization. Most religious houses were built by families or groups of citizens forming partnerships ("consortia") who constructed churches to serve the needs of their local community. Neither the prince nor the bishop of Salerno took much interest in the foundation, administration, or supervision of these churches. Diverse religious practices also characterized the region; documents specifically stated that priests and abbots were to officiate in houses according to local custom. Religious practices not only differed from one town to another but also from one church to another within the same town or region. Moreover, the Principality of Salerno had both Latin and Greek ecclesiastical foundations, as well as religious houses that combined the two traditions. Other religious categories also merged and overlapped. Ecclesiastical foundations were often not devoted to one type of religious activity or lifestyle, and many houses contained priests, monks, and anchorites living side-by-side. The duties of the clergy varied from one ecclesiastical foundation to another, and clerical titles did not reflect precise functions or specific lifestyles. Clerics claimed no special status or legal rights as a result of their calling, and their lives differed little from laymen. There was, in fact, little distinction between the clergy and laity in early medieval Salerno. In many ways, the categories and vocabulary used to describe the Catholic Church today—or even the Catholic Church of the thirteenth century—do not apply well to the religious landscape of early medieval Salerno.

The ecclesiastical system of early medieval Salerno should not be viewed as decadent, chaotic, or impoverished, despite its uniqueness and divergence

---

[4] On the switch from Christianity to Christendom in the High Middle Ages, see Dominique Iogna-Prat, *Order and Exclusion: Cluny and Christendom Face Heresy, Judaism, and Islam (1000–1150)*, trans. Graham Robert Edwards (Ithaca and London: Cornell University Press, 1998), 1–2.

from later Catholic practice. Documents show that priests and clerics took their pastoral duties seriously; inventories from churches and monasteries reveal wealthy foundations with rich decorations and garments imported from as far away as Constantinople and Africa. Religious foundations were built not only in major towns and cities but also in rural areas. There is no evidence that the Principality of Salerno had a shortage of churches or priests. In fact, many participants in legal transactions held clerical titles, such as *presbiter, sacerdos, clericus, diaconus, subdiaconus, monachus, abbas, ancilla dei*, to name a few. Moreover, the laity participated intensely in the church organization and religious life of their communities, exercising roles that would later be reserved for the clergy alone. The ecclesiastical system of early medieval Salerno, although radically different from the Catholic church of the later Middle Ages, functioned satisfactorily and provided well for the religious needs of the population.

The ecclesiastical system of Salerno should also not be seen as an anomaly or exception, portraying a number of unusual characteristics on account of its being in a frontier region never formally integrated into the Carolingian or Byzantine worlds. While it is true that Salerno lacked many features typical of Carolingian church organization, such as a strong episcopal authority and a system of parish churches, recent studies have shown the pervasiveness of diverse religious practices and church organization even within the Carolingian empire itself. Local traditions rather than a Rome-centered ecclesiastical hierarchy guided religious practices, and questions regarding liturgy, canonization, clerical discipline, doctrine, and religious law were decided regionally.[5] Prelates and rulers did not concern themselves too much with liturgical homogeneity.[6] Conciliar legislation sought mainly to increase episcopal power over church organization and lay society, while rulers such as Charlemagne and Louis the Pious, although they promoted the spread of specific religious ceremonies designed to propagate a royal ideology, did not seek to thwart local traditions.[7] In addition, the power of bishops differed from one location to another. In Brittany, for example,

[5] J.M. Wallace-Hadrill, *The Frankish Church* (Oxford: Clarendon Press, 1983), 1, 110–12, 118–21; Yitzhak Hen, *The Royal Patronage of Liturgy in Frankish Gaul to the Death of Charles the Bald (877)* (Woodbridge: Boydell & Brewer, 2001), 3–7.

[6] Hen, *The Royal Patronage*, 7, 78–81; Wilfried Hartmann, *Die Synoden der Karolingerzeit im Frankenreich und in Italien* (Paderborn: Ferdinand Schöningh, 1989), 408–09.

[7] See, in particular, the canons of the Council of Verneuil held in 755, the Council of Frankfurt held in 794, and the legislation of Louis the Pious issued in 818–19. Hartmann, *Die Synoden*, 68–72, 105–15, 415, 433–35; Hen, *The Royal Patronage*, 86–95; Wallace-Hadrill, *The Frankish Church*, 170–71; Michael McCormick, *Eternal Victory*.

community churches similar to the ones found in Salerno were the norm.[8] Village dwellers rather than bishops or powerful lay families built and supervised religious houses administered by clergy who lived locally. Bishops had little contact with these churches, and the reforms of the Carolingian bishops did not reach the area. Similarly, in the Abruzzi private churches built by *consortia* provided pastoral care in many rural areas in the ninth century, even after the region's integration into the Carolingian empire.[9] In both places, these types of community churches fulfilled not only religious functions, but also served as public spaces for a variety of activities, including feasts, ordeals, commercial transactions, and court cases.[10]

In southern Italy too church organization exhibited much variety. Naples, for example, had an ecclesiastical system that resembled Rome in many ways, with a well-organized hierarchy of clerics and churches within the city walls under the authority of the archbishop.[11] Calabria and Sicily modeled their church organization on Constantinople rather than Rome. Their Sees were directly dependent on the patriarch of Constantinople from the eighth century onward, and their bishops attended councils held in Byzantine territories.[12] In some regions, such as in Capua, bishops exercised strong authority over church organization and played an important role in political activities.[13] In other areas, including Apulia, bishops were weak and

Triumphal Rulership in Late Antiquity, Byzantium and the Early Medieval West (Cambridge: Cambridge University Press, 1986), 342–77.

[8] Wendy Davies, *Small Worlds: The Community in Early Medieval Brittany* (Berkeley: University of California Press, 1988), 11–26.

[9] Laurent Feller, *Les Abruzzes médiévales: Territoire, économie, et société en Italie centrale du IXe au XIIe siècle* (Rome: Ecole Française de Rome, 1998), 805–9.

[10] Also in late Anglo-Saxon and early Norman England, churches were built and administered by groups of citizens, in particular, families and craftsmen. Although some were large and well-endowed, the majority were small and poor, with space for a limited number of worshipers. C. N. L. Brooke, "The Church in Towns, 1000–1250," in *The Mission of the Church and the Propagation of the Faith*, vol. 6 of *Studies in Church History*, ed. G. J. Cuming (Cambridge: Cambridge University Press, 1970), 59–83. James Campbell, "The Church in Anglo-Saxon Towns," in *The Church in Town and Countryside*, vol. 16 of *Studies in Church History*, ed. Derek Baker (Oxford: Blackwell, 1979), 119–35.

[11] Nicola Cilento, *Civiltà napoletane del medioevo nei secoli VI–XIII* (Naples: Edizioni Scientifiche Italiane, 1969), 149–60; Vitolo, "Vescovi e Diocesi," 107–08; Martin, "L'ambiente," 213–14.

[12] Martin, "L'ambiente," 206–07.

[13] Stefano Palmieri, "Duchi, principi, e vescovi nella Longobardia meridionale," in *Longobardia e longobardi nell'Italia meridionale: Le istituzioni ecclesiastiche. Atti del 2° Convegno internazionale di studi promosso dal Centro di cultura dell'Università cattolica del*

had little power over religious or political life.[14] In fact, most areas of southern Italy in the Lombard period lacked either a strong episcopal authority or a system of parish churches. In some areas, such as where the abbeys of Montecassino and San Vincenzo al Volturno arose, an episcopal power was completely absent. As a result, monasteries and private religious houses were generally the main source of pastoral care in Lombard southern Italy. Even in northern and central Italy, ecclesiastical organization in the Lombard period, before the Carolingian conquest, was often centered on religious foundations outside of episcopal control.[15] The experience of Salerno was thus in many ways typical for Lombard regions of Italy in the early Middle Ages. Moreover, Salerno's religious landscape exhibited many features characteristic of Christianity in the eastern Mediterranean in late antiquity, including a weakened episcopate, a lack of religious unity, a regionalized ecclesiastical network that lacked a pyramid structure, an emphasis on the holy ascetic as opposed to the saintly bishop, and a dichotomy between desert and world, or regular and secular clergy, rather than a distinction between laypeople and clerics.[16] Even the traits unique to Salerno's ecclesiastical organization can be seen as normal for the time since diversity was, in fact, the rule for Christian organization in the period from 500 to 1000.

Sacro Cuore, Benevento, 29–31 May 1992, ed. Giancarlo Andenna and Giorgio Picasso (Milan: Vita e Pensiero, 1996), 88; G. A. Loud, *Church and Society in the Norman Principality of Capua* (Oxford: Clarendon Press, 1984), 33–35.

[14] Jean-Marie Martin, *La Pouille du VIe au XIIe siècle* (Rome: Ecole Française de Rome, 1993), 242.

[15] Antonio Rigon, "Le Istituzioni ecclesiastiche della Cristianità," in *La società medievale*, ed. Silvana Collodo and Giuliano Pinto (Bologna: Monduzzi, 1999), 224–25; Maureen Miller, *The Formation of a Medieval Church: Ecclesiastical Change in Verona, 950–1150* (Ithaca: Cornell University Press, 1993), 144–47.

[16] Brown, chap. 7 in *The Rise of Western Christendom*, 112–32.

CHAPTER 1

Society and Government before the Normans

The Province of Salerno in the Roman Period

The province of Salerno is a large and geographically diverse region, stretching from the western tip of the Amalfi coast down through the plain of Paestum and the rolling hills of Cilento to the gulf of Policastro in the south. Inland the province extends from the Irno River Valley down along the Picentino mountains to the plain of Eboli and from there through the Alburni mountains into the Tanagro River Valley and the Valley of Diano. On the coast, fertile plains and low hills provide good agricultural soil, while the interior lands are characterized by mountains, forests, and valleys.

The Romans conquered the area at the end of the fourth and beginning of the third centuries BC, after which they built colonies in various places, including Picentia in 297 BC and Salerno and Buxentum (Policastro) at the end of the second century BC.[1] In the first and second centuries AD Nocera,

<hr />

[1] For Salerno and its province in the Roman period, see Giuseppe Camodeca, "L'età romana," in *Storia del Mezzogiorno*, ed. Giuseppe Galasso (Naples: Edizione del Sole, 1986), 1/2: 7–79; Giovanni Avagliano, "Impianto urbano e testimonanze archeologiche," in *Guida alla storia di Salerno e della sua provincia*, ed. Alfonso Leone and Giovanni Vitolo (Salerno: P. Laveglia, 1982), 33–51; Werner Johannowsky, "Caratteri e fasi delle culture pre-istoriche e classiche," in *Guida alla storia di Salerno*, 415–31; Vittorio Bracco, *Salerno Romana* (Salerno: Palladio Editrice, 1979); Angela Greco Pontrandolfo and Emanuele Greco, "L'Agro picentino e la Lucania occiden-tale," in *Società romana e produzione schiavistica*, ed. Andrea Giardina and Aldo Schiavone (Bari: Laterza, 1981), 1: 137–151; Kathryn Lomas, *Rome and the Western Greeks*

Paestum, Velia, and Atena (Teanum) received colonists.[2] Salerno, Nocera, and Eboli were all *municipia*, and traces of Roman structures have been found in Rota, Vietri, Cava, Teggiano, Atena, Consilinum, Forum (Polla), Marcellianum, and Buccino. Archaeologists have also uncovered the rudiments of approximately twenty Roman villas, most of them located in the Sele plain or Valley of Diano.[3] In the late third century AD, the emperor Diocletian assigned the territory south of Salerno to the "corrector Lucania et Bruttiorum," making Salerno and Reggio the administrative centers.

The Via Popilia, the Capua-Reggio branch of the Via Appia built in 133 BC, passed through the province, extending from Capua to Nocera, Salerno, Eboli, and the Valley of Diano.[4] Salerno had an active port throughout the period, and a port also arose at the mouth of the Picentino river in Roman times.[5] Picentia and Salerno were located in the fertile "Ager Picentinus" region, and further north the "Campania Nucerina," which stretched from Nocera to Sarno, was an important agricultural site.[6]

Despite its agricultural and commercial possibilities, the region was never an important Roman center, neither for agriculture nor for commerce. The cities in the area were small by Roman standards, the port of Salerno and Capua-Reggio road were never very active, and few large villas have been discovered in the province.[7] Nocera alone, connected to the im-

---

350 BC–AD 200: Conquest and Acculturation in Southern Italy (London/New York: Routledge, 1993); Augusto Fraschetti, "La vicende storiche," in *Storia del Vallo di Diano*, ed. Nicola Cilento (Salerno: P. Laveglia, 1982), 205–15.

[2] Camodeca, "L'età romana," 16; Johannowsky, "Caratteri," 429.

[3] For a list of Roman villas in the area, see Greco Pontrandolfo and Greco, "L'Agro picentino" and Stephen L. Dyson, *The Roman Villas of Buccino: The Wesleyan University Excavation of Buccino, 1969–72* (Oxford: B. A. R., 1983).

[4] Johannowsky, "Caratteri," 429; Avagliano, "Impianto urbano," 47–49. There is a debate among historians and archeologists over the exact path of the Nocera-Reggio road from Nocera to Salerno. Some think it passed from Nocera to Camerelle, Sopr'arco, S Pietro, S Croce, and Fossa Lupara to the Porta Nucerina. Others claim it went via Rota and the Irno Valley. A few hypothesize that it traveled through Cava and Vietri on its way to Salerno. See Avagliano, "Impianto urbano," 47–49; Huguette Taviani-Carozzi, *La Principauté Lombarde de Salerne (IXe–XIe): Pouvoir et Société en Italie lombarde méridionale* (Rome: Ecole Française de Rome, 1991), 302–03; Giulio Schmiedt, "Le fortificazioni altomedievali in Italia viste dall'aereo," in *Ordinamenti militari in occidente nell'alto medioevo: Settimana di studi del centro italiano di studi sull'alto medioevo, 30 March–5 April 1967* (Spoleto: Centro Studi sull'Alto Medioevo, 1968), 15: 921.

[5] Avagliano, "Impianto urbano," 36.

[6] Camodeca, "L'età romana," 15; Donato Cosimato and Pasquale Natella, *Il Territorio del Sarno: Storia, società, arte* (Cava dei Tirreni: Di Mauro, 1981), 12.

[7] Camodeca, "L'età romana," 15, 61; Francesco Starace, "L'Ambiente ed il paes-

portant Vesuvian region, was a prominent Roman city, with an extensive complex of Roman urban structures and evidence of large-scale agricultural activity after the Gracchi distributed lands to colonists in the region in the second century BC.[8]

Historians and archeologists have generally viewed the late antique period, and in particular the sixth and seventh centuries, as a time of generalized crisis throughout Italy and indeed all the western provinces of the Roman empire.[9] International commerce in the Mediterranean declined, population levels fell, and many cities either contracted in size or disappeared. In southern Italy, historians have generally attributed the upheaval to a combination of the Byzantine-Gothic war, plague, famine, and coastal flooding. In the province of Salerno, disruption is most noticeable in the southern parts of the province, such as in Cilento, where many maritime cities disappeared or were relocated in late antiquity, and in the Valley of Diano, where the Via Popilia ran. However, the changes took place over a long span of time and affected areas differently.

Recent archaeological studies have shown that southern Italy in late antiquity was made up of diverse micro-regions that responded in vastly different ways to the political and economic transformations characteristic of the era.[10] Both intra- and extra-regional trade along sea routes continued, and even if a dramatic drop in the level of commercial activity in the Mediter-

---

saggio dai Latini a Ruggerio d'Altavilla," in *Storia del Mezzogiorno*, ed. Giuseppe Galasso (Naples: Edizione del Sole, 1986), 1/2: 223; Greco Pontrandolfo and Greco, "L'Agro picentino," 143–49; Andrea Giardina, "Allevamento ed economia della selva in Italia meridionale: Trasformazioni e continuità," in *Società romana*, 1: 87–88, 93–94.

[8] Johannowsky, "Carrateri," 429–30; Camodeca, "L'età romana," 34–35, 40.

[9] Two good recent syntheses on this topic are Michael McCormick, *The Origins of the European Economy: Communications and Commerce, AD 300–900* (Cambridge: Cambridge University Press, 2001) and Gian Pietro Brogiolo and Sauro Gelichi, *La città nell'alto medioevo italiano: Archeologia e storia* (Rome/Bari: Laterza, 1998). For studies related directly to Campania and the province of Salerno, see Nicola Cilento, "Centri urbani antichi, scomparsi e nuovi nella campagna medievale," in *Atti del Colloquio internazionale di Archeologia Medievale, Palermo-Erice, 20–22 September 1974* (Rome: S. Sciascia, 1976), 155–63; Paolo Peduto, "Insediamenti altomedievali e ricerca archeologica," in *Guida alla storia di Salerno*, 441–73; and Jean-Marie Martin, "Settlement and the Agrarian Economy," in *The Society of Norman Italy*, ed. G. A. Loud and A. Metcalfe (Leiden: Brill, 2002), 17–23.

[10] See, in particular, Ghislaine Noyé, "Villes, économie et société dans la province de Bruttium-Lucanie du IVe au VIIe siècle," in *La Storia dell'Alto Medioevo Italiano (VI–X secolo) alla Luce dell'Archeologia. Convegno internazionale, Siena, 2–6 December, 1992*, ed. Riccardo Francovich and Ghislaine Noyé (Florence: Edizioni all'Insegno del Giglio, 1994), 693–733.

ranean can be detected by the late sixth century, which caused the economy of southern Italy to become more localized and self-sufficient, such a change did not necessarily mean economic depression or an end to regional trade.[11] This is particularly true for areas like the province of Salerno, which did not participate heavily in long-distance trade. The abandonment of Roman sites and cities occurred at various points of time between the sixth and ninth centuries, and no single period of urban abandonment can be detected.[12] Furthermore, rather than disappearing completely, cities in general either shrunk in size or were moved.[13] In fact, the sixth through eighth centuries have recently been interpreted as a time of veritable urban renewal as new fortified villages and hilltop sites emerged throughout southern Italy.[14] Roman roads, moreover, continued to function throughout the medieval period, and three major roads ran through the Principality of Salerno: the Via Nucerina, extending from Stabia to Nocera and Vietri, and the Via Popilia, a branch of the Appia, stretching from Capua to Salerno and then splitting into two separate roads, one traveling along the coast to Paestum and Policastro and the other traveling inland to Eboli and the Valley of Diano.[15] Not to deny the important changes that took place over the long period referred to as late antiquity, but for areas such as the southern part of Campania, which was never an important center for Roman economy or administration, transformations were less dramatic than in principal Roman centers, such as northern Campania.

Historians have long debated whether small property-holders or latifundia dominated the economic system of late antique Salerno.[16] No direct ev-

---

[11] Noyé, "Villes, économie et société," 697–700.

[12] The descriptions of various late antique/early medieval sites summarized by Peduto clearly suggest that cities and towns alike in the region had vastly different experiences. Peduto, "Insediamenti altomedievali," 441–73.

[13] Brogiolo, *La città nell'alto medioevo*, 45.

[14] Noyé, "Villes, économie et société," 723–28.

[15] Taviani-Carozzi, *La Principauté*, 302–3.

[16] Lizier claimed that large property holdings ("ville," "curtes," and "casales") predominated in southern Italy, while Peduto also has asserted that Roman latifundia continued to dominate the landscape in early medieval Salerno. Carucci, to the contrary, contended that Roman latifundia were divided in the early medieval period, and Sparano argued that small holdings were characteristic of the early Lombard period, but then disappeared in the tenth and eleventh centuries, replaced by large concentrated properties. Ebner believes that there were latifundia in the Tanagro River Valley and Valley of Diano and "villae rusticae" in the plains near Paestum and Velia, while Jean-Marie Martin has asserted that both latifundia and small landholdings existed throughout southern Italy, although he insists that large estates here were not as central to the economy as in Francia. Augusto Lizier, *L'Ecomonia rurale dell'età prenormanna nell'Italia meridionale: Studi su documenti editi dai secoli IX–XI*

idence for landholding patterns exists for either the Roman or the late antique period. However, most historians have assumed that in the ancient period agriculture predominated on the plains, whereas livestock were raised
in the hill regions and that both activities produced goods destined for
trade.[17] Although there is no evidence to support the view, the existence of
large Roman estates worked by slaves is taken for granted by many historians, especially scholars specialized in periods either before or after the
Roman period. In fact, few Roman villas of any size have been found in the
province of Salerno, suggesting that large-scale agricultural production was
not a prominent feature in the area. Although the Valley of Diano and Tanagro River Valley located near the Capua-Reggio road exhibited signs of increased agricultural activity in the Roman period, the areas of Paestum and
Velia actually witnessed a decline in material culture and economic
activity.[18]

Most likely the economic lifestyle of the majority of the population in the
province of Salerno changed little from the Roman to the early medieval period, consisting of a mixed economy based on agriculture and a silvo-
pastoral regime. It is possible that some latifundia devoted to cereal cultivation developed in the fifth century, when southern Italy became the major
grain supplier to Rome after the loss of Africa. Archaeological research on a
number of sites in southern Italy, including San Giovanni di Ruoti in Lucania, has shown an increase in grain cultivation in some areas formerly characterized by a silvo-pastoral regime.[19] However, if such a development did

---

(Palermo: Reber, 1907), 14; Peduto, "Insediamenti altomedievali," 464; Carlo
Carucci, *La provincia di Salerno dai tempo più remoti al tramonto della fortuna normanna: Economia e vita sociale* (Salerno: Il Tipografio Salernitano, 1922), 129–31; Antonella Sparano, "Agricoltura, industria e commercia in Salerno," *Annali della facoltà
di lettere e filosofia, Università di Napoli* 10 (1962–63): 181–217; Pietro Ebner, chap. 3 in
Economia e società nel Cilento medievale (Rome: Edizioni di Storia e Letteratura, 1979);
Jean-Marie Martin, "Città e Campagna: Economia e società (sec. VII–XIII)," in *Storia del Mezzogiorno*, 3: 271–77 and "Le régime domanial dans l'Italie méridionale
Lombarde. Origines, caractères originaux et extinction," in *Du Latifondium au Latifondo: un heritage de Rome, une création médiévale ou moderne? Actes de la Table ronde in-
ternationale du CNRS organisée à l'Unversité Michel de Montaigne-Bordeaux III, 17–19
December 1992* (Paris: Diffusion de Boccard, 1995), 289–95.

[17] Lizier, chap. 3 in *L'economia rurale*; Carucci, chap. 6 in *La provincia di Salerno*;
Ebner, *Economia e Società*, 154–55; Johannowsky, "Caratteri," 425, 428; Giardina, "Allevamento," 87–89; Nicola Acocella, "Il Cilento dai Longobardi ai Normanni (secoli
X e XI): Struttura amministrativa e agricola," *Rassegna Storica Salernitana* 22 (1961):
45–49.

[18] Greco Pontrandolfo and Greco, "L'Agro Picentino," 138–42.

[19] Noyé, "Villes, économie et société," 715–17.

occur in southern Campania, it was ephemeral. Evidence from the early Lombard period points to a preponderance of small holdings and the widespread existence of common use lands. As in the Roman period, the agricultural regime was based on the classic form of *cultura promiscua*, in which vines grew on trees, beneath which cereals were sown.[20] In addition to cultivated foods, the population utilized a wide variety of other food sources, including domestic and wild animals, salt- and freshwater fish, wild nuts and fruits, and the large abundance of other food supplies, both animal and vegetable, found in forests. Trade in food stuffs most likely existed, although it was probably of a more local nature in comparison with the Roman era.[21]

The Lombard Conquest and the Establishment of the Principality of Salerno

Little is known about the early history of the Lombards, who arrived in Italy sometime in the late sixth century. Although historians formerly interpreted the Lombard invasion as a well-organized campaign of conquest, recent historiography has emphasized the protracted and fragmented nature of the Lombard takeover, which met little resistance in its early phases.[22] Nonetheless, the era of the Lombard conquest is generally seen as a watershed in Italian history, causing the decisive break between the ancient and medieval eras. For one, it was the beginning of a long period of political fragmentation that continued well into the modern age.[23] In addition, it marked the emergence of a warrior aristocracy who based their wealth on landholding and booty.[24] The second half of the sixth century also witnessed

[20] Martin, "Settlement," 38.

[21] Noyé, "Villes, économie et société," 698; McCormick, *Origins of the European Economy*, 115–16.

[22] Gian Piero Bognetti, "Tradizione longobarda e politica bizantina nelle origini del ducato di Spoleto," in *L'età longobarda* (Milan: Giuffrè, 1967), 3: 441–57; Vera von Falkenhausen, "I Longobardi meridionali," in *Storia d'Italia: Il Mezzogiorno dai Bizantini a Federico II* (Turin: UTET, 1983), 3: 251–52; Stefano Gasparri, *I Duchi Longobardi*, vol. *102* of *Studi Storici dell'Istituto Storico Italiano per il Medio Evo* (Rome: Istituto Storico Italiano per il Medio Evo, 1978), 86–87; Taviani-Carozzi, *La Principauté*, xiii; Neil Christie, *The Lombards: The Ancient Longobards* (Oxford: Blackwell, 1995), 73–79.

[23] Chris Wickham, *Early Medieval Italy: Central Power and Local Society, 400–1000* (Ann Arbor: The University of Michigan Press, 1981), 28.

[24] Nicholas Everett, *Literacy in Lombard Italy, c. 568–774* (Cambridge: Cambridge University Press, 2003), 5; Stefano Gasparri, "The Aristocracy," in *Italy in the Early Middle Ages*, 64.

a slowing down of long-distance Mediterranean trade and drastic changes in settlement patterns, which included the end of the villa system, the shrinkage and simplification of urban centers, and the emergence of fortified hilltop towns.[25] Most historians, however, now view the arrival of the Lombards as the consequence of many of these changes rather than their cause. Changes in settlement patterns and the merging of civil and military administration had begun well before the Lombards entered Italy, and it appears that the new Lombard rulers cooperated much more closely with the native Roman aristocracy than was previously thought.[26] Moreover, the nature and extent of the economic crisis of the sixth century continues to be hotly debated among historians and archaeologists alike.[27]

The new Lombard rulers inherited a secular political system that had an institutional basis and espoused a public ideology of the state. Rather than relying on church officials, they administered their kingdom through a system of lay officials, both dukes and gastalds, who were placed in urban centers and were responsible for collecting dues and rents within a specific territory as well as overseeing the local courts.[28] As early as 643, the Lombard kings began to issue written edicts that served as the basis for the legal system that encompassed all the inhabitants of their kingdom, Lombard and Roman alike.[29] In Lombard Italy, written charters always held more power than oaths in law courts, and the mention of specific edicts issued by Lombard kings proves time and again that royal law held force.[30] One important change, however, was the abandonment of the land tax. Unlike the Roman rulers who preceded them, the Lombard kings relied upon tolls, tribute, and landed estates to fund their administration.[31]

Much controversy surrounds the religious orientation of the first Lombard rulers, and historians continue to debate over whether they were Catholic, Arian, or pagan.[32] The common view has been that the Lombards en-

---

[25] Riccardo Francovich, "Changing Structures of Settlements," in *Italy in the Early Middle Ages*, 150–54; Brogiolo, *La città nell'alto medioevo italiano*, 55; Everett, *Literacy in Lombard Italy*, 15–17.

[26] Everett, *Literacy in Lombard Italy*, 5, 73–74; Francovich, "Changing Structures," 152.

[27] For a good summary of the debate, see Brogiolo, chap. 2 in *La città nell'alto medioevo italiano*.

[28] Wickham, *Early Medieval Italy*, 35–36; Everett, *Literacy in Lombard Italy*, 82–83.

[29] François Bougard, "Public Power and Authority," in *Italy in the Early Middle Ages*, 50–51.

[30] Everett, *Literacy in Lombard Italy*, 176–86.

[31] Wickham, *Early Medieval Italy*, 40; Everett, *Literacy in Lombard Italy*, 78.

[32] For good summaries of the debate, see Steven C. Fanning, "Lombard Arianism Reconsidered," *Speculum* 56 (April, 1981): 241–58 and Everett, *Literacy in Lombard Italy*, 59–65.

tered Italy as Arians and then were converted to Catholicism sometime at the beginning of the seventh century. Some historians have also claimed, based on evidence from later sources such as Paul the Deacon, that they set up a rival Arian church and persecuted Catholics. Contemporary sources, however, characterize the Lombards as either pagan or Catholic, and most likely the bulk of Lombards who entered Italy professed some form of Christianity while at the same time retaining some of their pagan beliefs and practicing some non-Christian rituals. The Lombard leaders, however, used religious affiliation to create and advance political alliances, and thus some appear as Catholics and some as Arians.[33] There is no evidence that they promoted Arianism or persecuted Catholics, and overall Arianism played a relatively unimportant role among the Lombards, as compared to the Visigoths in Spain.[34] Moreover, the religious experience of the Lombards was not really so different from that of the indigenous population of Italy at that time: Arianism itself had deep roots in the region, dating back to the fourth century, and many converts to Christianity continued to engage in "pagan" practices and rituals.[35]

The Lombard Duchies of Benevento and Spoleto were established around the same time as the Lombard kingdom based in Pavia, and although historians previously believed that the Lombards who settled in southern Italy were sent by the king in Pavia, most evidence supports the theory that from the beginning the Lombard Duchies of Benevento and Spoleto both functioned independently of the Lombard kings in northern Italy. Moreover, Lombard southern Italy was always administered separately from the Lombard Regno based in Pavia, despite intermarriage and close alliance at times.[36] Nonetheless, the dukes in Benevento and Spoleto in the seventh century constructed a political system similar to the kings in Pavia. It was dominated by a warrior aristocracy and relied on secular officials, both gastalds and judges, to collect rents and dues and to administer justice.[37]

A variety of hypotheses surround both the origin and settlement of the Lombards in southern Italy.[38] Some believe that they were Byzantine mer-

---

[33] Christie, *The Ancient Longobards*, 57–58.

[34] Fanning, "Lombard Arianism," 256–57.

[35] Everett, *Literacy in Lombard Italy*, 60, 64–65.

[36] Gasparri, *I Duchi*, 86–87; Taviani, *La Principauté*, xii–xiii; von Falkenhausen, "I Longobardi," 252–53.

[37] The most detailed descriptions of Lombard administration in southern Italy are found in René Poupardin, *Les institutions politiques et administratives des principautés lombardes* (Paris: H. Champion, 1907), 3–61 and Taviani-Carozzi, *La Principauté*, 440–513.

[38] For an excellent summary of the theories surrounding the arrival of the Lombards in southern Italy, see Palmieri, "Duchi," 53–59.

cenaries who were placed in various *castra* in central Italy after the defeat of the Byzantine general Baduarius in 575/76 and then gradually took power in their own right as Byzantine political authority weakened. Another theory suggests that they belonged to a group of Lombard soldiers under the leadership of Zottone who were recruited by the Byzantines to fight the Lombard general Alboin during his siege of Pavia from 569 to 572. After Alboin's assassination in 572, the Byzantine officials sent Zottone and his followers away to southern Italy due to the fear that they would try to take power for themselves in the north. Finally a source from the tenth century recounts how some Lombards under Zottone were invited to settle in Benevento by the general Narses, after his break with Constantinople. The local population, however, was unwilling to receive them, so instead the Lombards built a small settlement of their own nearby, named "kastron micron," or "civitas nova" in Latin, from which they eventually besieged and occupied Benevento. Despite the lateness of this source, it does support the idea that a group of Lombards led by Zottone came to southern Italy at the invitation of a Byzantine leader. This group of Lombards was sent there either to provide military support to the Byzantine army and population, or alternatively to prevent them from aiding the Lombards in northern Italy who were intent on establishing their own kingdom. In the end, the paucity of sources will make it unlikely that we will ever know the exact details surrounding the arrival of the Lombards and Zottone in southern Italy c. 570.

When the Carolingians conquered the Lombard Kingdom of Pavia in 774, Duke Arechis II (758–87) of Benevento responded by crowning himself prince, re-fortifying the cities of Benevento and Salerno, and establishing a separate political identity for himself and his duchy. He was heavily influenced by Byzantine models: he built the famous church of Santa Sofia in Benevento in imitation of the Hagia Sofia in Constantinople, adopted aspects of Byzantine ceremonial for his court, and began to mint his own money, something that was again based on Byzantine examples.[39] Soon after, Charlemagne led an expedition to southern Italy in 786–87. After defeating Arechis' army, Charlemagne made a pact with the prince, forcing him to become his vassal and to raze the walls of Conza, Acerenza, and Salerno as an act of submission. In addition, Arechis' son, Grimoaldus, be-

[39] *Chron. Sal.*, 10–15, chaps. 9–10; Nicola Cilento, *Le origini della signoria capuana nella Longobardia minore* (Rome: Istituto Storico per il Medio Evo, 1966), 73; Gasparri, *I Duchi*, 98–100; von Falkenhausen, "I Longobardi," 257–59; Michelangelo Schipa, *Storia del Principato Longobardo di Salerno*, in *La Longobardia meridionale (570–1077)*, ed. Nicola Acocella (Rome: Edizioni di storia e letteratura, 1968), 95–96; Palmieri, "Duchi," 78–80.

came Charlemagne's hostage and grew up at the imperial court of Pavia.[40] Nonetheless, Charlemagne and his successors never established direct rule over the Principality of Benevento, as they did over the Kingdom of Pavia in northern Italy.

The Principality of Salerno emerged as a separate political unit in 839, when a succession crisis broke out in the Principality of Benevento between Rachelchis, based in Benevento, and Siconolf, based in Salerno, both of whom vied for the crown after Prince Sicard was assassinated. In 849 the two parties agreed to end their dispute peacefully by splitting up between them the territories that made up the Principality.[41] Although both rulers kept the title "prince of the Lombards" ("Langobardorum gentis princeps"), Siconolf took over the southern regions of the Principality, including Taranto, Latiano, Cassano, Cosenza, Laino, Lucania, Conza, Montella, Rota, Sarno, Cimiterio, Furculo, Capua, Teano, Sora, one-half of Acerenza, and Salerno, which he made his capital, while Radelchis received Molise, Apulia, and the region north of Taranto in addition to the area in and around Benevento, which he made his capital.

Indeed, southern Italy in the early Middle Ages was a mosaic of kingdoms and city-states whose territories were constantly in flux. The Byzantine empire continued to hold lands in Apulia throughout the early medieval period, and in the second half of the tenth century the emperors expanded their power into Calabria and Basilicata.[42] Similarly a small number of Byzantine cities in Campania, including Naples, Amalfi, and Gaeta, while nominally clinging to Byzantine over-lordship established autonomous power in the early Lombard period.[43] Lombard territories from the

[40] *Chron. Sal.*, 13–18, chaps. 10–11; Gasparri, *I Duchi*, 98–100; von Falkenhausen, "I Longobardi," 258–59.

[41] MGH, *Legum*, 4: 221–25; Jean-Marie Martin, Errico Cuozzo, Stefano Gasparri, and Matteo Villani (eds.), *Regesti dei Documenti dell'Italia Meridionale* (Rome: Ecole Française de Rome, 2002), 367–70. Schipa, *Storia*, 101–11; von Falkenhausen, "I Longobardi," 263–65; Cilento, *Le origini*, 93–97; Taviani-Carozzi, bk. 2, chap. 1 in *La Principauté*.

[42] von Falkenhausen, "I Longobardi," 271–73; G. A. Loud, "Southern Italy in the Tenth Century," *The New Cambridge Medieval History*, ed. Timothy Reuter (Cambridge: Cambridge University Press, 1999), 3: 631–33. For the history of the Byzantines in southern Italy, see Jules Gay, *L'Italie méridionale et l'Empire Byzantin depuis l'avènement de Basile Ier jusqu'à la prise de Bari par les Normands (867–1071)* (Paris: A. Fontemoing, 1904), Vera von Falkenhausen, *La dominazione bizantina nell'Italia meridionale dal IX all'XI secolo* (Bari: Ecumenica Editrice, 1978), and Martin, *La Pouille*.

[43] For information on these cities, see Cilento, *Civiltà napoletane*; Mario Del Treppo, *Amalfi: Una città del Mezzogiorno nei secoli IX–XIV* (Naples: Giannini, 1977);

mid-ninth century onward were not only divided into the two Principalities of Benevento and Salerno, but also included the county of Capua that became independent over the course of the ninth century as Count Landolfus (815–43) and his son Landolfus turned their city into a fortified center and began to administer their lands autonomously of the princes in Benevento and Salerno.[44] Other cities, such as Avellino, also were often ruled independently of the princes.[45] In addition, Muslims both conducted raids and established centers of political power in southern Italy over the course of the ninth and tenth centuries. In 848 some Muslim raiders founded an emirate in Bari, which survived over twenty years, and in Lombard territories Muslim colonies arose in both Garigliano and Agropoli, from which numerous raids were made into neighboring regions up through the early tenth century.[46] Only with the Norman takeover in the eleventh century would southern Italy and Sicily slowly become integrated into a single political unit.

The Political and Economic Structures of the Principality of Salerno, 850–1050

From the establishment of Salerno as an independent Principality in 849 until its integration into the Norman Duchy of Apulia by Robert Guiscard in 1077, two dynasties ruled the Principality of Salerno, the first established by Guaiferius in 860 and the second founded by John II in 983. (See figure 1.) Although brief periods of political unrest that occurred in the 850s, the 970s, and the 1050s produced short-reigning princes from other families or neighboring kingdoms, these rulers did not reign for long nor did they establish lasting dynasties. Yet despite the remarkable degree of dynastic stability, and the tradition of naming sons co-rulers, succession from father to son was not a given. Chronicle evidence suggests that the death of a prince was

---

Patricia Skinner, *Family Power in Southern Italy: The Duchy of Gaeta and its Neighbours, 850–1139* (Cambridge: Cambridge University Press, 1995).

[44] Cilento, chaps. 3 and 4 in *Le origini*.

[45] *Chron. Sal.*, 154–56, chap. 147*.

[46] For the history of the Muslim Emirate of Bari, see Giosuè Musca, *L'Emirato di Bari, 847–71*, 2d ed. (Bari: Dedalo, 1967). For the Muslims in the Principality of Salerno, see *Chron. Sal.*, 142–62, chaps. 129–54; Schipa, *Storia*, 128–31, 141–45; von Falkenhausen, "I Longobardi," 270. Also see Cava documents CDC I: 109–11, no. 86 and CDC I: 123–24, no. 97, which mention that in 882 the Muslims surrounded and besieged Salerno.

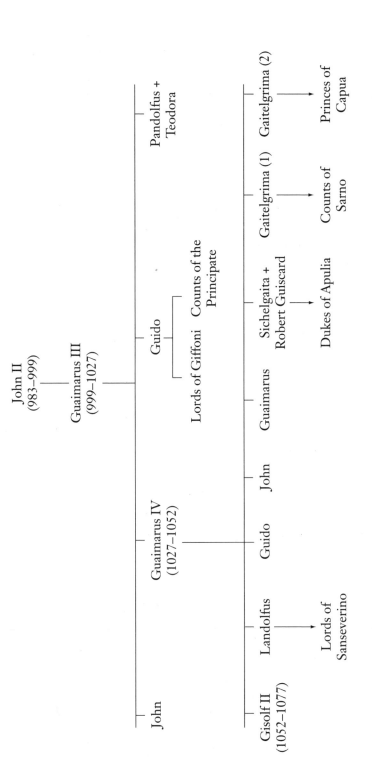

Figure 1. The Princely Family of Salerno: The Dynasty of John II

Sources: Cava Archives; *Catalogus Baronum*; Loud, "Continuity and Change" and *Age of Robert Guiscard*; Drell, *Kinship and Conquest*

often followed by a period of crisis in which different candidates were put forward.[47] Moreover, the eventual winner was always "elected," meaning that he had to gain the consent of the Salernitans and the nobility in order for his succession to be legitimate.

Charters from Salerno give evidence for both palace officials and administrative units. Gastalds and counts were the two most important officials, although the exact functions and duties of each are unclear. Documents from the tenth century suggest that gastaldates were territorial units, although they give no clue to the type of authority that gastalds exercised within their gastaldates.[48] They did not serve as judges or military commanders but could possibly have been in charge of collecting dues and services owed on palace lands (*res publica*), as was the case in the Lombard kingdom in northern Italy.[49] Count (*comes*), however, appears to have been an honorific title that simply meant a connection to the princely family, without any sort of territorial component or even any precise administrative duties connected to it.[50] In the end most palace officials seem to have had no well-defined functions. They were simply close relatives of the prince who could provide aid in a number of different ways.[51]

In addition to gastaldates, documents speak of "actus," or centers of document redaction, in Sarno, Nocera, Salerno, Rota, and Forino and later in Stricturia (Giffoni), Apudmontem (Roccapiemonte), Capaccio, Lucania, Metiliano (Cava), Montoro, and Cilento.[52] Most of these places were also fortified centers (*castra* or *castella*) in the Lombard period, and villages and

---

[47] The author of the Anonymous Chronicle of Salerno even made the remark, after the death of Guaimarius II in 943, that the Salernitans began immediately to fight one another as was usual in such circumstances. *Chron. Sal.*, 167, chap. 160.

[48] For example, the gastald Eghinus son of Eghenardus, in a charter from 902, speaks of lands located inside "his gastaldate of Nocera" ("rebus . . . de locum nuceria quod illius eghini essent partinentes de ipso suo gastaldatum"), while two gastalds in 928 mentioned that they resided in "our gastaldate of Nocera" ("dum resideremus nos guaiferius et petrus gastaldei in locum nuceria nostrum gastaldatum"). CDC 1: 144–46, no. 115; CDC 1: 189–91, no. 148.

[49] Taviani-Carozzi, *La Principauté*, 447; Gasparri, *I Duchi*, 21.

[50] Taviani-Carozzi, *La Principauté*, 481–82, 568–69; Loud, "Southern Italy in the Tenth Century," 638–39. Loud claims, however, that in the Principality of Benevento and Capua the title took on a territorial meaning in the tenth century.

[51] Taviani-Carozzi, *La Principauté*, 458.

[52] "Actus" Forino is first mentioned in 792, "Actus" Rota in 798, "Actus" Salerno in 799, "Actus" Sarno in 819, and "Actus" Nocera in 822. CDC 1: 1–2, no. 1; CDC 1: 2–3, no. 2; CDC 1: 3–4, no. 3; CDC 1: 9, no. 8; CDC 1: 13–14, no. 12. "Actus" Stricturia is first mentioned in 920, "In locum" Roccapiemonte in 956, "Actus" Capaccio in 974, "Actus" Lucania in 994, "Actus" Montoro in 1002, "Actus" Metiliano in 1009, and "Actus" Cilento in 1034. CDC 1: 178, no. 138; CDC 1: 249–51, no. 194;

towns surrounding them are often described as being in their territory ("in finibus" or "in pertinentiis"). However, once again the exact meaning of both "actus" and "in finibus" is uncertain. Perhaps some sort of territorial power existed in the province under Lombard rule, based on "actus," fortifications, or gastaldates; however, the paucity of documents makes it difficult to reconstruct the administrative system of the Lombard princes in any detail.

Other than charters, the only other extensive information on Salerno in the Lombard period comes from the Anonymous Chronicle of Salerno, a history of the Principality of Salerno written by an anonymous cleric at some point in the late tenth century.[53] The author of the chronicle drew extensively from the earlier Lombard chronicles of Paul the Deacon and Erchempertus, but also incorporated information from a variety of sources including the *Chronicon S. Benedicti Casinensis*, the *Liber Pontificalis*, the *Life of S. Trophimena*, letters, archives, and oral sources. Although the author's description of the early history of the Lombards in southern Italy presents a highly idealized portrait of the distant past, people and events of the ninth and tenth century are portrayed in a more detailed and nuanced light.

In the Anonymous Chronicle, the Lombard princes of Benevento and Salerno exercised power in a way typical of other early medieval rulers. They wielded limited authority over other members of the ruling class, forming what one historian has referred to as a "condominium" with the aristocracy, whose members the author of the Anonymous Chronicle called the prince's "consanguinei" and "fideles."[54] Like their counterparts in Pavia and Francia, they relied heavily on negotiation and gift-giving in order to gain and hold onto power.[55] The idea of mutual obligation was strong, not only between the prince and his entourage, but also with the leading citizens of the cities over which he ruled. The prince was required to gain consent

---

CDC 2: 83–4, no. 277; CDC 3: 16–17, no. 470; CDC 4: 12–13, no. 545; CDC 4: 139, no. 618; CDC 5: 251–52, no. 864.

[53] For biographical information on the author, see Westerbergh's introduction, xii–xiii and Taviani-Carozzi, *La Principauté*, 87–91. Taviani-Carozzi believes the chronicle was written by an abbot named Radoald. Also see Taviani-Carozzi, *La Principauté*, 172–237 for a comprehensive analysis of the text.

[54] Loud, "Southern Italy in the Tenth Century," 637. *Chron. Sal.*, 83, chap. 83 and 105, chap. 105.

[55] Taviani-Carozzi, *La Principauté*, 451. *Chron. Sal.*, 91–92, chap. 91; 105–6, chap. 105. Recently some historians have begun to refer to this system of kingship as a "government of favors." See, for example, Bougard, "Public Power and Authority." Like most historians, Bougard sees this type of government as an effective one, helping rulers to govern and providing dynastic stability.

from the urban populaces of the various cities of his principality, and on numerous occasions the Anonymous Chronicle shows citizens rejecting his decision or even his right to rule.[56] Since citizens and nobles alike could and
did act on their own, the princes had to form alliances with these groups and
gain their consent for their actions, sometimes through gifts or negotiation,
and sometimes by sheer force.[57] In at least one case, a prince used the policy
of "divide and rule," whereby he encouraged infighting among his *fideles* in
order to control them better.[58] In the end, the political system of Lombard
southern Italy stressed influence over direct control. Moreover, the princes
most likely exercised little authority over the more remote areas of their
principalities, and places such as Taranto, Cosenza, and Cassano would be
completely lost in the late ninth and tenth centuries when they became integrated into the new Byzantine administration in the area.[59] In the case of the
Principality of Salerno, the prince's power was mostly felt in the main urban
centers located close to Salerno itself, such as Nocera, Sarno, Rota, and
Forino, even if at times the prince did give cities to others to rule in far off
places such as Conza and Marsico.[60]

The prince's primary revenue base appears to have been fiscal lands, referred to as "res publica" in the charters. Although the size of these landholdings is unknown, in some areas, such as Cilento, the princes seem to
have possessed quite extensive properties.[61] Moreover, the fiscal lands could
increase over time either when land was confiscated or when it reverted to
the prince when a man died without any heirs. The prince also collected
tolls and commercial dues, and most likely earned revenue from justice and
minting rights.[62] However, there is no evidence for a universal land tax. In
addition, war represented an important income source, and military opera-
tions more often than not were specifically aimed at taking booty or impos-

---

[56] *Chron. Sal.*, 101–3, chaps. 100–101; 142, chap. 129; 145–46, chap. 136; 156–57,
chap. 149; 162–63, chap. 155; 166–67, chap. 159; 167, chap. 160; 179–80, chap. 176.

[57] See, for example, *Chron. Sal.*, 65–66, chap. 68; 87, chap. 85; 87, chap. 86; 91–92,
chap. 91; 99–101, chap. 99; 169–70, chap. 164 for the use of gifts and negotiation and
Chron. Sal., 66–67, chap. 69; 73, chap. 75; 75, chap. 77; 77–79, chap. 80; 102–03, chap.
101; 104, chap. 103; 162–63, chap. 155 for the use of violence and force. Gifts came in
the form of luxury items, lands, castles, and cities, while force could result in everything from exile and tonsuring to imprisonment, torture, or death.

[58] *Chron. Sal.*, 58–59, chaps. 59 and 61–62.

[59] Loud, "Southern Italy in the Tenth Century," 637; von Falkenhausen, *La dominazione bizantina*, 21–28.

[60] *Chron. Sal.*, 179–80, chap. 176.

[61] See, for example, CDC 6: 89–90, no. 931.

[62] Poupardin, *Les institutions*, 20–21.

ing tribute rather than capturing a city.[63] The ransoming of prisoners was also commonly practiced.[64]

The prince had oversight over the legal system of the Principality of Salerno, which functioned efficiently and was available to all denizens of the region, rich and poor alike. As in the case of the Lombard Kingdom of Pavia, the justice system was a key factor in the effectiveness and stability of princely power.[65] It was based on both Lombard and Roman law, written evidence, and a professional class of lay judges and notaries. The law was personal in Lombard Salerno, meaning that people followed the law of their ancestors. Both Lombard and Roman law were practiced, and in charters people at times stipulated which of the two laws they followed. Nonetheless, evidence also points to a mixing of traditions, especially as it related to women and marriage, making it difficult if not impossible to discern a neat distinction between a Lombard and a Roman legal tradition, except, perhaps, with regard to inheritance laws.[66]

Most people who appeared in the charters in the Principality of Salerno followed Lombard law, and although it is unclear whether all the edicts issued by Lombard kings in the seventh and eighth centuries were either known or adhered to, certain statutes and customs are specifically mentioned in charters and were consistently applied. For example, church property was considered inviolable, according to an edict of Aistulf, and could be alienated only if the religious houses benefited.[67] Charters of exchange involving church property specifically mentioned Aistulf's edict and then gave

[63] *Chron. Sal.*, 57–58, chap. 57; 60–62, chaps. 63–64; 65–66, chap. 68; 72, chap. 73; 93–94, chap. 93; 147–48, chap. 140.

[64] Marriage contracts found at Cava, for example, sometimes stipulated that the husband had to provide for at least some of the ransom if his wife was captured or taken away. See, for example, CDC 4: 125–26, no. 609 and CDC 4: 83–84, no. 590.

[65] On the Lombard Kingdom of Pavia, see Bougard, "Public Power and Authority," 54–58.

[66] Wickham, *Early Medieval Italy*, 69; Taviani-Carozzi, *La Principauté*, 515–20; Joanna Drell, *Kinship and Conquest: Family Strategies in the Principality of Salerno during the Norman Period, 1077–1194* (Ithaca: Cornell University Press, 2002), 79–80; Everett, *Literacy in Lombard Italy*, 173–75.

[67] According to Edict 16 of Aistulf, lands, buildings, and servants belonging to ecclesiastical foundations could only be exchanged if a representative of the prince, the pope, or a judge, or three honest or oath-worthy men decided that the religious house gained in the transaction. "Si vero communtatione fecerint de casis, terres, vel familias, et fuerit intermissus regis, vel pontifici, seu iudici, aut tales homines tres quorum fides ammittitur, et res meliorates ei paruerit, tunc quando ipsa commutatio facta fuit, quod pars religiousi suscipiant, nullo tempore postea ab eorum successoribus removeatur." Aistulf, Edict 16, edition in CDC 3: 219.

proof that the religious house would benefit. Moreover, the prince's permission was often sought, or if not, other men were called in to make sure the religious houses gained.[68] In addition, the use of guarantors and the tradition of the laungilt, or counter-gift, were widespread. For women, the custom of guardianship ("mundium") was practiced, and during legal transactions women would appear with their guardian ("mundoalt") who would approve the action and protect the women. Also common was the tradition of the Morgengabe, or morning gift, in which a wife received one-quarter of all her husband's property the day after the consummation of a marriage.

The legal system of the Principality of Salerno relied heavily on written documentation that recorded a wide variety of activities, including sales, leases, donations, agricultural contracts, Morgengabe agreements, wills, and loans. Although the charters to a large extent recorded oral transactions that required witnesses, oaths, and guarantors, as well as notaries, judges, and/or *boni homines* to be valid, the parchments themselves were carefully preserved and brought forward as evidence when needed. Even humble citizens had a cache of charters, and when a piece of land was transferred, all the charters relating to it were passed on to the new owner. In the case of disputes, decisions reached were based almost exclusively on written evidence, and sometimes the number of charters produced by the parties involved could be quite large indeed.[69] If a person showed up without written evidence, he or she almost inevitably lost the case.[70] Witnesses rarely were used to decide cases involving property.[71] Disputes tended to end with judgments rather than compromises, although in the case of questions regarding land borders, judges often tried to reach a compromise suitable to the disputing parties if written evidence did not clearly spell out the exact rights of the parties involved.[72] In fact in many cases these types of property disputes seem more

[68] CDC 1: 193–94, no. 150; CDC 2: 289–95, no. 422; CDC 2: 320–21, no. 442; CDC 3: 20–22, no. 473; CDC 4: 25–27, no. 554; CDC 4: 59–64, no. 577; CDC 4: 152–54, no. 625; CDC 6: 191–93, no. 996; CDC 7: 248–49, no. 1200.

[69] In 928, for example, one party to a dispute produced 55 charters (15 *brebri et iudicate* and 40 *cartule*). CDC 1: 189–91, no. 148. For other disputes with large numbers of charters see, CDC 1: 228–30, no. 177; CDC 2: 207–13, no. 368; CDC 4: 103–17, no. 602.

[70] See, for example, CDC 1: 205–7, no. 161; CDC 2: 1–2, no. 211; CDC 2: 240–41, no. 387.

[71] I have found only one example where a witness rather than a charter provided evidence. CDC 3: 89–90, no. 522.

[72] See, for example, the 982 dispute between Peter son of Madus and the church of San Massimo in which San Massimo received the lands under dispute, but in return the abbot gave the defendant Peter other lands in the same area. CDC 2: 164–65, no. 337.

like an opportunity to define land borders or ownership rights rather than to resolve a true disagreement.[73]

Judges and notaries were almost exclusively members of the laity in the Principality of Salerno and they appear to have been a professional class of people, although we have no information on their training. The fact that many had similar names suggests that both may have been hereditary professions.[74] Nonetheless the prince had oversight of the legal system: judges took decisions in the prince's name and the majority of disputes decided in Salerno took place in the prince's palace. Moreover, in charters the princes spoke of "our judges," suggesting that at least some judges had a close connection to princely authority; however, it is not clear whether the prince directly appointed the judges who served in Salerno and other cities.

Cities, *consortia*, and kinship groups were the primary organizational units of society in Lombard southern Italy. The political system of Lombard southern Italy was urban based, just as in Roman times, and the aristocracy resided in cities, from where they administered and protected the surrounding countryside.[75] Even before the arrival of the Lombards, siege warfare had become widespread throughout southern Italy and possession of a city became key for seizing and holding onto political power. Urban fortifications grew up rapidly over the course of the sixth century and battles during the Lombard period were almost always focused on besieging and capturing cities.[76] Rulers would assign cities to their followers to administer for them, and documents for the Principality of Salerno were all redacted in urban centers, generally in Salerno but also in places such as Nocera, Rota, and Sarno. In addition, denizens of cities possessed political power. In Salerno the leading citizens not only participated actively in decisions taken by the prince, but they also played a decisive role in the selection of princes.[77] Sim-

---

[73] CDC 1: 173–75, no. 135; CDC 1: 268, no. 209; CDC 2: 22–3, no. 230; CDC 2: 45–6, no. 248; CDC 2: 120–21, no. 304; CDC 2: 207–13, no. 368; CDC 2: 245, no. 392; CDC 2: 289–95, no. 422; CDC 3: 42–43, no. 489; CDC 3: 63–64, no. 502; CDC 3: 73–75, no. 509; CDC 3: 89–90, no. 522; CDC 4: 75–76, no. 584; CDC 5: 28–29, no. 724; CDC 5: 256–57, no. 867; CDC 6: 89–90, no. 931.

[74] Taviani-Carozzi, *La Principauté*, 559–61, 586.

[75] Palmieri, "Duchi," 69.

[76] Noyé, "Villes, économie e société," 724–28.

[77] For example, in 861, the citizens of Salerno imprisoned and then deposed Prince Ademarius, according to the author because of his avaricious and domineering behavior. When Ademarius' nephew Dauferius tried to take his uncle's place without the consent of the Salernitans, the citizens met to discuss the matter, after which they imprisoned Dauferius and proclaimed Guaiferius prince. *Chron. Sal.*, 101–03, chaps. 100–01. In another example, the author of the chronicle described how the Salernitans, tired of the rule of Guaimarius I (880–900), asked first

ilarly when the prince assigned other cities in his principality to men to rule, consent of the citizens was required.[78] Cities and villages also represented an important form of identity for people. Charters regularly specified the place where people lived or were born, and in chronicles citizens of specific cities, such as Salerno, Benevento, Capua, and Naples, acted as groups on a regular basis. Citizens often constructed complicated histories for their cities, such as the case of the Amalfians who supposedly began life as merchants from Constantinople and then, after a shipwreck in Slavic lands and various perambulations in both Slavic and Italian territories, slowly made their way to the Amalfi coast.[79] Moreover, archival and archaeological evidence from cities such as Salerno suggest a highly sophisticated urban landscape, with stone houses, markets, aqueducts and drainage systems, and, in at least one case, an indoor latrine.[80]

Kinship groups were another important form of legal and political identity. In the Lombard laws family members were legally responsible for one another, and in charters they often appear together in possession of a common inheritance. Also in chronicles extended families acted as cohesive groups, and their fortunes rose and fell together.[81] The issue of family honor looms large in both the law codes and in chronicles. Many of the edicts issued by Lombard princes related to marriage, adultery, and the proper conduct concerning female members of the family. Even minor insults to female honor could result in retaliation and even death, such as the example of a nobleman who saw Prince Sicard's wife bathing her feet in a

---

Siconolf, ruler of Benevento, and then Guaimarius' son, Guaimarius II, to replace him as prince. Thus in 900 Guaimarius II ascended the throne, sending his father to San Massimo to live out the rest of his days as a monk. *Chron. Sal.*, 156–57, chap. 149 and 162–63, chap. 155. Similarly after Guaimarius' death, the Salernitans argued over whether to elect as prince his son, Gisolf I or Atenolfus prince of Benevento. *Chron. Sal.*, 167, chap. 160. The same held true for other cities under Lombard rule, such as Benevento and Capua. See, for example, *Chron. Sal.*, 142, chap. 129; 145–46, chap. 136; 166–67, chap. 159.

[78] For example, when Prince Gisolf I of Salerno (943–78) gave Conza to Atenolfus, the citizens of the city rejected his choice and refused to let him enter the city. *Chron. Sal.*, 177–79, chap. 175. In another case, however, when Prince Grimoaldus IV of Benevento (806–17) assigned Sicone to Acerenza, Sicone was allowed to stay since the city's population liked him. They even defended his right to continue to rule over the city later on against Grimoaldus IV, who was trying to eject Sicone forcibly. *Chron. Sal.*, 177–79, chap. 175. *Chron. Sal.*, 43–47, chap. 43–44.

[79] *Chron. Sal.*, 87–90, chaps. 87–89.

[80] Paolo Delogu, *Mito di una città meridionale (Salerno, secoli VIII–IX)* (Naples: Liguori, 1977), 127–39.

[81] See, for example, *Chron. Sal.*, 146, chap. 138; 147–48, chap. 140.

river. The princess demanded vengeance, and so her husband, the prince, captured the man's wife and paraded her around naked. The nobleman, in turn, sought his revenge and ended up killing the prince along with a group of his *fideles*.[82] Finally documents speak of *consortia*, groups of people who owned goods in common or banded together for specific activities, such as building a church or managing lands.[83] Although at times *consortia* were made up of blood relatives, in many cases they were not.

During the Lombard period, princes and aristocrats built or refortified *castra* in order to guard and protect their territories.[84] Lines of fortresses, linked to one another by sight or signal, stretched north from Salerno to Nocera, west to Angri, Castellamare, and Gragnano, north to Roccapiemonte, Lanzara, San Giorgio, west to Sarno and east to Rota, then north to Montoro, Solofra, Serino, and Forino and southeast to Giffoni, Montecorvino, Campagna, Olevano, Eboli, and Capaccio. In addition, seaside fortresses were erected in the southern region, with remains in Agropoli, Ascea (Castellamare della Bruca), Camerota, Velia, and Policastro. In the hills of Cilento *castra* appeared in Laurino, Roccacilento, Ogliastro, Vatolla, Melilla, and Roccaglorioso and in the Valley of Diano in Atena, Teggiano, and Sala Consilina.

According to most historians, these fortified centers arose in response to Muslim attacks that became frequent in the ninth century.[85] In the tenth century there is evidence that the *castra* appearing in the regions of Benevento and Capua not only provided protection, but also served as centers of lordship and as points of agricultural colonization.[86] Further north the

[82] *Chron. Sal.*, 73–75, chap. 76.

[83] Taviani-Carozzi has also stressed the importance of consortial communities in her study of Salerno in the Lombard era. Taviani-Carozzi, *La Principauté*, 917–18.

[84] For information on *castra* in the Lombard period, see Lucio Santoro, "Le difese di Salerno nel territorio," in *Guida alla storia di Salerno*, 481–540; Vittorio Gleijeses, *Castelli in Campania* (Naples: Società Editrice Napoletana, 1973); Schmiedt, "Le fortificazioni altomedievali," 920–22; Pasquale Natella and Paolo Peduto, *Il castello di Mercato S. Severino* (Naples: Hermes, 1965); Giovanni Vitolo, "Da Apudmontem a Roccapiemonte. Il castrum come elemento di organizzazione territoriale," *Rassegna Storica Salernitana*, n.s. 6 (December 1986): 129–142 and "Organizzazione dello spazio e vicende del popolamento," in *Storia del Vallo di Diano*, 43–77.

[85] von Falkenhausen, *I Longobardi*, 300–02; Vitolo, "Da Apudmontem a Roccapiemonte," 135; Taviani-Carozzi, *La Principauté*, 280–85; Bruno Figliuolo, "Morfologia dell'insediamento nell'Italia meridionale in età normanna," *Studi Storici* 32 (1991): 26–27.

[86] Mario Del Treppo, "La vita economica e sociale in una grande abbazia del Mezzogiorno: San Vincenzo al Volturno nell'alto medioevo," *Archivio storico per le province napoletane*, n.s. 35 (1956): 31–110; Cilento, *Le origini*, 22–44; Loud, "Southern Italy in the Tenth Century," 637–38.

abbeys of both Montecassino and San Vincenzo al Volturno similarly established compact lordships at this time, as did counts, secular lords, and large abbeys in the Abruzzi.[87] However, there is no evidence for this type of development in the Principality of Salerno. Fortresses built here in the ninth and tenth centuries represented neither centers of seigneurial power, as seen by Duby in the Mâconnais, nor concentrated population centers for agricultural colonization, as described by Toubert for Lazio.[88] Instead the *castra* had purely strategic functions, and they did not serve as centers of familial power, as they would in the twelfth century and beyond.[89] Although some of the *castra* may also have had administrative functions, linked to gastaldates and "actus," archaeological studies have shown the early medieval structures to be small and purely defensive, and thus the *castra* and *castella* which appeared before 1000 may rightly be called "fortifications."

Beginning in the late tenth century, the amount of land under cultivation in the Principality of Salerno began to increase.[90] Due mainly to the initiative of large property holders, tracts of uncultivated lands, often located in marshy areas in need of drainage or in wooded areas in need of clearance, were leased out to tenants under favorable terms. The tenants promised to ameliorate the property and often they were required to plant crops such as vines and olive trees that took years to become productive.

As large landholders in the Principality of Salerno began to expand agriculture into regions formerly vacant, they also started to restrict access to uncultivated lands. They began to define the boundaries of their property more clearly and prevent others from entering their lands for food or wood.[91] Formerly people had been allowed to engage in a number of economic activities on uncultivated lands free of charge. They hunted, col-

---

[87] Martin, "Settlement," 22–23.

[88] Georges Duby, *La société aux XIe et XIIe siècles dans la région mâconnaise* (Paris: A. Colin, 1953), 137–262; Pierre Toubert, *Les Structures du Latium Médiéval: Le Latium méridionale et la Sabine du IXe à la fin du XIIe siècle* (Rome: Ecole française de Rome, 1973), 305–549.

[89] Taviani-Carozzi, *La Principauté*, 280–85; Vitolo, "Da Apudmontem a Roccapiemonte," 135; Valerie Ramseyer, "Territorial Lordships in the Principality of Salerno, 1050–1150," *Haskins Society Journal* 9 (2001): 83–84.

[90] Both historical and archaeological records report the increase in cultivated lands. See the articles by Giovanni Vitolo, "La conquista normanna nel contesto economico del Mezzogiorno," *Rassegna storica salernitana*, n.s. 9 (June 1988): 7–22, "Il castagno nell'economia della Campania medievale," *Rassegna storica salernitana*, n.s. 11 (June 1989): 21–34, and "Produzione e commercio del vino nel Mezzogiorno medievale," *Rassegna storica salernitana*, n.s. 10 (December 1988): 65–76.

[91] For a more detailed study of this phenomenon, see Ramseyer, "Territorial Lordships," 88–89.

lected food and wood, masted pigs in forests, kept a variety of animals in pastures, and fished in the rivers and the sea, all without paying a fee. Evidence suggests that the inhabitants of Lombard Italy relied heavily upon the abundant food sources of the Italian forests and waterways to meet their nutritional needs.[92] During the period of agricultural expansion in the late tenth and early eleventh century, as concepts of land ownership changed, common-use lands became less prevalent. Although non-agricultural products remained an important part of the diet, the population no longer had the right to utilize uncultivated land free of charge.[93] In the second half of the eleventh century, large landholders, both lay and ecclesiastical, would increase their economic power further, and tenants would become progressively tied to the land and dependent on large landholders. Small holdings appear less frequently in the documents and tenant agriculture slowly became the chief economic activity for the population.

Southern Italy and the Arrival of the Normans

Throughout the early Middle Ages, both Greek and Latin emperors conducted military campaigns in southern Italy and claimed authority over Lombard territories. In addition to Charlemagne, the Carolingian emperor Louis II launched a major expedition in southern Italy in 866–68 and put the Lombard kingdoms under his power. His successes were short-lived, however, and already by 871 rebellions against Carolingian authority had begun.[94] The Byzantine armies, though, had more lasting success in southern Italy at this time. In 871 they captured Bari and large parts of Apulia and Calabria. By 876 most of Apulia was under Byzantine control, and in 888 the Byzantines had enough lands in southern Italy to create a new theme of Longobardia. During this period of Byzantine successes, the Lombard princes of Benevento and Salerno became vassals of the Byzantine emperor

[92] Massimo Montanari, *L'Alimentazione contadina nell'alto medioevo* (Naples: Liguori Editore, 1979); Vito Fumagalli, *Terra e società nell'Italia padana* (Turin: Einaudi, 1976); Chris Wickham, "European Forests in the Early Middle Ages: Landscape and Land Clearance," in *L'ambiente vegetale nell'alto medioevo: Settimana di Studio del centro italiano di studi sull'alto medioevo, 30 March–5 April, 1989*, 37/2: 479–548 (Spoleto: Centro italiano di studi sull'alto medioevo, 1990).

[93] Not just in the Principality of Salerno but throughout southern Italy in the Norman period, lords began to collect dues from the peasants who used their forests to procure wood or pasture animals. Martin, "Settlement," 43.

[94] Schipa, *Storia*, 125; von Falkenhausen, "I Longobardi," 269–70.

and swore oaths of fealty to him.[95] In 888 the prince of Salerno even traveled to Constantinople to receive his lands from the emperor, who bestowed the title of "patrikios" on him, and for a brief time at the end of the ninth century the Byzantines actually established direct rule over Benevento.[96] Finally the Saxon emperor Otto I traveled to Lombard regions in 962 and attempted to assert control over them. Both Gisolf of Salerno and Pandolfus of Benevento swore oaths of fealty to him before he left Campania to campaign in Apulia; however, like the oaths to other emperors, these promises of fealty were short-lived.[97] Thus, although Lombard rulers at times put themselves under the nominal authority of Latin or Byzantine emperors, their kingdoms were never incorporated into any larger empire. Moreover, the iconography and ceremonial of the Lombard princes in southern Italy clearly show that they saw themselves as independent rulers, equal to both the Frankish and Byzantine emperors.[98]

Beginning in the early tenth century, the Lombard rulers in Salerno, Benevento, and Capua started to consolidate their power, often allying together against Muslims and Byzantines. In 915, a united imperial-papal-Lombard army defeated the Muslims of Garigliano, and although Muslim piracy still remained a problem afterward, Muslim offensives in Lombard territories became less frequent. In 929, Guaimarius II allied with Landolfus, prince of Benevento, against the Byzantines. Together their army defeated a Byzantine army in Apulia, asserting Lombard authority once again in the region. In 934–35 further revolts against the Byzantines in Apulia took place, and Guaimarius II participated in these as well.[99]

Atenolfus, count of Capua, captured Benevento in 900 and united Capua and Benevento under his rule. This marks the beginning of Capua's rise to power, which would culminate in the rule of Pandolfus I Iron Head, who briefly united the southern Italian Lombard regions under his leadership between 974 and 981. The key to Pandolfus' success lay in his alliance with Emperor Otto I, who sought to place southern Italy under more direct imperial rule.[100] In 967 Otto conceded to Pandolfus the duchy of Spoleto and the margravate of Camerino, and shortly thereafter Otto and Pandolfus led an army against Byzantine Apulia. The campaign in Apulia did not accom-

---

[95] Mark Whittow, *The Making of Byzantium, 600–1025* (Berkeley and Los Angeles: University of California, 1996), 298–309.

[96] von Falkenhausen, "I Longobardi," 271; Cilento, *Le origini*, 143; *Chron. Sal.*, 144, chap. 133; 150, chap. 143.

[97] von Falkenhausen, "I Longobardi," 277–79.

[98] Taviani-Carozzi, *La Principauté*, 216–18.

[99] Schipa, *Storia*, 153–57; von Falkenhausen, "I Longobardi," 275–77.

[100] Loud, "Southern Italy in the Tenth Century," 629.

plish much, however, and after Otto returned to northern Italy, Pandolfus was even taken prisoner and sent to Constantinople. Nonetheless, shortly after his return to southern Italy, Pandolfus once again went on the offensive. In 970 he marched on Salerno, although his siege of the city was unsuccessful. Events in 972, however, helped Pandolfus to attain his goal of capturing the city: a rebellion broke out in Salerno that year, led by Landolfus and Landolfus (father and son), who captured and deported Prince Gisolf and his wife Gemma to Amalfi and declared themselves princes of Salerno.[101] Less than a year later, the citizens of Salerno, unhappy with the rule of the two Landolfuses, asked Pandolfus for aid. He captured Salerno with the citizens' aid, killed the two Landolfuses, and made himself prince. Soon after, Prince Gisolf returned to Salerno from Amalfi and threw Pandolfus out. However, in 978 the Beneventan prince captured Salerno for a second time, and for another three years, Lombard southern Italy was once again unified under Pandolfus' rule.[102]

After Pandolfus' death in 981, his kingdom soon fell apart. The Principality of Salerno became independent once again in 983 when John, a palace count, became prince and established a dynasty that would last until the Norman conquest in 1077. During this time Salerno grew in size and wealth as both agriculture and commerce expanded. The Principality of Salerno also increased its territory with successful military campaigns in Campania, Apulia, and Calabria. Under Guaimarius III (999–1027) and Guaimarius IV (1027–52), Salerno reached the apex of its power when the Principality expanded to include Amalfi, Sorrento, Apulia, and Calabria. The rapid growth of Salerno was due largely to the abilities of Norman soldiers, who arrived in southern Italy in the late tenth century and began to offer their services to various rulers in the area, including the princes of Salerno. Prince Guaimarius III hired Norman mercenaries in 999 and again in 1015 when Muslims besieged Salerno, and under Prince Guaimarius IV, a combined Salernitan-Norman army took the offensive. In 1038 it captured Amalfi and Sorrento. In 1042 a combined Norman-Lombard army took large parts of Apulia. Although the army was under the command of Atenolfus, brother of the Prince of Benevento, when the conquests were made, the Norman soldiers soon had a falling out with Atenolfus and acknowledged Guaimarius as their sovereign. In addition to territories taken for the Salernitan prince by the Normans, the German emperor Conrad added to Prince Guaimarius's power in 1038 when he gave him control over Capua in order to punish the

---

[101] *Chron. Sal.*, 180–84, chaps. 178–83. Cilento, *Le origini*, 149; Schipa, *Storia*, 162–67.

[102] Schipa, *Storia*, 168–70; von Falkenhausen, "I Longobardi," 277–79.

Capuan prince Pandolfus, who had captured Gaeta and molested the imperial abbey of Montecassino. Between 1043–47, Guaimarius IV signed his documents as "prince of Salerno and Capua, duke of Amalfi and Sorrento, and duke of Calabria and Apulia."[103]

Guaimarius IV's extensive power was more illusory than real, based on the abilities and generosities of others, and by 1050 he had lost almost all the territories gained. In 1047, Henry III came to Italy, took Capua from Guaimarius, and gave it back to Pandolfus. In addition, the emperor gave Norman leaders the lands they had conquered in Campania, Apulia, and Calabria, including some areas in the southern part of the Principality of Salerno.[104] By this time, the Normans' political power had grown considerably, as their leaders slowly established themselves as rulers in their own right. In 1030 Rainolf received Aversa from the duke of Naples, and in 1042 the Normans divided conquered lands in Apulia and Calabria among themselves, acknowledging Guaimarius IV as their sovereign but exercising power independently.[105] Henry's concession of territories to the two Norman leaders, Rainolf and Drogo, merely served to legitimize the power which the two already possessed. The Normans were slowly taking control of southern Italy, and it was only a matter of decades before Drogo's brother, the powerful Robert Guiscard, would oust Prince Guaimarius IV and add the Principality of Salerno to his newly formed Duchy of Apulia, ending the rule of Lombard princes forever.

---

[103] For a description of the reigns of Princes Guaimarius III and IV, see Ferdinand Chalandon, *Histoire de la domination normande en Italie méridionale et en Sicile* (Paris: A. Picard, 1907), 48–52, 80–87, 104–15; von Falkenhausen, "I Longobardi," 283; and G. A. Loud, *The Age of Robert Guiscard: Southern Italy and the Norman Conquest* (Harlow: Pearson, 2000), 74–77, 102–9.

[104] von Falkenhausen, "I Longobardi," 284; Loud, *The Age of Robert Guiscard*, 106–07.

[105] Loud, *The Age of Robert Guiscard*, 74–75, 97–107.

CHAPTER 2

Religious Authority and Ecclesiastical Organization before Centralization

Christianity in Late Antiquity

Little is known about the spread of Christianity and the establishment of bishops in the cities of southern Campania. Before the Lombard conquest at the end of the sixth century, there are scattered references to bishoprics in a few cities, including Salerno, Paestum, Nocera, Marcellianum, Velia, Buxentum (Policastro), and Agropoli.[1] Papal estates spread throughout southern Italy, including parts of Lucania, provided important revenues to the papacy and required the help of local clerics to oversee.[2] Nonetheless, Christianization appears to have been a slow process in the province of Salerno, especially outside of urban areas. The small number of bishops and churches in late antiquity points to limited episcopal influence outside of major cities and a rural population that was either still pagan or only nominally Christian. Overall the evidence points to an ecclesiastical organization that was both fragile and incomplete, and there is no evidence for a well-organized episcopal hierarchy in the late Roman period.[3]

As in other areas of Italy, widespread Christianization in southern Italy dates from the Lombard period. Pope Gregory I sent missionaries to the region in the 590s, while local hagiographical sources attribute mass conver-

---

[1] C. D. Fonseca, "Aspetti istituzionali dell'organizzazione ecclesiastica meridionale dal VI al IX Secolo," in *Particolarismo Istituzionale e Organizzazione Ecclesiastica del Mezzogiorno Medievale* (Galatina: Congedo Editore, 1987), 5.

[2] Jeffrey Richards, *The Popes and the Papacy in the Early Middle Ages, 476–752* (London: Routledge and Kegan Paul, 1979), 312.

[3] Vitolo, "Vescovi e Diocesi," 86–89.

sions to bishops such as Barbatus of Benevento and Decorosus of Capua, who began a crusade against paganism in the second half of the seventh century.[4] In the Principality of Salerno, evidence for Christianity in rural areas comes to light in the eighth and ninth centuries with the appearance of anchoritic communities in caves and forests, often founded by ascetics from Byzantine regions, and of small religious houses in both city and countryside, constructed mostly by local families and *consortia* for the religious needs of their communities. As a result, the bishops of Salerno were not necessarily the primary factor in the spread of Christianity to the rural population. Moreover, the religious organization that arose in the province in the Lombard era, similar to other regions of southern Italy, had little connection to the ecclesiastical institutions of the Roman period.[5]

In many cities throughout Europe and the Mediterranean, bishops in the late antique period took over important political functions which formerly had been exercised by civil administrators. The letters of Pope Gregory I, for example, show the Roman bishop paying imperial troops, appointing military commanders, negotiating treaties, ransoming prisoners, and providing aid to the population of Italy in times of crisis. Also in other cities in Italy and Gaul bishops filled the power gap when secular Roman administrative offices disappeared.[6] Justinian's Code itself gave bishops oversight over local administration and allowed them to participate in the selection of provincial governors. It also required bishops to oversee prisoners, orphans, foundlings, and the mentally deranged; to supervise civic expenditure, public works, aqueduct maintenance, and public order; to supply the troops with food; to report criminals and lawbreakers to the emperor; and to bring the complaints of the people to the emperor.[7] In Frankish territories, bishops were given authority over a broad range of issues within their dioceses, including economic policy, lay morality, and the legal system, and as a result the episcopate in Frankish regions developed into an extremely powerful office during the late antique and early medieval era, with bishops exercising political, religious, and economic power simultaneously.[8]

---

[4] Palmieri, "Duchi," 62; Vitolo, *Vescovi e Diocesi*, 92.

[5] Martin, "L'ambiente," 197.

[6] Richards, chap. 19 in *The Popes and the Papacy*; Azzara, "Ecclesiastical Institutions," 87–8; Wallace-Hadrill, *The Frankish Church*, 2; Wickham, *Early Medieval Italy*, 18–19.

[7] Richards, *The Popes and the Papacy*, 323. Also in his Pragmatic Sanction for Italy, Justinian required bishops to participate in the choice of new provincial governors.

[8] See, in particular, the Council of Aachen held in 789 and the Synod of Paris held in 829. Later Carolingian councils reinforced and expanded episcopal authority. Wallace-Hadrill, *The Frankish Church*, 279; Emile Amann, *L'époque carolingienne*, vol.

In southern Italy, in contrast, bishops in late antiquity saw their office weaken or disappear. Numerous episcopates documented in the Roman period did not survive into the sixth and seventh centuries.[9] In the Principality of Salerno five out of seven bishoprics vanished, while the bishop of Peastum was forced to relocate inland to Capaccio sometime in the ninth or tenth century.[10] The cathedral church of Salerno alone had an uninterrupted history. Thus, with very few exceptions, the bishops of southern Italy failed to establish and consolidate their power with the disappearance of Roman imperial government. Although in northern and central Italy bishoprics also disappeared in many places, most of these were re-established under Carolingian rule, and were then used by kings and emperors to help administer their kingdom.[11] In southern Italy, by contrast, Lombard rulers did not place bishops in positions of power, and many of the episcopal seats remained vacant until the eleventh century, while some were never resurrected.

Traditionally historians blamed the Lombards for the destruction of the episcopate, claiming that their adherence to the Arian faith led to an anti-Catholic program and the construction of a rival Arian church organization. Today most historians date the disappearance of the majority of bishoprics to before the Lombard conquest and link it to the abandonment of cities.[12] The five bishops that vanished in the province of Salerno—in Nocera, Marcellianum, Velia, Buxentum (Policastro), and Agropoli—all resided in towns that were abandoned in late antiquity. Yet as the populations of these cities moved to new areas, the question remains why the bishops did not move with them, as occurred with the bishop of Paestum when his town relocated

---

6 of *Histoire de l'Eglise depuis les origines jusqu'à nos jours* (Paris: Bloud and Gay, 1937), 75; R. W. Southern, *Western Society and the Church in the Middle Ages* (Harmdonsworth: Penguin Books, 1970), 173–77; Hartmann, *Die Synoden*, 103–04, 463–67.

9 Gian Piero Bognetti, "La continuità delle sedi episcopali e l'azione di Roma nel Regno longobardo," in *Le Chiese nei regni dell'Europa occidentale e i loro rapporti con Roma sino all'800: Settimana di studi del centro italiano di studi sull'alto medioevo, 7–13 April 1959*, (Spoleto: Centro Italiano di Studi sull'Alto Medioevo, 1960), 7: 415–54; Raffaele Calvino, *Diocesi scomparse in Campania* (Naples: F. Fiorentino, 1969); Fonseca, "Aspetti istituzionali," 3–13; Vitolo, "Vescovi e Diocesi," 75–86. For a detailed look at the episcopate in Apulia, see Martin, *La Pouille*, 242–46. For the Abruzzi, see Feller, *Les Abruzzes*, 118.

10 The bishop in Capaccio, however, continued to refer to himself as bishop of Paestum up through the mid-twelfth century. Paolo Delogu, "Storia del sito," in *Caput Aquis Medievale* (Salerno: P. Laveglia, 1976), 23–24.

11 Bognetti, "La continuità delle sedi episcopali," 415–16; Miller, *The Formation*, 144–46.

12 Bognetti, "La continuità delle sedi episcopali," 419; Fonseca, "Aspetti istituzionali," 3–13; Vitolo, "Vescovi e Diocesi," 75; Palmieri, "Duchi," 46.

to the hilltop village of Capaccio. The example of Nocera is particularly telling. When the city was torn down and then rebuilt soon after, the cathedral church was not resurrected in the new location.[13] Either the populations of these episcopal cities were not heavily Christianized, or the Christians did not feel it necessary to have bishops to minister to their religious needs in their new homes.

Papal policy may also have played a role in the disappearance of bishoprics.[14] In southern Italy and Sicily the activities of bishops were closely connected to the papacy and the management of papal estates, and up through the end of Gregory I's reign, popes actively participated in the day-to-day affairs of these bishoprics. They supervised episcopal elections, ordained newly elected bishops, and at times even involved themselves directly in the election of a new bishop, handpicking a local or Roman candidate. They served as judges for the clergy and decided almost all the important cases that involved clerics. They called councils that included prelates from all areas of Italy, including Salerno and other cities that were later conquered by the Lombards. They also appointed rectors to manage their vast patrimony in the region as well as to oversee religious matters such as ecclesiastical appointments and clerical discipline.[15]

Beginning in the seventh century, popes began to turn their backs on southern Italy, and only sporadic contact occurred between the papacy and southern Italian prelates in the eighth and ninth centuries, especially in Lombard territories. Many reasons account for this lack of interest, including the conquest of southern Italy by the Lombards in the late sixth and early seventh century, as well as the threat posed by the new Lombard rulers based in Pavia, who continually attacked papal territories throughout the seventh and eighth centuries. Equally important was the loss of the papal estates in southern Italy and Sicily, which had been a vital source of revenue in the time of Gregory I.[16]

---

[13] Peduto, "Insediamenti altomedievali," 441–43.

[14] Brown, *The Rise of Christendom*, 113–14.

[15] For information on the early medieval papacy, see Richard, *The Popes and the Papacy*; R. A. Markus, *Gregory the Great and His World* (Cambridge: Cambridge University Press, 1997); Peter Llewellyn, *Rome in the Dark Ages* (London: Faber, 1971); Walter Ullmann, *A Short History of the Papacy in the Middle Ages*, 2nd ed. (London/New York: Routledge, 2003); Thomas F. X. Noble, *The Republic of St. Peter: The Birth of the Papal State, 680–825* (Philadelphia: University of Pennsylvania Press, 1984). Useful short studies include Arnaldi, "Profilo di storia della Chiesa," and Claudio Azzara, "The Papacy," in *Italy in the Early Middle Ages*, 102–17.

[16] Most historians place the date of the confiscation to 732–33. Richards, *The Popes and the Papacy*, 309–13; Llewellyn, *Rome in the Dark Ages*, 168–69; M. V. Anastos, "The Transfer of Illyricum, Calabria, and Sicily," *Studi Bizantini e Neoellenici* 9

These estates had allowed popes to exercise important political and economic power in Sicily, Calabria, Lucania, and Campania, and as the papacy lost control over them in the seventh and eighth centuries, because of the Lombard conquests as well as the policy of the emperors in Constantinople, the region as a whole became less significant. It also meant that bishops in areas such as the province of Salerno lost a primary function. Finally, as Byzantine emperors in the seventh and eighth centuries began to concentrate their military resources in eastern provinces, because of the danger posed by Arab armies that were threatening Constantinople itself, the papacy was left to fend for itself. With the loss of imperial support and pressure from the Lombards mounting, the papacy asked Frankish rulers for aid in the mid-eighth century.[17] From this point forward, popes turned their attention north toward the Carolingian empire, and as a result they had little contact with southern Italian territories in the eighth through tenth centuries. Bishops in the area thus lost their primary patron.

Throughout the early Middle Ages, the pope theoretically could claim control over key aspects of church organization in southern Italy, including the authority to judge southern Italian clerics and the right to supervise episcopal elections and consecrate in Rome the bishops elected by the clergy and *populus*.[18] Before the eleventh century, however, the pope rarely, if ever, exercised either right. Moreover, Roman synods seldom included clergy from southern Italian territories and papal representatives hardly ever traveled south. The bishops of Salerno did not participate in Roman councils before the eleventh century, nor is there any evidence that they attended local councils held in southern Italian Lombard territories. In addition, the clerics and bishops in the Principality of Salerno did not follow the rules laid down by popes in councils. As a result papal regulations regarding church organization and clerical behavior did not influence religious life in the Principality of Salerno in the early medieval period. From the death of Gregory I in 604 until the 980s when the pope raised Salerno to the rank of a metropolitan, little contact or communication took place between the bishops in Salerno and the papacy.[19] Instead bishops and clerics in southern

---

(1954): 14–31. The pope, however, did retain estates in northern Campania, in and around Naples, Gaeta, Misenum, and Sorrento, and on Capri.

[17] As early as 577, Emperor Justin II suggested to Pope Benedict I (575–79) that he seek aid from disgruntled Lombards or from the Franks who ruled in Gaul. Richards, *The Popes and the Papacy*, 165.

[18] Richards, *The Popes and the Papacy*, 333–34.

[19] Norbert Kamp has aptly called the early Middle Ages the time of "papal passivity" in southern Italy. Norbert Kamp, "Vescovi e diocesi nell'Italia meridionale nel passaggio della dominazione bizantina allo stato normanno," in *Il passaggio dal do-*

Italy relied on local support for privileges and aid, and traditions and customs developed regionally, often in contrast to papal ideas and trends in Carolingian territories.

Bishops under Lombard Rule

When the Lombards conquered and settled in southern Italy, they did not integrate bishops into the political or religious structures of their kingdom as Frankish rulers did. Instead the Lombard dukes used secular officials to administer their realms, and the gastalds, who were their main officials, were generally placed in cities that never had a bishop at all. The dukes themselves personally provided guardianship over the religious houses and clergy in their Duchy; additionally, they created ecclesiastical networks that mostly bypassed bishops and cathedral churches, relying instead upon princely foundations, proprietary churches, and monasteries to provide for pastoral care.[20]

It is unclear why, exactly, the Lombard dukes did not integrate bishops into their new administration. It could have been because they professed a different form of Christianity or because they were only nominally Christian when they arrived, still hanging on to old pagan beliefs and practices while at the same time venerating the Christian God.[21] However, the same is also true of the Merovingian kings, who nonetheless developed a close relationship to bishops and episcopal power early on. Perhaps it was because bishops in southern Italy refused to acknowledge the Lombards as rulers at the beginning, or as a consequence of the antagonism between the Lombards and the papacy.[22] However, bishops in southern Campania may have never developed the type of political power characteristic of bishops in Gaul and other places, where the landed aristocracy took over the government of urban churches in the late Roman era.[23] As a result, the Lombard conquerors, while not necessarily persecuting the bishops, may have simply ignored them as they began to organize the governmental and religious structures of their new kingdom because of the weakness of the episcopate in

---

minio bizantino allo stato normanno nell'Italia meridionale. Atti del II Convegno internazionale di studi sulla civiltà rupestre medioevale nel Mezzogiorno d'Italia, Taranto-Mottola, 31 October–4 November 1973 (Taranto: Amministrazione provinciale, 1977), 166.

[20] Martin, *La Pouille*, 235–38, 242; Palmieri, "Duchi," 65.

[21] Palmieri, "Duchi," 60–62.

[22] Ibid., 59–60; Everett, *Literacy in Lombard Italy*, 82–83.

[23] Brown, *The Rise of Christendom*, 64, 134.

most cities in southern Italy by the time of their arrival.[24] Although the motivations are obscure, the results are clear: bishops took on key roles in neither the religious nor political sphere.

After the Lombard dukes of Benevento converted to Catholicism at the end of the seventh century, ducal and episcopal power became more closely linked. Duke Romoaldus I (671–87), for example, placed the important Lombard sanctuary of San Michele in Gargano under the authority of the bishop of Benevento, and in the eighth century, perhaps in response to the Carolingian conquest of the Kingdom of Pavia, bishops in the Lombard capital began to preside over important religious ceremonies in Benevento in imitation of Byzantine observances, and even began to participate in coronations. Under Prince Arechis II (758–87) the bishop of Benevento took on the title of "orator," meaning the one who prays for the prince and the Lombard people.[25] Bishops from this time on were generally drawn from princely families or the aristocracy, and in a few instances rulers in the ninth century even combined religious and political authority.[26] Yet examples of bishops in Lombard southern Italy occupying positions of political power are rare. The number of bishoprics in the area remained small throughout the Lombard period, and bishops never stood at the center of religious life or organization, except within their city walls.

In the Carolingian empire, a centralized and hierarchical church organization emerged in which, at least in theory, archbishops exercised control over suffragan bishops, who then looked after the priests and clerics in their dioceses.[27] Bishops were also given a monopoly on certain religious functions, such as baptism, penance, and the collection of the tithe. For example, the Synod of Pavia, held in c. 845–50, gave bishops in the Kingdom of Italy power over lesser churches, called "minores tituli," or parish churches, all of which contained a baptistery. The archpriests who operated these baptismal churches administered the penitential system and had authority over other rural priests in their districts in the same way the bishops exercised power over them. Moreover, laypeople were specifically forbidden from holding these baptismal churches, giving the bishop alone the right to oversee the administration of this sacrament. In addition, the Carolingian rulers as-

---

[24] Palmieri, "Duchi," 60–62.

[25] Ibid., 70–76, 78–83.

[26] For example, Landolfus II simultaneously held the offices of both count and bishop in Capua from 851 to 879 and Athanasius was both duke and bishop in Naples from 878 to 898. Palmieri, "Duchi," 84; Carmela Russo Mailler, *Il Medioevo a Napoli nell'età ducale (sec. VI–1140)* (Salerno: Università degli Studi di Salerno, 1988), 66.

[27] See, for example, the Council of Verneuil in 755, the Council of Herstal in 779, and the Council of Frankfurt in 794. Hartmann, *Die Synoden*, 68–72, 99–101, 105–15.

signed a compulsory tax, or tithe to the bishops in the Kingdom of Italy, owed by all inhabitants.[28] As a result, legislation in northern and central Italy gave bishops authority over a system of parish churches in their dioceses, assigned them a tithe to support their activities, and granted them a monopoly over certain religious rites, such as baptism and penance. Even if the reality did not always fit the ideal, and evidence does, in fact, show that at times proprietary churches outside episcopal authority functioned as baptisteries and received tithes—at least, the bishops had a theoretical claim to these rights.[29]

In Lombard southern Italy, bishops were never given authority over a system of parish churches or a monopoly over certain religious functions. Instead Lombard rulers relied on other types of institutions to oversee religious life. In some cases they endowed and empowered monasteries to oversee religious organization. Large abbeys in northern Campania, such as Montecassino, San Vincenzo al Volturno, and Santa Sofia of Benevento, all rose to prominence at this time due to the patronage of the Lombard dukes.[30] Smaller monasteries in many areas of southern Italy, including the southern part of the Principality of Salerno, similarly took on a prominent role in the religious life and organization of their territories, providing for the pastoral needs of rural areas.[31] In other cases, either princely foundations or private churches provided pastoral care. Although regional variations did exist, nowhere in southern Italy did the bishops enjoy the powers that their counterparts in Carolingian territories did. Cathedral churches throughout Lombard southern Italy tended to be small and weak with extremely limited economic resources, and bishops never created networks of parish churches, never established a universal tithe in their diocese, and never built up large patrimonies as occurred in northern and central Italy.[32]

---

[28] Catherine E. Boyd, *Tithes and Parishes in Medieval Italy: The Historical Roots of a Modern Problem* (Ithaca: Cornell University Press, 1952), 58–59, 80–82.

[29] Boyd, *Tithes and Parishes*, 64, 81–82.

[30] For the foundation of Montecassino, see H. E. J. Cowdrey, *The Age of Abbot Desiderius: Montecassino, the Papacy, and the Normans in the Eleventh and Twelfth Centuries* (Oxford: Clarendon Press, 1983), 2–3 and von Falkenhausen, "I Longobardi meridionali," 316–18; for San Vincenzo al Volturno, see Richard Hodges, *Light in the Dark Ages: The Rise and Fall of San Vincenzo al Volturno* (Ithaca: Cornell University Press, 1997), 23–29, and for Santa Sofia, see G. A. Loud, "A Lombard Abbey in a Norman World: St Sophia, Benevento, 1050–1200," *Anglo-Norman Studies* 19 (1996): 278–79.

[31] This is true for Apulia, the Abruzzi, and various parts of Campania. In Apulia, in fact, the office of abbot-bishop emerged as early as the eleventh century. Martin, *La Pouille*, 659; Feller, *Les Abruzzes*, 819–20; Loud, "A Lombard Abbey," 273.

[32] For general studies of southern Italian dioceses in the early medieval period, see Martin, "L'ambiente"; Hans-Walter Klewitz, "Zur Geschichte der Bistumsor-

Monasteries, princely foundations, and proprietary houses became the main foci of religious life in the Lombard period.

Bishops in southern Italy also did not as a rule form the backbone of political administration since Lombard rulers relied on secular officials to govern their realms. Although they were found among the court elite whose role it was to advise and aid the princes, and were in many cases close relatives of the princes, they were never given specific political duties in their cities or dioceses.[33] They could, at times, take on political roles.[34] However, such a situation depended upon the ambition and abilities of one particular man, rather than a well-established tradition of precise political functions. Moreover, bishops in Lombard southern Italy, as other clerics, were legally integrated into secular society, and although they exercised spiritual prestige, at least from the second half of the seventh century onward, they received no special legal privileges in the Lombard law codes.[35] The never formed a separate *ordo*, and, as a result, never developed a group identity or acted as a cohesive force, as occurred in Carolingian territories.[36] There are few examples of episcopal saints in Italy before 800, and the image of the charismatic holy man, typical of the Mediterranean region in late antiquity, remained the ideal in southern Italy up through the eleventh century.[37]

Rulership in southern Italy was of a secular nature, resembling the Byzantine more than the Carolingian empire where a theocratic ideal emerged. Whereas ritual in Francia was first and foremost sacred, in Constantinople political celebrations were organized by lay officials and set in secular surroundings.[38] Carolingian kings received unction at the hands of the bishops and used liturgy—in particular, grand scale prayers and mass celebrations in honor of the king and his family—to bind together their empire and promote the concept of a *populus Christianus*.[39] Lombard princes in southern Italy, to the contrary, did not use Christianity as a unifying factor in the same way; they did not push their subjects to convert to Christianity or adhere to certain liturgical practices. Moreover, in Salerno and Lombard southern Italy in general, bishops do not appear as intermediaries in the leg-

---

ganisation Campaniens und Apuliens im 10. und 11. Jahrhundert," *Quellen und Forschungen aus italienischen Archiven und Bibliotheken* 24 (1932–33): 1–61; and Vitolo, "Vescovi e Diocesi."

[33] Martin, "L'ambiente," 218–19; Palmieri, "Duchi," 77.

[34] Palmieri, "Duchi," 79–84.

[35] Ibid., 77.

[36] Wallace-Hadrill, *The Frankish Church*, 176.

[37] Brown, *The Rise of Western Christendom*, 116–18; Antonio Vuolo, "Agriografia beneventana," in *Longobardia e longobardi*, 199–237; Martin, *La Pouille*, 248–49.

[38] McCormick, *Eternal Victory*, 366.

[39] Hen, *The Royal Patronage*, 89–99.

ends and rituals surrounding princely power. Direct signs from God, either miracles or military victory, demonstrated a ruler's divine favor.[40] Although the princes of Salerno did portray themselves as the protectors of churches and clerics, as well as the builders of religious houses and the guardians of saints and their relics, religious unity and liturgical celebrations played a secondary role. Even as late as the eleventh century, and even in the writings of the great church reformer, the archbishop of Salerno Alfanus I, the almost purely secular nature of rulership can be seen. In his eulogies written for Prince Gisolf II and his brother Guido, Alfanus alluded solely to ancient Roman precedents and political ideals, claiming that all virtue found in the world stemmed from Roman integrity and law. He encouraged Gisolf to repeat the acts of Caesar and even declared that under his father's rule Salerno came to outshine ancient Rome itself. No religious or biblical references are found in the poems at all.[41]

The situation of the bishop of Salerno was thus typical for the region. He never took over political power in his city and never played an important administrative role in the Principality. Episcopal power rarely extended beyond the city, and bishops did not claim supervisory rights over the churches or clerics in their diocese. Although bishops occupied a special place in the religious life of the city, they neither headed a territorial diocesan system nor controlled a system of parish churches, acting instead as a leader of the faithful as opposed to the head of a territory. In fact the vast majority of ecclesiastical foundations were outside his authority and only a few churches were directly dependent on him. Moreover, no precise definition of episcopal responsibilities emerges in the documents for early medieval Salerno, and it appears that the episcopal office at this time carried with it no well-defined duties. In addition, the wealth of the cathedral church of Salerno paled in comparison with bishops in northern and central Italy. Up until the eleventh century, the cathedral church in Salerno remained an extremely weak institution, and the limited powers and activities of the bishops are reflected in the almost complete lack of documentation in the episcopal archives before 1100.[42] Only in the second half of the eleventh

---

[40] Taviani-Carozzi, *La Principauté*, 209–11.

[41] Alfanus I, *I Carmi di Alfano I*, ed. Anselmo Lentini and Faustino Avagliano, vol. 38 of *Miscellanea Cassinese* (Montecassino: M. Pisani, 1974), 143–44, no. 17 and 150–52, no. 20.

[42] The archbishop had no chancery prior to the eleventh century, and his written acts carried no real institutional authority since they differed little from charters written at the request of laypeople. Galante, "La documentazione vescovile," 226–30. For a chronological study of the early bishops of Salerno, including discussions of the available sources, see Giuseppe Paesano, vols. 1–2 of *Memorie per servire alla storia della chiesa salernitana* (Naples: V. Manfredi, 1846) and Generoso Crisci, vol. 1

century would the archbishop of Salerno begin to claim authority over religious organization in his diocese and to take on administrative functions for the new Norman rulers, a situation familiar in the Carolingian world but novel for Salerno and its surrounding territories.

Bernard, who headed the See of Salerno c. 849–60, provides a good example of a typical early medieval bishop in Salerno. Our information on Bernard comes from the Anonymous Chronicle of Salerno, whose author depicts Bernard as a pious man who spent his days reciting the holy office and his nights in prayer. He also spent much time and energy on building activities and the translation of saints' bodies to Salerno. He finished the lavish church dedicated to John the Baptist that his predecessor Radoaldus had begun, providing it with a new ciborium and decorating it with beautiful paintings. He constructed a church dedicated to San Salvatore and added a bell tower to the cathedral church. He brought the bodies of the martyrs Fortunatus, Gaius, and Anthes to the city when a Muslim attack threatened them in their resting place on the Irno river. He also retrieved the bodies of Cirinus and Quingesius from Faianus and brought them to Salerno, building a new church for them as well. The city rejoiced as both saints began to perform miracles for the population. Moreover, Bernard himself joined the ranks of the elect upon his death, and he even had a vision of this while praying in the cathedral church one evening: the Virgin Mary came to him and told him that she had interceded on his behalf, asking Christ her son and God to accept him among the saints. Afterward she took him on a visit to heaven. A large crowd witnessed this miraculous event and when Bernard awoke from his vision he was picked up off the church floor and carried back to his house with great joy and reverence. For the author Bernard was worthy of veneration because of his piety, his building activity, and his translations of relics to the city.[43]

Bishop Bernard did not participate in political events, with the exception of a minor protest he embarked upon when Prince Sico (849–56) received a Muslim ambassador in the city. According to the chronicler, when the bishop heard of the ambassador's imminent visit to Salerno, and the prince's plan to lodge the ambassador in the bishop's residence, he became angry and left the city for Rome. The prince begged the bishop to come back, and Bernard agreed to do so, but only on the condition that the prince build him

---

of *Il cammino della Chiesa salernitana nell'opera dei suoi vescovi* (Naples/Rome: Libreria Editrice Redenzione, 1976). For a list of documents relating to the cathedral church of Salerno in the Lombard period, see Antonio Balducci, *L'Archivio Diocesano di Salerno: Cenni sull'Archivio del Capitolo Metropolitano* (Salerno: Camera di Commercio, Industria e Agricoltura, 1959), 1:3–9 and Galante, "La documentazione vescovile," 247–50.

[43] *Chron. Sal.*, 97–99, chaps. 97–98.

a new house.[44] In the end, the prince received the ambassador but also built a new house for the bishop to appease him. Thus Bernard's protest did not influence the prince's political activity.

Similarly, other bishops of Salerno in the Anonymous Chronicle rarely participated in political affairs, and when they did, they served in a purely advisory role. The bishops clearly belonged to the prince's entourage, the group of men referred to as *consangunei*, *fideles*, and *optimates* by the chronicle's author, which included counts, gastalds, generals, ambassadors, and other leading citizens, as well as bishops. These men served the prince in the highest military and political capacities and participated actively in his decisions. However, the office of the bishop was not the most prominent one, and rarely do we see bishops acting decisively in the Anonymous Chronicle, as counts and gastalds did. The image of the ideal bishop that emerges in early medieval literature in Salerno is one based on an ascetic lifestyle and mystical powers, and bishops never turn up as political or military figures, as they do in Frankish chronicles, nor do they appear as protectors of the city. Even during the brutal siege of Salerno by Muslims in 871, described in great detail in the Anonymous Chronicle, the bishop took no role.[45] Advice to the prince or a weak show of protest marked the limits of episcopal influence over politics in the Anonymous Chronicle of Salerno.

Although the bishop played a prominent role in the religious life of Salerno itself, outside the city limits, the bishop of Salerno did not actively participate in ecclesiastical affairs. The majority of religious houses were founded and administered by others. Only in a few cases did the bishop show up in possession of religious foundations outside the city, and when he did so it was generally in order to give them to others to restore.[46] As in other regions of southern Italy, bishops claimed power over dependent churches in the same manner as laypeople who built and administered proprietary houses.[47] Nonetheless, the bishops of Salerno and Paestum did grant emancipation charters to a small number of ecclesiastical foundations in the early medieval period, mostly in the late tenth to mid-eleventh century.[48] In these charters, the bishops and archbishops exempted the religious

---

[44] *Chron. Sal.*, 99–101, chap. 99.

[45] *Chron. Sal.*, 123–32, chaps. 111–18.

[46] In 940, for example, the bishop of Salerno gave a dilapidated church to three brothers from Amalfi to restore and administer, while in 979 the bishop of Salerno handed over an abandoned church on a hill above Salerno to a nun named Sosanna to restore and turn into a convent. CDC 1: 212–18, no. 169; CDC 2: 137–38, no. 317.

[47] Martin, *La Pouille*, 242.

[48] Seven *chartae libertatis* issued by the bishops and archbishops of Salerno survive, dated between 882 and 1050, while two emancipation charters from the mid-eleventh century, redacted by the bishop of Paestum, remain. For the bishops and

houses from episcopal authority, giving the church owners and their heirs the authority to appoint clergy and to administer the foundation's patrimony, and promising to demand neither dues nor services from the clergy or the owners. In at least one case, a bishop specifically stated that he could not excommunicate the church's clergy.[49] The only rights the bishops reserved for themselves in the emancipation charters were the duties to reconsecrate contaminated altars and to provide the consecrated host, chrism, and holy oil on certain religious holidays free of charge.

In their emancipation charters the bishops and archbishops conceded many rights usually reserved exclusively for parish churches in northern Italy. For example, in 983 the bishop of Salerno granted the priests of Santa Maria in Vietri the authority to baptize, visit the sick, and bury the dead, while in 1005 he gave similar rights to the clergy of the church of San Nicola in Pontecagnano. In at least four cases, the clergy exercised the full functions of a cathedral church. Documents for Santa Maria de Domno, Santa Maria in Vietri, San Preparazione in Corneto, and San Matteo in Subarci specifically mentioned that the clergy would perform baptisms, communions, burials, and visitations, bless and sanctify water and baptismal fonts, lead processions, and sprinkle holy water and place crosses in nearby houses.[50] In the case of San Preparazione, the clerics were also given the right to lead the solemn procession of penance during the period of Easter, one of the most important religious ceremonies in the region beginning in the eighth century. For other ecclesiastical foundations, the large invento-

---

archbishops of Salerno: CDC 1: 111–12, no. 87 issued in 882 to San Massimo; CDC 2: 64–6, no. 263 issued in 970 to SS Matteo and Tomaso; CDC 2: 272–74, no. 412 issued in 989 to Santa Maria de Domno; CDC 6: 40–42, no. 898 issued in 1005 to Santa Maria in Vietri, with date corrected by Galante, *La Datazione*, 57–58, no. 36; CDC 4: 132–35, no. 614 issued in 1009 to San Nicola in Tostaccio (Nocera); Mensa register, I, 589–91, a seventeenth-century copy of a 1005 *charta libertatis* issued to San Nicola in Pontecagnano (edition in Maria Galante, "La documentazione vescovile salernitana: aspetti e problemi," in *Scrittura e produzione documentaria nel Mezzogiorno longobardo. Atti del Convegno internazionale di studio, Badia di Cava, 3–5 October 1990*, ed. Giovanni Vitolo and Francesco Mottola (Salerno: Edizioni 10/17, 1991), 251–53); CDC 7: 147–49, no. 1146 issued in 1050 to Santa Lucia in Balnearia. Also a 996 document for San Nicola of Gallocanta mentions a *chartula libertatis* issued from the bishop of Salerno to Marinus, the founder, in 989. CDC 3: 59–54, no. 494 (Cherubini, 126–29, no. 30). For the bishops of Paestum: CDC 7: 49–50, no. 1086 issued in 1047 to San Preparazione in Corneto; CDC 7: 221–23, no. 1194 issued in 1054 to San Matteo in Subarci. For a paleographical analysis of the emancipation charters, see Galante, "La documentazione vescovile," 227–29 and 234–35.

[49] CDC 7: 221–23, no. 1194.

[50] CDC 2: 272–74, no. 412, CDC 6: 40–42, no. 898, with date corrected by Galante, *La Datazione*, 57–58, no. 36, CDC 7: 49–50, no. 1086, CDC 7: 221–23, no. 1194.

ries of gowns, books, and other religious items suggest that they, too, performed similar duties. San Giovanni in Vietri, San Giovanni in Tresino, Santa Maria in Vietri, Sant'Adiutore in Nocera, San Nicola in Priato, Sant'Andrea in Arcelle, Sant'Angelo in Capaccio, SS Maria and Nicola in Mercatello, San Michele Arcangelo in Passiano, and San Nicola in Gallocanta all contained either antiphonaries or liturgical gowns associated with parish churches.[51] An archaeological excavation of the church of San Lorenzo in Altavilla Silentina has revealed a baptismal font, giving proof of another baptismal church outside episcopal authority.[52]

In many cases proprietary churches exercising the full range of parochial duties were located outside the cities of Salerno and Paestum, so perhaps the bishops had no churches there to perform these functions. However, the churches of San Massimo, SS Matteo and Tomaso, and Santa Maria de Domno were all located in Salerno not far from the cathedral church itself, and like ecclesiastical foundations outside the city they were granted a wide range of religious functions. Particularly striking is the case of the princely foundation of Santa Maria de Domno, whose abbots were allowed to baptize, give communion, found other churches, visit the sick, give last rites, and bury the dead.

Although the bishops and archbishops of Salerno and Paestum renounced almost all authority over the ecclesiastical foundations and their clergy in these emancipations charters, by issuing the charters they also claimed the right to grant such privileges. Before the late tenth century, no ecclesiastical foundations sought episcopal permission or consecration, with the exception of the princely foundation of San Massimo. As a result, the *chartae libertatis* issued by the bishops and archbishops at this time represent the growth of episcopal authority in Salerno. They show the bishops taking an active interest in at least some of the new religious houses being built in their city and diocese. As a result, the exemptions can be seen as a mechanism of power enhancement, as has been shown to be the case in Frankish territories.[53] With regard to the princely foundations they demonstrate the important link between episcopal and princely power. Nonetheless, the small number of emancipation charters points once again to the weak authority of bishops in Salerno vis-à-vis their counterparts in Francia. Even

[51] CDC 2: 233–34, no. 382, CDC 4: 71–73, no. 582, CDC 6: 182–83, no. 990, CDC 7: 22–23, no. 1070, CDC 7: 33–34, no. 1077, CDC 7: 198–200, no. 1178, CDC 8: 38–40, no. 1258 (Cherubini, 197–200, no. 77), CDC 8: 208–12, no. 1345.

[52] Peduto, "Insediamenti altomedievali," 449–52.

[53] Barbara H. Rosenwein, *Negotiating Space: Power, Restraint, and Privileges of Immunity in Early Medieval Europe* (Ithaca: Cornell University Press, 1999), 6–8 and chapter 5.

taking into account the possibility that some emancipation charters issued by bishops and archbishops in the eighth through eleventh centuries have been lost, clearly not all of the founders of the hundreds of ecclesiastical foundations found in the Cava documents sought episcopal permission.[54] Although it is unclear why some churches received exemptions from bishops while others did not, what is clear is that the bishops of Salerno exercised little to no authority over the vast majority of religious houses in their diocese, and even in Salerno itself most religious foundations were under the power of others, often laypeople, who had little or no connection to the cathedral church.

The cathedral church was not a powerful economic force in early medieval Salerno, and the bishops in Salerno and Paestum played a negligible role in the expansion of agriculture which occurred in the Principality of Salerno in the late tenth and early eleventh century. For the bishop of Salerno, one agricultural contract alone survives, dated 978, on lands in Fuenti.[55] For the bishop of Paestum a single charter, dated 1020, mentions lands belonging to the cathedral church that were leased out.[56] Although the bishops, who tended to come from noble families and were often relatives of the prince, clearly had their own private wealth and led comfortable lives, the two cathedral churches had limited economic resources, especially in comparison with their counterparts in Carolingian territories. Similar to other regions of southern Italy in the Lombard era, the cathedral church of Salerno neither administered a vast patrimony nor had access to important economic resources.[57]

The bishop of Salerno in the early medieval period, as other bishops in southern Italy, did not operate on a territorial basis, but instead exercised his office through sacraments and liturgy.[58] Nonetheless sporadic evidence suggests that a nascent concept of territorial episcopal power developed among some prelates of early medieval southern Italy. For example, the 849 divi-

---

[54] Even as late as 1100 a document tells how Teodora, the widow of Pandolfus son of Prince Guaimarius, rebuilt the church of Santa Sofia in Salerno without episcopal consecration, because the church was old and in ruin. ("et ipsa ecclesia sancte sophie olim monasterium fuit et ob vetustate, cum in ruina posita esset ipsa genitrix mea divino adiuta auxilio a fundamenta eam delere et in meliorem et ampliore statu reedificare fecerat absque episcopali consecratione") Cava D, 28 (edition in P. Fedele, "I Conti del Tusculo ed i principi di Salerno," *Archivio della reale società romana storia patria* 28 (1905): 19–21).

[55] CDC 2: 119–20, no. 303.

[56] CDC 5: 24–26, no. 722.

[57] Martin, *La Pouille*, 242.

[58] Fonseca, "Aspetti istituzionali," 19–20; Vitolo, "Vescovi e Diocesi," 75; Palmieri, "Duchi," 77.

sion of the Lombard Duchy of Benevento between Radelchis and Sichenolf required all bishops and clerics to return to their dioceses, with the exception of those dependent on the palace. It also called for the return of all ecclesiastical revenues belonging to episcopal churches, monasteries, and ecclesiastical hospices (*xenodochia*) to their mother institutions ("ubi capita sunt earum"), with the exception of the imperial monasteries of Montecassino and San Vincenzo and abbeys pertaining to the palace.[59] In addition, a council held in the mid-ninth century somewhere in Lombard southern Italy insisted that churches be made subject to "plebes."[60] Although the precise meaning of "plebes" in this context is unclear, generally historians have translated it as either parishes or parish churches based on the word's meaning in other times and places. Two other regional synods held in the second half of the ninth century, the first one in either Siponto or Benevento sometime between 840 and 880 and the second one called in October of 887 by Teodosius the bishop of Oria, issued similar regulations,[61] and at the Benevento-Siponto council priests from one "plebs" were forbidden from collecting dues in a different "plebs."[62] At the same time, bishops throughout Lombard southern Italy began to issue emancipation charters, again suggesting the expectation that bishops should exercise some sort of author-

[59] MGH, *Legum* 4: 221–25. This has led at least two historians to hypothesize that ecclesiastical organization in southern Italy had a bipartite structure in the early Lombard period, with parish churches placed under episcopal authority and private foundations dependent on the prince. Fonseca, "Particolarismo istituzionale e organizzazione ecclesiastica delle campagne nell'Alto Medioevo nell'Italia meridionale," in *Cristianizzazione ed organizzazione ecclesiastica delle campagne nell'Alto Medioevo: espansione e resistenze: Settimana di studio del centro italiano di studi sull'alto medioevo* (Spoleto: Centro Italiano di Studi sull'Alto Medioevo, 1982), 28: 1169–70; Vitolo, "Vescovi e Diocesi," 98–99.

[60] ". . . aut plebetaniis in titulo subdantur, aut plebis nomine constituantur." "Un concile inédit tenu dans l'Italie méridionale à la fin du IXe siècle," ed. D. Germain Morin, *Révue Benedictine* 17 (1900): 147, canon XI. Both the date and the place of the council are unknown, although most historians place it in the mid-ninth century, based on paleographical analysis and the reference to the division of the Duchy. Most scholars have put the council in Benevento, while more recently Vitolo has argued for Capua and Martin for Naples. Vitolo, "Vescovi e Diocesi," 96–97; Martin, "L'ambiente," 214–15; Taviani-Carozzi, *La Principauté*, 652–54.

[61] For editions of the canons of the councils, see A. Amelli, "Acta Synodi Sipontinae Ecclesiae" and "Synodus Orietana," in *Spicilegium Casinense* (Montecassino, 1898), 1:388–93 and 1:377–81 and Charles Joseph Héfèle, *Histoire des Conciles d'après les documents originaux*, trans. H. Leclercq (Paris: Letouzey et Ané, 1910), 3/2: 1222–32.

[62] Amelli, "Acta Synodi," 392. For an excellent discussion and analysis of all three councils, see Vitolo, "Vescovi e Diocesi," 96–101.

ity over the churches in their dioceses.[63] In 839 the bishop of Benevento even claimed in a court case that the church of San Felice, a baptismal church, belonged to him by law, since church councils had legislated that all baptismal churches in a diocese were to be dependent on the bishop.[64] Unfortunately, the judge disagreed with him, and San Felice did not go under episcopal control.

Although the examples above suggest that starting in the mid-ninth century some bishops in Lombard southern Italy began to express an idea of territorial jurisdiction over churches in their dioceses, most likely because of renewed contact with the papacy, these claims were neither constant nor prevalent. Not only do all the documents mentioned assume the existence of religious houses outside episcopal control, but archival evidence shows that the vast majority of churches in southern Italy, including baptismal ones, remained outside episcopal authority. Bishops in southern Italy rarely opposed the numerous ecclesiastical foundations outside their power, and they issued few emancipation charters and consecrated few churches.[65] Whereas in northern Italy, bishops insisted on authority over baptismal churches, referred to as "plebes" in the documents, in southern Italy the exact meaning of "plebs" is difficult to establish on account of inconsistent usage.[66] As a result, in the documents from Salerno, episcopal claims over churches called "plebes" did not necessarily mean a claim over a system of parish churches. For example, when Prince Sichenolf conceded the "plebs" of Santa Maria in Nocera to the bishop of Salerno in 841, the reasons behind the donation are not expressed, and no evidence suggests that the bishop received the church based on a universal right to administer baptismal churches in his diocese.[67] Moreover, there is no evidence that the bishop of Salerno attended the ninth-century councils held in southern Italy

[63] Fonseca, "Particolarismo," 1170–73; Vitolo, "Vescovi e Diocesi," 95–101.

[64] Vitolo, "Vescovi e Diocesi," 103–4; Fonseca, "Particolarismo," 1163–65, 1174.

[65] For the most complete studies on episcopal emancipation charters in medieval southern Italy, see H.E. Feine, "Studien zum langobardisch-italienischen Eigenkirchenrecht," pt. 2, *Zeitschrift der Savigny-Stiftung für Rechtsgeschichte* 31 (1942): 1–105 and Bruno Ruggiero, "Per una storia della pieve rurale nel Mezzogiorno medievale," in *Potere, istituzioni, chiese locali: Aspetti e motivi del Mezzogiorno medievale dai Longobardi agli Angioini* (Bologna: Centro Salentino di Studi Medioevali Nardò, 1977), 59–87.

[66] According to Jean-Marie Martin, "plebs" did not refer to a regular institution, but rather was used to designate a church that theoretically could be dependent on a bishop. Martin, "L'ambiente," 222. Feller calls the word "polysèmique." Feller, *Les Abruzzes*, 800.

[67] Muratori, 3:77–78.

where some sort of territorial claims were put forth by the bishops in attendance. For Salerno no evidence from before 1000 shows the bishop asserting territorial jurisdiction over ecclesiastical foundations in his diocese.

The Religious Authority of Princes

The prince of Salerno in many ways exercised more authority over the ecclesiastical system of his principality than did the bishop. He served as protector for all the churches and monasteries throughout his principality and had the duty of safeguarding ecclesiastical patrimonies since, according to Lombard Law, alienation of ecclesiastical lands could be undertaken only through necessity, and the churches involved in exchanges or sales had to gain through the transaction. The prince often gave his permission when a religious house wished to exchange or sell land, and these charters specifically mentioned that the alienation would be beneficial to the religious house, as Lombard law demanded.[68] However, the prince's permission was not always necessary for such transactions.[69]

The bishops of Salerno and Paestum were also under the prince's protection, and in charters from Cava, the bishops consistently sought the prince's permission before proceeding with certain transactions. Land alienations as well as consecrations of new churches or monasteries required the prince's consent ("solutio," "absolutio"), and up until the mid-eleventh century, every sale or exchange executed by the bishops and all the consecrations of religious houses included the prince's authorization.[70] The prince, moreover, would send a representative to oversee the process, who was required to ensure that the action would be beneficial for the bishop before giving his approval.[71]

[68] See CDC 2: 34, no. 239; CDC 2: 289–95, no. 422; CDC 4: 59–64, no. 577; CDC 6: 191–93, no. 996; CDC 6: 240–43, no. 1025.

[69] See, for example, CDC 1: 193–94, no. 150; CDC 2: 41–2, no. 244; CDC 2: 320–21, no. 442; CDC 3: 6–7, no. 463; CDC 3: 20–22, no. 473; CDC 3: 105–07, no. 533; CDC 4: 152–54, no. 625.

[70] For the bishop of Salerno: CDC 1: 170–72, no. 133; CDC 1: 212–18, no. 169; CDC 1: 219–20, no. 170; CDC 2: 64–6, no. 263; CDC 2: 109–11, no. 297; CDC 2: 175–76, no. 345, with an edition in Galante, *La Datazione*, 186–91, no. 14; CDC 2: 185–86, no. 352; CDC 4: 132–35, no. 614; CDC 6: 40–42, no. 898, with date corrected by Galante, *La Datazione*, 57–58, no. 36; CDC 2: 325–27, no. 446. For the bishop of Paestum: CDC 1: 253–55, no. 197, with date corrected by Galante, *La Datazione*, 32, no. 11; CDC 2: 106–8, no. 296; CDC 2: 11–13, no. 299; CDC 2: 263–65, no. 406.

[71] According to the documents, the prince had to make sure that the transaction "was beneficial to our bishop" ("quod vonum ad pars nostri episcopii hebenirent").

Literary sources from Salerno depict the Lombard princes actively participating in ecclesiastical appointments. In the Anonymous Chronicle, for example, princes often appointed bishops, who were at times direct relations.[72] According to the *Life of the First Four Abbots of Cava*, Alferius, the founder of the abbey of Cava, served as head of all the monasteries of Salerno at the bequest of Prince Guaimarius IV before building his monastery in the hills above Salerno.[73] Prince Gisolf II was said to have recalled Alfanus I from Montecassino in order to name him archbishop of Salerno in 1058.[74] However, the princes did not possess unlimited power in appointing bishops and other prelates. The consent of the clergy and people remained imperative, and papal consecration bulls, which became common starting at the end of the tenth century, always acknowledged this fact. The Anonymous Chronicle of Salerno also demonstrates how the prince did not have unchecked authority to appoint whomever he liked. For example, when Prince Ademarius named his son Peter the new bishop of Salerno, the citizens of Salerno rose up against him since they objected to the prince wanting power over both the clergy and laity. They imprisoned and then blinded Ademarius, after which they proclaimed Guaiferius their new prince. Bishop Peter fled the city in fear soon after Guaiferius' election, retiring to the monastery of San Michele Arcangelo on Mt. Aureo.[75] Clearly consent from both the clergy and the *populus* of Salerno was necessary to avoid violent confrontations such as this one. Thus Salerno followed the traditional guidelines for episcopal elections that stretched back to the earliest days of Christianity in which an obvious candidate was brought forward and then approved of unanimously by the people and clergy of the city. Controversial elections did, of course, occur, but the choice was a joint one made by the ruler, the clergy, and the people of the city. The prince clearly had influence, but represented only one component of the formula.

As in the case of the bishops, the documentation reveals no precise duties or specific powers consistently exercised by the princes in the Lombard period, but rather certain matters over which they could have influence, as well as limits to their rights in other matters. Moreover, the prince's authority was never absolute, and the clerics of their principality, as well as the *populus* of Salerno, participated in their decisions, either through influence or by the outright refusal to accept a new appointee or policy. Like the bishop, the ability of the princes to participate in ecclesiastical matters depended

---

[72] *Chron. Sal.*, 101–2, chap. 100; 105–6, chap. 105; 169, chap. 163.
[73] *VQPA*, 6.
[74] *Chron. Cas.*, 354–55, bk. 2, chap. 96.
[75] *Chron. Sal.*, 101–3, chap. 100–101.

both on the personality and popularity of a particular prince as well as his ability to obtain a consensus for his decision.

The princes of Salerno built and administered some of the most powerful churches in the city. Both Guaiferius and John II, who founded the two dynasties that ruled Salerno during the Lombard period, established dynastic churches on their property in Salerno. Guaiferius built the church of San Massimo in c. 868 while John II built the church of Santa Maria de Domno c. 984. The bishops issued exemptions for both houses shortly after their foundation. These two churches were by far the largest and wealthiest ecclesiastical foundations in the Principality. They exercised all the important spiritual functions, including baptisms, burials, and last rites, and owned numerous properties in Salerno and throughout the province, which the abbots leased out for profit. Because of their size, wealth, and longevity, the two princely foundations were unique. Unlike the majority of religious houses in the Principality of Salerno, which were humble affairs, possessing limited lands and resources, San Massimo and Santa Maria had numerous clerics connected to them, possessed holdings which stretched throughout the Principality, and were some of the oldest churches in the region to survive into modern times. Both were later given to the abbey of Cava, and they are two of the best documented ecclesiastical foundations in the Cava archives.

Guaiferius announced the foundation of San Massimo in 868. He had built the church on property next to his palace ("casa") and then provided the church with a generous patrimony of lands in and around Salerno, Rota, and Sarno.[76] He also gave the church a servant and his wife, clerics to help administer the church along with separate lands to support them, and rights over all the revenues collected by and donations offered to the church.

Guaiferius reserved the power to appoint the church's clergy for himself and his heirs, explicitly denying the bishop of Salerno any power to invest San Massimo's priests or clerics. If his heirs were negligent or acted contrary to the good of the church, Guaiferius stipulated that they would forfeit the right to invest the church's rectors. However, the power of investiture was to devolve not onto the bishop, but onto the abbot of Montecassino. If similarly the abbot of Montecassino acted negligently, the right to invest passed to the abbot of San Vincenzo al Volturno.

[76] CDC 1: 79–84, no. 64. For a complete history of the church of San Massimo, see Bruno Ruggiero, *Principi, nobiltà e chiesa nel Mezzogiorno longobardo: l'esempio di S. Massimo di Salerno* (Naples: Università di Napoli, 1973). Also see Taviani-Carozzi, *La Principauté*, 409–39.

Guaiferius relinquished all rights over the lands, revenues, and people donated, which were to remain forever in the possession of San Massimo and its rectors. If Guaiferius or his heirs tried to subtract lands from the church's patrimony or appropriate any dues owed to the church, the church's rectors could take the usurper before a judge and demand their return. In addition to returning the lands and/or revenues, the usurpers were also required to pay a penalty of one hundred *solidi*.[77]

Fourteen years later, in March of 882, the bishop of Salerno issued an emancipation charter to the church of San Massimo.[78] In addition to giving Guaiferius and his heirs complete freedom to appoint and invest the church's clergy, he exempted the clerics themselves from episcopal jurisdiction and relinquished all claims to any dues or services owed to the church. He gave the church the power to found other churches or altars which would remain strictly under San Massimo's control. In his own words, the bishop claimed that "neither I, Bishop Peter, nor my successors will have any power whatsoever over the church of San Massimo" ("nec nos supradictus petrus episcopus, nec nostris successoribus abeamus ibi in ipsa ecclesia sancti maximi potestatem aliquid faciendum"), and he promised to pay a penalty of one hundred gold Byzantine *solidi* if he failed to fulfill the terms of the agreement.

San Massimo remained part of the founding family's patrimony, and descendants of Guaiferius inherited portions of the church and participated in San Massimo's activities up through the late tenth century. Guaiferius's son Guaimarius I (880–900) and his son Guaimarius II (900–943) both made donations to the church, in one case a gift of a certain Lupus and his family who had apparently allied with the Muslims during the siege of the city. Gisolf I (943–978) confirmed the church's property in a March 959 charter.[79] The princes were often present during disputes involving the church, and in some cases they actively defended San Massimo's rights.[80] Family members also served as advocates of the church: Guaiferius and Dauferius, the sons of Arechis, who himself was the son of Prince

[77] Byzantine gold *solidi*, weighing 4.45 grams, were the most common form of currency found in southern Italy at this time. Some came from Byzantine territories, while others were minted locally by Lombard rulers, including the princes of Salerno in the ninth century. Lucia Travaini, *La Monetazione nell'Italia Normanna* (Rome: Istituto storico italiano per il Medio Evo, 1995), 6, 8–11.

[78] CDC 1: 111–12, no. 87.

[79] CDC 1: 139–40, no. 111; CDC 1: 147–48, no. 117; CDC 1: 260–61, no. 202.

[80] CDC 1: 173–75, no. 135; CDC 1: 224–25, no. 174; CDC 1: 268, no. 209; CDC 2: 22–3, no. 230; CDC 2: 29–30, no. 235.

Guaiferius, appeared as advocates for at least three transactions, while their brother Peter appeared once. Guaimarius, son of Guido, brother of Guaimarius II, appeared as an advocate as well.[81]

Despite the family's active interest, the rectors of San Massimo administered the property and performed the religious duties of the church autonomously. The palace itself contained a private chapel, dedicated to Saint Peter, which most likely served as the family's major religious center.[82] Generally the owners appeared only to appoint new abbots or to help protect the church's landed patrimony. Moreover, the number of partial owners increased dramatically as time went on, since all legitimate heirs received a portion of the church. By the late tenth century, numerous people in the documents referred to themselves as "lords" or "one of the lords" of San Massimo.[83] Multiple ownership, however, did not affect the church's fate, since the church's fortunes were not directly linked to the owners, but lay in the hands of the abbots. San Massimo not only survived the founding family's extinction, but its greatest period of economic expansion occurred under Abbot Maius (995–1029), in the generation immediately after the founding family's demise.

Documents from the tenth and eleventh centuries show that San Massimo had a large staff of clerics connected to it, who carried a wide variety of titles and exercised diverse duties. San Massimo's community included priests and clerics engaged in pastoral duties, clerics who lived on benefices, and monks who may or may not have lived a common life.[84] However, the documents do not specify the precise duties of the priests and clerics, do not

[81] See Taviani-Carozzi, *La Principauté*, 429–30.

[82] Unfortunately only limited documentation remains for the chapel. See CDC 2: 42–3, no. 245; CDC 4: 89–91, no. 594; CDC 4: 143–46, no. 621; CDC 4: 171–73, no. 636; CDC 5: 114–16, no. 779.

[83] In 976, 977, and 980, Truppoaldus, an advocate and gastald, was one of the lords, while Guido, a gastald and advocate, was called so in 979 and 992, Guaiferius, an advocate, in 982, 984, 985, and 988, Alfanus, a gastald, in 978, Landoarius, a count, in 980, 989, 990, and 991, and Guaimarius, a gastald, in 982. Also the abbots Maius (995–1029) and Alferius (1033–55) claimed in the documents that they were "one of the lords of the church." See CDC 2: 99, no. 290; CDC 2: 105–6, no. 295; CDC 2: 147–48, no. 325; CDC 2: 131–32, no. 313; CDC 2: 334–45, no. 452; CDC 2: 339, no. 454; CDC 2: 168–69, no. 340; CDC 2: 218–19, no. 372; CDC 2: 219–21, no. 373; CDC 2: 260–62, no. 403; CDC 2: 121–23, no. 305; CDC 2: 141–42, no. 320; CDC 2: 267–69, no. 409; CDC 2: 303–05, no. 428; CDC 2: 313–14, no. 435.

[84] Only one charter speaks of monks in San Massimo: an 895 charter from a man who gave money and lands to San Massimo and became "a monk and servant of God" in the church. CDC 1: 136–37, no. 108.

speak about their lifestyles, and do not explain the differences connected to the various titles. The one remaining investiture charter for a new rector, dated February 904, stated only that the abbot would live in a house on church lands and that he would have authority to supervise, govern, and reign over the church, the clergy, and other men of the church.[85] The foundation charter of San Massimo mentioned that the clerics had to use the profits from the land to aid the poor, the weak, and widows, but did not specify how they were to do so.

Most clerics attached to San Massimo held benefices outside of Salerno, often far away in places such as Nocera, Montoro, Angri, and Roccapiemonte, and it is unclear what types of services they provided for the church. These clerics generally appear in the documents only when leasing out church land to sharecroppers.[86] They lived on the benefices, often with their wives and children, and their sons had the right to inherit the benefices when their father died.[87] The abbots, however, kept a close watch over the property, and all benefice-holders were required to seek the abbot's permission before renting out lands. San Massimo even had a cellar in "Pareti" near Nocera, where sharecroppers of that region brought the wine and produce they owed. Because of the distance, these benefice-holders obviously did not travel regularly to San Massimo to perform religious duties, which suggests they served an economic rather than religious function for the church.[88]

In addition to a large staff of clerics, San Massimo also had other ecclesiastical foundations dependent upon it. San Gennaro, San Nicola in Priato, and Sant'Andrea in Arcelle all pertained to San Massimo, and the abbots had the right to choose the foundations' rectors and collect an annual rent from them.[89] Priest investitures from the mid-eleventh century for San Nicola and Sant'Andrea demonstrate that the abbots of San Massimo

---

[85] CDC 1: 150–51. no. 119.

[86] Out of approximately one hundred and fifty sharecropping agreements which survive for San Massimo, seventy-seven came from benefice-holders. During Maius's abbacy (993–1029), forty-seven of the seventy-five sharecropping contracts were issued by benefice-holders.

[87] CDC 1: 141–43, no. 113, with date corrected by Galante, *La Datazione*, 79–81, no. 55; CDC 2: 339, no. 454; CDC 4: 97–98, no. 598. For a fuller discussion of this, see Ruggiero, *Principi, nobiltà*, 126–41.

[88] Martin, in his study of early medieval Apulia, has also remarked that the economic role of princely foundations is seen much more clearly than their religious role. Martin, *La Pouille*, 238.

[89] See, for example, CDC 1: 141–43, no. 113, with date corrected by Galante, *La Datazione*, 79–81, no. 55; CDC 7: 22–23, no. 1070; CDC 7: 275–76, no. 1220; CDC 7: 33–34, no. 1077.

treated their dependencies as other lay owners in the region, placing the religious and economic administration of the ecclesiastical foundations completely in the hands of the clergy they appointed. The abbots of San Massimo required only that the rectors perform certain unspecified religious duties, keep the church and its lands in good condition, and pay an annual rent to the rectors of San Massimo.[90] As a result, San Massimo's dependencies operated autonomously, and San Massimo never exercised control over a centralized network of dependent houses. The rectors of San Massimo administered their dependencies in the same manner as laypeople who owned proprietary houses.

The foundation and emancipation of the church of Santa Maria de Domno, founded by Prince John II in c. 984, followed along the same lines as those for San Massimo. However, the descendants of Prince John took a more active role in the activities of Santa Maria than did the owners of San Massimo. Not only did the owners appear during disputes, but certain transactions were performed by the abbots with their permission ("per absolutionem").[91] Count John, son of Prince John and brother of Prince Guaimarius, and his son Iohannacius showed up beside the abbots in a number of transactions between 1030 and 1060.[92] Moreover, another member of the princely family, also named John, became abbot of the church sometime before 1077.[93]

The abbots administered the new princely foundation of Santa Maria much in the same way as the abbots of San Massimo. The church had a large landed patrimony both in Salerno and outside, as well as three dependent churches, Sant'Eustasio in Liciniano, San Stefano in Roccapiemonte, and Santa Maria in Roccapiemonte, although the relationship between Santa Maria and its dependencies is unknown.[94] The abbots both leased out property directly for profits and gave lands to benefice-holders, who then rented them out to others for rent or a share of the produce.[95] As a result, the ab-

---

[90] CDC 7: 22–23, no. 1070; CDC 7: 33–34, no. 1077; CDC 7: 275–76, no. 1220. In the case of San Nicola, for example, the annual rent was composed of one-third of the offerings ("botationes" et "cingitura") given to the church on Christmas, Easter, and the feast of San Nicola as well as an unspecified gift. In addition, the priests had to give a percentage of all the profits from the *chartula fraternitatis*, one-fourth in the 1047 investiture and one-fifth in the 1056 one.

[91] CDC 3: 61, no. 500; CDC 3: 68–70, no. 505; CDC 3: 98, no. 528.

[92] CDC 5: 211–12, no. 841; CDC 7: 268–69, no. 1214; CDC 7: 261–62, no. 1209.

[93] CDC 10: 228–30, no. 93; CDC 10: 239–42, no. 98.

[94] CDC 2: 297–300, no. 425.

[95] In a 1078 document, for example, the abbot of Santa Maria, John, gave out church lands "in beneficio" to a cleric and doctor named Alfanus son of Arechis. Alfanus received lands and a house in Salerno for twenty-two years, and was required

bots of both San Massimo and Santa Maria de Domno administered their vast properties and dependent churches by placing them in the hands of clerics in return for rents and services. They never developed a hierarchical system to administer their holdings or dependencies, and the princes neither gave them a central role in the religious life of the Principality nor granted them any special powers over other religious foundations in the region. This meant that although San Massimo and Santa Maria were the wealthiest ecclesiastical foundations in the region before the mid-eleventh century, with vast patrimonies stretching throughout the region, they never claimed a supervisory role over the ecclesiastical system of the Principality of Salerno as whole and never stood at the head of a centralized network of churches and lands, as the archbishop of Salerno and the abbey of Cava would do from the twelfth century on.

Thus, no one authority emerged to exercise power over the ecclesiastical system in the Principality of Salerno in the early medieval period. Instead, control of ecclesiastical foundations and influence over religious practices and clerical discipline fell under the purview of numerous individuals and communities, including popes, bishops, princes, clerics, and laypeople. Theoretically the popes had the right to appoint bishops in the region, who were required to come to Rome for consecration. However, bishops and clergymen from the region rarely if ever went to Rome for consecration or to attend councils and popes participated minimally in the religious and political affairs of southern Italy up through the end of the tenth century. The bishops had the right to consecrate new churches in their dioceses and to exempt religious houses from episcopal control. However, they rarely did either, and most ecclesiastical foundations operated independently of episcopal power and had no contact with the bishops. The princes founded and owned some of the most powerful churches in the city of Salerno and served as protectors for other smaller religious houses. However, they rarely participated in the activities of their churches and were infrequently called upon to defend the rights of other ecclesiastical foundations. Moreover, neither the bishop nor the prince developed an ecclesiastical hierarchy or a system of dependent churches to administer other foundations or direct religious life, which meant that no centralized authority oversaw ecclesiastical administration and appointments or supervised religious practices and clerical discipline.

---

to live in the city and perform religious services in the church. He gave an annual rent of eight *tarì* and would pay a further four *tarì* a year if he remained outside of the city for more than two years. CDC 10: 239–42, no. 98. Also see CDC 3: 17–18, no. 471; CDC 3: 29–30, no. 478; CDC 4: 7–9, no. 542.

Families and Consortia

In early medieval Salerno most ecclesiastical foundations were built and administered by local families or groups of citizens, sometimes referred to as *consortia* in the documents, who pooled their resources together specifically for the purpose of establishing a religious house in their community. Charter evidence from Salerno suggests that founding a house was simply a matter of having enough land and wealth to sustain the church and its clergy and to outfit the church with the necessary books, garments, and ornaments. In some cases individuals built religious houses on their property. For example, a woman by the name of Adelaita built a church some time in the early tenth century on land she owned in Salerno.[96] In general, however, groups of people came together to build and administer religious foundations. For example, sometime around 986, a certain Ligorius, son of John, built a church on his property in Tresino (Cilento) dedicated to Saint John. Along with his brother, Leo, Ligorius provided for the upkeep of the church by giving lands and animals and appointing a priest to officiate.[97] Like Ligorius and Leo, family members frequently joined together to build and maintain religious houses. In 974 two brothers constructed a church dedicated to Saint John on property they owned in Vietri.[98] Another church dedicated to Saint John in Vietri, San Giovanni di Staffilo, was erected in 1036 by two sets of brothers, and the heirs of these men continued to administer the house throughout the eleventh century.[99] Count Alfanus son of Landone with his nephew Landone gave a piece of their property between the Sele and Calore rivers to an abbot named Leo in 1018 in order to found and administer a monastery there dedicated to Sant'Onofre.[100]

In addition to families, groups of people, joining together in a *consortium*, often restored and built neighborhood churches. Members of *consortia* included relatives, neighbors, co-heirs, and clerics, and the houses they founded included both small rural churches as well as larger village ones which exercised a wide range of functions. In 965, for example, a *consortium* of fourteen men formed in Avellino to build a church in a village nearby, called Gauldo.[101] Andrea, son of Guilsemarus, donated a portion of his land

---

[96] CDC 1: 193–94, no. 150.

[97] CDC 2: 241–42, no. 388.

[98] CDC 2: 81–82, no. 276.

[99] CDC 6: 60–61, no. 910; CDC 7: 64–65, no. 1096; CDC 9: 107–11, no. 32.

[100] CDC 4: 288–89, no. 707.

[101] CDC 2: 23–5, no. 231. The fourteen were: Gualdus (son of Sindolfus), Gualdus's sons Marundus, Risus, and Sandolfus and his nephew Gaulus, John (son of Angelus), Fossemarus, Truppoaldus, and Marus (all sons of John), John, a priest son of

and then, together with fourteen other "parentes et consortes," he built a church. The church owners and their heirs were to appoint the priests and monks jointly. In 1024 a *consortium* of eight men, including a judge, a priest and his two brothers, and group of four brothers, built the church of Sant'Adiutore in Nocera and outfitted it with both books and ecclesiastical garments.[102] In 985 a group of six men sharing a common inheritance restored a church dedicated to Sant'Adiutore on their lands in Puciano, near Metiliano.[103] The six men referred to themselves as "brothers and co-heirs" ("fratres et sortifices"), although they had different fathers. This church represents an interesting mix of dynastic foundation and ecclesiastical *consortium*, since the restorers, although not necessarily blood relations, shared in a joint inheritance where they rebuilt the church.

In all these cases, the building or restoration of religious houses came from individual initiative and the only parties involved were the church founders and the clergy appointed by them. Owners needed no special permission from the bishop or the prince in order to build their churches. The only requirement, aside from land and wealth, was finding a priest or abbot to administer the house. Thus no ecclesiastical hierarchy oversaw the building or administration of religious houses in the region. Private initiative rather than centralized planning formed the basis of the ecclesiastical system of the Lombard Principality of Salerno.

Not just in Salerno but throughout Latin Christendom and the Byzantine empire, individuals and families, rather than bishops or other prelates, built and administered most religious houses. These ecclesiastical foundations have traditionally been referred to in English as "private" or "proprietary" churches, a translation of the German term "Eigenkirchen" coined in the late nineteenth century by the historian Ulrich Stutz.[104] Stutz invented the term *Eigenkirche* to reflect the fact that the lay owners exercised complete proprietary rights over their foundations, without any interference on the part of a bishop or lay ruler. Stutz also traced the origins of the practice back to pagan German customs and property laws, in which families built and administered cult centers over which they had complete control. In the mid-twentieth century, H. E. Feine used Stutz's ideas as the basis for a study

---

Foscemarus and nephew of this John, Domnandus a smith ("magister ferrarius"), Angelus (son of Peter), Amancius, and Marinus (son of Sofia).

[102] CDC 5: 82–84, no. 757. Potonus is specified as giving the church a book containing the lives of SS Stephen, Felice, Barbara, and Geronimo, a collection of the visions of Saint Paul, along with liturgical garments (a chasuble and an amice), while John Corbinus gave an antiphonary.

[103] CDC 2: 224–25, no. 376.

[104] Ulrich Stutz, *Geschichte des kirchlichen Benefizialwesens* (Berlin: Müller, 1895; reprint, Aalen: Scientia, 1965).

of ecclesiastical organization in early medieval Italy. Like Stutz, Feine claimed that the introduction of *Eigenkirchen* by the Lombards radically changed church organization in Italy, because they were based on "Germanic" ideas concerning private cult centers. Although Feine admitted that private churches existed before the Lombards, he claimed that they were regulated by Roman church law which required that they be part of episcopal organization and within the bishop's power to supervise. The new Lombard-style *Eigenkirchen*, however, remained completely outside episcopal oversight.[105] Consequently, Feine believed that the establishment of *Eigenkirchen* destroyed the episcopal system in Italy, which before the Lombard period had been centralized and efficient.

In fact, documents show the existence of proprietary churches exempt from episcopal control long before the establishment of Germanic subkingdoms in the Roman empire, and most historians no longer discuss the "national" origins of the practice. Nonetheless many historians continue to oppose "private" churches to "public" ones and view the phenomenon of proprietary churches as a usurpation of episcopal authority, characterizing the early medieval period as a constant struggle on the part of the bishops to gain back their rightful authority over all ecclesiastical foundations within their dioceses. Such a view, however, overlooks the symbiotic relationship between bishops and lay church owners found in the earliest days of Christianity.[106] Bishops had neither the resources nor the institutions necessary to build, maintain, and supervise all the religious foundations in their dioceses and thus they both sanctioned and promoted private church building, especially in remote areas. In the early Middle Ages, lay and religious leaders alike continued to rely upon laypeople to construct and maintain religious foundations, and councils held in various places, in southern Italy, the Byzantine empire, and even in Frankish territories, encouraged and exhorted laypeople to build churches and monasteries with the only stipulations being that they do so with episcopal approval and that they place the clergy under episcopal supervision.[107] In the early medieval period, the laity

---

[105] H. E. Feine, "Studien zum langobardisch-italischen Eigenkirchenrecht," *Zeitschrift der Savigny-Stiftung für Rechtsgeschichte* 30 (1941): 1–95; 31 (1942): 1–105. Also see his "Ursprung, Wesen, und Bedeutung des Eigenkirchentums," *Mitteilungen des Instituts für österreichische Geschichtsforschung* 57 (1950): 195–208 which speaks of *Eigenkirchen* in Europe in general.

[106] See, for example, Thomas' study on private religious foundations in the Byzantine Empire and Ruggiero's examination of private churches in the Principality of Salerno. John Philip Thomas, *Private Religious Foundations in the Byzantine Empire* (Washington D. C.: Dumbarton Oaks, 1987); Ruggiero, "Per una storia."

[107] For southern Italy, see canon 9 of the council held in either Siponto or Benevento sometime between 840 and 880, "Un concile inédit," ed. Morin, 147. For the

and clergy were partners in ecclesiastical administration, and laypeople participated in a broad range of religious activities which later would be prohibited to them.

Similarly, in the Principality of Salerno, both bishops and princes encouraged families and *consortia* to build and maintain religious houses. In 940, for example, the bishop of Salerno gave a decayed church in Fuenti, dedicated to San Felice, to three Amalfians to restore.[108] According to the agreement, Lupenus son of Ursus, a cleric Leo, and Ursus son of Maurus de Rini, were to restore the church, appoint priests, and put the land under cultivation in return for an annual rent of one gold *tarì*.[109] Sometime between 1018 and 1027, Princes Guaimarius III and Guaimarius IV gave their church in Lucania dedicated to Santa Lucia to a *consortium* of eight men to administer, renouncing "in perpetuum" all rights over the church, along with its vines, vacant lands, three mills, cells, and houses. They granted the church immunity from taxes or services to the princes, stating that the church would now perform services and pay taxes to the "men of Lustra and Trocclara."[110] However, unlike Carolingian regions, princes and prelates in Salerno did not insist that proprietary houses be under the supervision of bishops. Moreover, the ability to found ecclesiastical foundations in early medieval Salerno was not reserved for a wealthy, noble class alone, and religious foundations, as a rule, were not used by families to bolster their power.

Owners of religious houses in the Principality of Salerno had the right to appoint the clerics serving in their houses, without seeking the permission of the bishop or prince. They also received a rent from the church rectors administering their church, which in general consisted of either wax or an unspecified offering ("paria de oblata") but could also include a money rent

Byzantine Empire, see Thomas, *Private Religious Foundations*, 125–27, 133–35, 139–42. For Councils in Frankish territories, see Stutz, *Geschichte*, 95–111 and Hartmann, *Die Synoden*, 454–55. Only two councils during the Carolingian period, at Valence and at St-Laurent-lès-Mâcon both in 855, sought to abolish lay ownership of churches, insisting that founders relinquish control of their churches to the bishops. Hartmann, *Die Synoden*, 456.

[108] CDC 1: 212–18, no. 169.

[109] *Tarì* is the Latin term for the Arab *ruba'i*, or gold quarter dinar. A dinar legally weighed 4.25 grams, and thus a *tarì* weighed about one gram. Over the course of the tenth century, it slowly became a more popular form of currency than the gold Byzantine *solidus*, and rulers in both Salerno and Amalfi minted their own *tarì* in the eleventh century. Travaini, *La Monetazione*, 19–21.

[110] Cava XX, 114. This donation is found as an insert in a charter from 1118, and although the exact date of the earlier transaction is not recorded in the later document, it must have occurred between 1018 and 1027, when Princes Guaimarius III and IV were co-rulers.

or a share of the produce from church lands. In addition, the founders and their heirs had the power to sell or alienate the churches as they wished, again without the consent of the bishop or prince. They could even divide the church into parcels and alienate a portion of the church, while keeping the rest for themselves. Normal inheritance practices applied to the houses, and most dynastic foundations ended up with multiple owners. Usually the ecclesiastical foundations remained in the hands of one family; however, over time the heirs could become quite numerous, with many families related to the original founder three generations back or more each owning small portions of the church. In the second half of the eleventh century, for example, San Giovanni di Staffilo in Vietri had no fewer than sixteen owners, while Santa Maria, nearby, had at least fifteen.[111] Other foundations remained in the hands of fewer people. San Nicola of Gallocanta, for example, passed from Count Adelbertus, son of Count Lambertus, who purchased the church in 996, to his two sons, Count Landoarius and Count Lambertus, who then passed it on to their sons, Ebolus, Peter, Adelbertus, and Landoarius, sons of Count Lambertus and Landoarius, son of Count Adelbertus. In the late eleventh and early twelfth century, when the church gradually became dependent on the abbey of Cava, one half of the church belonged to Landoarius, son of Count Adelbertus, and his wife, Gemma, while the other half pertained to Ebolus, Landolfus, Constantine, and Lambertus, sons of Adelbertus and great-grandsons of the first Count Adelbertus.[112]

Despite the fact that specific individuals or groups of people claimed possession over portions of religious houses, ecclesiastical foundations were not "owned" in the modern sense of the word. In the Middle Ages, ownership

---

[111] For San Giovanni: CDC 10: 341–44, no. 142; Cava XIV, 58; Cava XIV, 80; Cava XV, 9; Cava XV, 21; Cava XV, 37; Cava XVIII, 9; Cava XVIII, 67. For Santa Maria: Cava XIV, 22; Cava XIV, 89; Cava XVI, 67; Cava XVI, 68; Cava XVIII, 53; Cava XVIII, 75; Cava XVIII, 80; Cava XIX, 107; Cava XX, 58; Cava XX, 99; Cava XX, 105.

[112] CDC 8: 66–68, no. 1270 (Cherubini, 193–96, no. 76); CDC 9: 3–9, no. 1 (Cherubini, 219–23, no. 88); Cava XIV, 14 (Cherubini, 260–62, no. 102); Cava XIV, 73 (Cherubini, 262–64, no. 103); Cava XIV, 78 (Cherubini, 264–65, no. 104); Cava XIV, 95 and 96 (Cherubini, 272–75, no. 107); Cava XIV, 116 (Cherubini, 275–77, no. 108); Cava XV, 48 (Cherubini, 286–87, no. 114); Cava XV, 72 (Cherubini, 290–91, no. 116); Cava C, 41 (Cherubini, 296–97, no. 119); Cava XV, 94 and 95 (Cherubini, 301–05, no. 122); Cava XVI, 70 (Cherubini, 305–07, no. 123); Cava XVIII, 111 and 112 (Cherubini, 309–13, no. 126); Cava XIX, 5 (Cherubini, 313–15, no. 127); Cava XIX, 31 (Cherubini, 315–17, no. 128); Cava XIX, 52 (Cherubini, 317–18, no. 129); Cava XIX, 90 (Cherubini, 319–20, no. 130); Cava E, 37 (Cherubini, 321–22, no. 132); Cava XX, 34 (Cherubini, 323–24, no.133); Cava XX, 38 (Cherubini, 324–26, no. 134); Cava XX, 59 (Cherubini, 326–28, no. 135).

did not relate so much to the substance of the property as it did to its utility ("dominium utile"), given that the ability to use was far more important than the authority to alienate.[113] As one historian has explained it, property consisted in multiple positions of economic utility that pertained to an unending chain of generations of *consortia*. The economic needs of the community counted more than the power of individuals over property, and as a result ownership in the Middle Ages denoted an aggregate of different powers exploiting property for different uses.

Ownership of religious foundations was even more complicated than landed property since these foundations were not seen as commodities, but as entities that served a variety of social, religious, and economic purposes. Owners had as many duties and obligations as they did privileges, and in the Principality of Salerno both regulations and custom restricted the rights of church founders. For one, the patrimonies attached to religious houses could not be taken away or utilized by owners for their own benefit. The prince served as protector of ecclesiastical patrimonies, and clerics had to seek his permission before selling or exchanging church property. In addition, owners were required to provide financial support for both the upkeep of the religious house and its clergy. Furthermore, although the owners personally appointed clerics to administer their foundations, they themselves rarely participated in the activities of their houses, leaving the supervision of both the religious and economic life in the hands of the clergy. Moreover, they did not receive any special treatment from the clergy, except for an annual or bi-annual rent paid by them. As a result, church owners exercised extremely limited authority over their foundations. Instead the clerics who served in the churches and the communities that worshipped in them exerted the strongest influence.

Thus Christianity in the Lombard Principality of Salerno remained a community-based phenomenon in the early Middle Ages, focused on communities of worshippers who attended ceremonies in modest religious houses built and maintained by themselves. It propagated the sentiments of many early Christians who defined "ecclesia" not as a place of worship but as a community of believers gathering to worship.[114] It also followed closely the regulations for private foundations set down in church councils in the late Roman period, which limited the property rights of owners, forbade

---

[113] Paolo Grossi, *Il dominio e le cose. Percezioni medievali e moderne dei diritti reali* (Milan: Giuffrè, 1992), in particular, "Tradizioni e modelli nella sistemazione post-Unitaria della proprietà," 439–570 and "La proprietà e le proprietà nell'officina dello storico," 603–65.

[114] Thomas, *Private Religious Foundations*, 7–8.

them from expropriating church property or secularizing religious houses, and required them to provide proper financial support for the clergy they appointed.[115] Moreover, it mirrored the experience of many eastern Mediterranean Christian communities at the time, where ecclesiastical networks were regionalized and often lacked any centralized authority or institutions to oversee religious houses and their clergy.[116] In the Byzantine empire, for example, bishops and emperors alike encouraged wealthy laypeople to construct places of worship outside episcopal networks, and in the ninth and tenth centuries evidence suggests that it was not at all uncommon for villagers to pool their resources together and build small communal churches on private property.[117] Until the very end, the empire relied on private philanthropy to meet the religious needs of the Christian population, especially in rural areas, and the only concern was that orthodox creeds be taught.[118] Christians throughout the region in the early Middle Ages remained united in belief, rather than by way of institutions or hierarchies.

[115] Ibid., 37–41, 53–55.
[116] Brown, *The Rise of Christendom*, 128–30.
[117] Thomas, *Private Religious Foundations*, 27, 160–61.
[118] Ibid., 17–19.

CHAPTER 3

Religious Houses and the Clergy before Reform

The vocabulary used to describe the religious houses and clergy of early medieval Salerno often lacked precision. For example, charters from the Lombard period vacillate between the terms "ecclesia" and "monasterium" when referring to an ecclesiastical foundation. San Massimo, SS Matteo and Tomaso in Salerno, San Magno in Cilento, Santa Maria in Vietri, and Santa Sofia in Salerno, to give only a few examples, were sometimes labeled as churches and sometimes as monasteries in the documents.[1] Other religious labels found in charters from Salerno, such as cleric ("clericus"), priest ("sacerdos"), monk ("monachus"), deacon ("diaconus"), and abbot ("abbas"), similarly lack precise meaning and are often used interchangeably. Abbots headed churches, exercising pastoral duties, as often as they did monasteries.[2] For some terms, such as "sacerdos" and "clericus," it is impossible to know the precise meaning. Even the meaning of "episcopus" at times is uncertain, as in the case of a bishop named Cennamus ("Domnus Cennamus Episco-

---

[1] CDC 2: 137–38, no. 317; CDC 5: 93–95, no. 764. In 979 the bishop of Salerno even gave a nun a "church" ("ecclesia") to administer, while the original foundation charter for the abbey of Cava referred to the monastery as the church of the Holy Trinity of Cava. CDC 2: 137–38, no. 317; CDC 5: 93–95, no. 764.

[2] Abbots headed San Massimo, Santa Maria de Domno, the palace chapel of San Pietro, Santa Maria in Nocera, Sant'Adiutore in Nocera, Santa Sofia in Salerno, Sant'Angelo in Capaccio, and San Nicola in Gallocanta, as well as the abbey of the Holy Trinity at Cava and other foundations in Cilento. In one case, in the mid-tenth century the bishop of Paestum is referred to as both bishop and abbot. Nicola Acocella, *La Traslazione di San Matteo: Documenti e testimonianze* (Salerno: Grafica di Giacomo, 1954), 111.

pus") who appears in 1010 at the head of San Michele Arcangelo on Mt. Aureo, and a bishop named Theodorus, who was referred to as both bishop and rector of Santa Sofia in Salerno between 1039 and 1063.[3] Neither of these foundations was ever a cathedral church.[4]

Throughout southern Italy the terminology found in early medieval documents for describing religious foundations and clerical lifestyles tends to be both imprecise and inconsistent. Foundations called monasteries did not necessarily refer to a community of monks, abbots at times administered secular churches, and foundations called churches sometimes lacked a priest.[5] In Byzantine regions of southern Italy, terminology makes it difficult to distinguish between churches and monasteries, since monks as well as priests could administer churches.[6] As discussed above, the precise meaning of "plebs" (generally translated as "parish church") in early medieval southern Italy has never been established because of inconsistent usage.[7] In Carolingian regions, also, vocabulary to describe different clerical lifestyles could at times lead to confusion; terms such as "fratres" and "coenobitae," for example, were used interchangeably to refer to both monks and canons.[8]

Earlier historians attributed this vacillation and imprecision to carelessness on the part of scribes or hypothesized that foundations included both a church and a monastery.[9] However, more recently historians have recog-

---

[3] Di Meo 7: 17–18; CDC 6: 120–21, no. 953; CDC 6: 137–38, no. 963; CDC 6: 146–47, no. 969; CDC 8: 256–58, no. 1359.

[4] Martin believes that the *episcopus* Cennamus, as well as one named Ursus who appears in a document from 1051, were sent by Byzantine officials as part of their continuing expansion into the region. Martin, "L'ambiente," 208 and "Cennamus episcopus. Aux avant-postes de l'Hellénisme sud-italien vers l'an mil," *Rivista di studi bizantini e neoellenici* 27 (1964): 89–99. Also see Nicola Acocella, "La figura e l'opera di Alfano I di Salerno," *Rassegna Storica Salernitana* 19 (1958): 39.

[5] Ruggiero, *Principi, nobiltà*, 100; Martin, *La Pouille*, 240.

[6] Vera von Falkenhausen, "Il Monachesimo italo-greco e i suoi rapporti con il monachesimo benedettino," in *L'Esperienza monastica benedettina e la Puglia: Atti del Convegno, Bari-Noci-Lecce-Picciano, 6–10 October 1980* (Galatina: Congedo, 1983), 130. Throughout the Byzantine empire in the ninth and tenth centuries, the distinction between monasteries and churches was blurred and monks often performed all the duties of parish priests. Thomas, *Private Religious Foundations*, 161.

[7] Martin, "L'ambiente," 222; Feller, *Les Abruzzes*, 800. Also see Bruno Ruggiero, "'Parrochia' e 'Plebs' in alcune fonti del Mezzogiorno longobardo e normanno," in *Potere, istituzioni, chiese locali: Aspetti e motivi del Mezzogiorno medievale dai Longobardi agli Angioini* (Bologna: Centro Salentino di Studi Medioevali Nardò, 1977), 175–81.

[8] Charles Dereine, "Chanoines," in *Dictionnaire d'Histoire et de Géographie Ecclésiastique*, 12:354.

[9] For San Massimo in Salerno, see the various theories of Lubin, Mabillon, Sinno, and Feine, summarized by Ruggiero, *Principi, nobiltà*, 100.

nized that the imprecise vocabulary represents an overlap in clerical duties.[10] In many parts of the Carolingian empire, for example, the distinction between monks and canons was blurred because the main duty of both was the recitation of the holy offices.[11] In the Byzantine empire, as well as in some Carolingian territories, monasteries in the countryside undertook all the duties of parish churches, thus obscuring the distinction between church and monastery, and between priest and monk.[12] It can also be hard at times to distinguish between laypeople and clerics who served together in the same churches because their duties overlapped, or even to clearly differentiate who is cleric and who is a layman because often they pursued mixed careers in state service and church administration or alternated between lay and religious lives.[13]

In the Principality of Salerno, the vast majority of ecclesiastical foundations in the early medieval period combined functions associated with both churches and monasteries. The duties performed by the various clerics serving in these religious houses were not clearly defined or differentiated. Most ecclesiastical offices did not come with precisely delineated duties, and the functions exercised by clerics did not always correspond to their titles. The regular clergy often did not live under a rule or in accordance with a specific religious lifestyle. Even the line separating the clergy from the laity was often blurred, and the laity participated intensely in the religious life and organization of their communities, performing duties later denied to them. In addition, since Christianity was a community-based phenomenon in the Principality of Salerno in the Lombard period, it exhibited a high degree of diversity with regard to religious practices, ecclesiastical foundations, and clerical lifestyles. Both "Western" and "Eastern" practices were found in the region, and evidence even suggests that Christians at times adopted Jewish and Muslim traditions as well. No attempt was ever made to standardize liturgy or clerical lifestyle, and holiness was connected to lifestyle rather than office-holding. Custom and community rather than an ecclesiastical hierarchy shaped the religious landscape of early medieval

[10] By far the best discussion of this phenomenon is found in Dereine's article, "Chanoines." Also see Pierre Toubert, "La vie commune des clercs aux XI–XIIe siècles: un questionnaire," *Revue Historique* 231 (1964): 15–20; Giseppe Forchielli, *La pieve rurale: Ricerche sulla storia della costituzione della Chiesa in Italia e particolarmente nel Veronese* (Rome: G. Bardi, 1931); and M. M. Hildebrandt, chap. 6 in *The External School in Carolingian Society* (New York: E. J. Brill, 1992).

[11] Dereine, "Chanoines," 358; 366.

[12] Ibid., 358–59; 391.

[13] Ibid., 363; Thomas, *Private Religious Foundations*, 73, 116.

Salerno, and this phenomenon is reflected in the imprecise use of terminology in the documents.

Community Churches

As discussed in the previous chapter, the vast majority of religious houses in early medieval Salerno was built by families and *consortia*, often of modest economic means. Like the owners themselves, the foundations also tended to be humble affairs, possessing limited lands and influence. Although often outfitted with expensive accoutrements and administered by a well-educated clergy, they were generally simple structures with small landholdings. They were community-based houses, owned and administered by local citizens and exercising religious, economic, and social functions for the neighboring population. Unlike the princely foundations and a few dynastic houses that had far-flung patrimonies and absentee clerics who provided economic rather than religious services, these community houses contained clerics who lived locally and served the religious, social, and economic needs of their communities. Most of them had short lifespans, generally not surviving beyond one or two generations. They appear only once or twice in the documents, and then disappear when the founder or founders died, perhaps resurfacing at a later time under a new ecclesiastical head or with the patronage of a new family member. Only a few remained active for a century or longer, generally due to a large patrimony which the church rectors administered well. Almost all, however, were local phenomena whose influence rarely extended beyond the immediate environs of the church. The clergy who served in the houses followed community religious practices, required to act "as was right" or "according to the custom of the place." As in the early days of Christianity, the churches were defined more by the community that worshipped in them than the physical structure of the building.

The archives of the abbey of Cava contain over twenty-five priest investitures from the pre-Norman period, in which church owners handed over their religious foundations to clerics to administer, and these charters provide a window onto the inner workings of churches in the Lombard period because they spelled out the various duties and obligations of both clergy and owners.[14] Although the terms of the investitures differed slightly from

---

[14] Investitures from the pre-Norman period survive for the following foundations: San Matteo in Salerno (971, 1050): CDC 2: 67–8, no. 265 and CDC 7: 126–28, no. 1131; San Giovanni in Vietri (974, 980, 986): CDC 2: 81–2, no. 276; CDC 2: 145–46, no. 323; and CDC 2: 233–34, no. 382; San Giovanni in Tresino (986, 1042): CDC 2: 241–42, no. 388 and CDC 6: 182–83, no. 990; Santa Barbara in Lucania (1005): CDC 6: 38, no. 896 with date corrected by Galante, *La Datazione*, 55, no. 34; Santa

one house to another, some general requirements set down for church rectors applied to most of them. First of all, the charters stipulated that the rectors live on ecclesiastical property, near the church, and that they perform their religious duties diligently. They required that a priest be present to perform the office day and night. In addition, the owners instructed the rectors to keep lands profitable and under cultivation, to maintain the church and other buildings in good repair, and to have the church lit at all times. Sometimes the owners specified the amount of money or time that rectors had to spend on the church's maintenance. For example, Bernard, the priest appointed to San Giovanni in Tresino, had to spend three *solidi* per annum on church upkeep.[15] In 1047, when the owners of the church of San Giovanni di Staffilo in Vietri appointed a new priest, Peter, as rector, they required him to do work for the church every year valued at two *tarì*.[16] Some owners required the priests to add to the church's patrimony, generally supplying books. The same Bernard, mentioned above, had to leave the church a book upon his death, while a priest named Stephen, who headed the church of San Giovanni di Staffilo in Vietri immediately before Peter did, was required to use church revenues to buy a book for the church every year.[17] Finally the investiture charters required the rectors to administer the churches according to local custom, stating that the clerics were to run their churches "as was right for a peasant church" ("sicut meruerit ecclesia billana"), "as was proper for a peasant priest" ("sicut decet presbiter billanus"), or "as was the custom of the place" ("sicut ipso locum meruerit et consuetudo ibi fuit").[18]

Maria in Vietri (1006): CDC 4: 71–73, no. 582; Santa Maria de Domno (1022): CDC 5: 51–52, no. 738; Sant'Adiutore in Nocera (1024): CDC 5: 82–84, no. 757; SS Maria and Nicola in Mercatello (1029, 1043, 1045, 1049, 1054): CDC 5: 170–72, no. 812; CDC 6: 225–27, no. 1016, CDC 6: 282–84, no. 1052; CDC 7: 111–13, no. 1121; and CDC 7: 254–56, no. 1205; San Giovanni di Staffilo in Vietri (1036, 1047, 1067): CDC 6: 60–61, no. 910; CDC 7: 64–65, no. 1096; and CDC 9: 107–11, no. 32; San Nicola in Priato (1047, 1056): CDC 7: 22–23, no. 1070 and CDC 7: 275–76, no. 1220; Sant'Andrea in Arcelle (1047): CDC 7: 33–34, no. 1077; San Venero in Corneto (1052): CDC 7: 191–93, no. 1174; Sant'Angelo in Velanzanu (1053): CDC 7: 198–200, no. 1178; San Felice in Felline (1057): CDC 8: 25–27, no. 1252; San Nicola in Gallocanta (1058, 1065): CDC 8: 38–40, no. 1258 (Cherubini, 197–200, no. 77); CDC 8: 66–68, no. 1270 (Cherubini, 193–96, no. 76); and CDC 9: 3–9, no. 1 (Cherubini, 219–23, no. 88); San Michele Arcangelo in Passiano (1063): CDC 8: 208–12, no. 1345.

15 CDC 2: 241–42, no. 388.

16 CDC 7: 64–65, no. 1096.

17 CDC 2: 241–42, no. 388. CDC 6: 60–61, no. 910.

18 This is the case for the vast majority of churches for which priest investitures remain, including San Giovanni in Vietri, San Giovanni in Tresino, Santa Maria in Vietri, Sant'Adiutore in Nocera, SS Maria and Nicola in Mercatello, Sant'Andrea in Arcelle, San Venero in Corneto, San Nicola in Priato, San Felice in Felline, and San

Rectors were required to make annual payments to church owners, which differed greatly from one church to another. Usually they paid an annual or bi-annual rent of wax or an unspecified offering ("paria de oblata").[19] Other payments given to the owners included a portion of the agricultural produce or animals, part of the ecclesiastical revenues, or an annual money fee. The priests assigned to run the church of San Giovanni in Vietri (in 974, 980, and 986) had to give part of the citrus fruit crop as well as some wine.[20] The priest appointed in 1054 to head SS Maria and Nicola in Mercatello gave one-third of all grain, wine, fruit, and animals to the owners.[21] The priest selected in 1052 to administer the monastery of San Venero in Corneto, dependent on Santa Sofia, had to give six pigs and a sheep every year.[22] Peter, a deacon appointed to the church of San Nicola in Priato in 1046, had to give the owners one-fourth of the profits of the *cartula fraternitatis*, presumably a list of anniversaries for people for whom the priests were to say prayers, while Stephen and Peter, appointed to the church of Sant'Andrea in 1047, gave one-half of the church profits to the owners.[23] A priest named Peter, chosen in 1056 to head San Nicola in Priato, gave one-half of all ex-voto offerings and rents, as well as one-fifth of the profits from the *charta fraternitatis*.[24] The priest appointed in 1042 to San Giovanni in Tresino paid an annual rent of four gold *tarì*.[25] Theophilus the rector of San Nicola in Gallocanta paid thirty gold *tarì* per annum to two of the owners and thirty-four *solidi* to two others.[26] Alfanus the abbot of Santa Maria de Domno paid eight gold *tarì* per annum.[27] Thus churches could be a source of revenue for the owners, although in general the payments were small and seem to have been symbolic.

Owners of larger religious houses sometimes specified the number of priests and clerics needed to administer the foundations, as well as indicat-

---

Nicola in Gallocanta. CDC 2: 145–46, no. 323; CDC 2: 241–42, no. 388; CDC 4: 71–73, no. 582; CDC 5: 82–84, no. 757; CDC 6: 60–61, no. 910; CDC 9: 107–11, no. 32; CDC 7: 33–34, no. 1077; CDC 7: 191–93, no. 1174; CDC 7: 275–76, no. 1220; CDC 8: 25–27, no. 1252; CDC 8: 66–68, no. 1270 (Cherubini, 193–96, no. 76).

[19] The documents give no clue as to what kind of donation a "paria de oblata" entailed, although sometimes the rectors were required to bring it to the owners' house. See, for example, CDC 7: 126–28, no. 1131.

[20] CDC 2: 81–2, no. 276; CDC 2: 145–46, no. 323; CDC 2: 233–34, no. 382.

[21] CDC 7: 254–56, no. 1205.

[22] CDC 7: 191–93, no. 1174.

[23] CDC 7: 22–23, no. 1070; CDC 7: 33–34, no. 1077.

[24] CDC 7: 275–76, no. 1220.

[25] CDC 6: 182–83, no. 990.

[26] CDC 8: 38–40, no. 1258 (Cherubini, 197–200, no. 77); CDC 8: 66–68, no. 1270 (Cherubini, 193–96, no. 76).

[27] CDC 10: 239–42, no. 98.

ing how to provide for them. For the church of SS Maria and Nicola in Mercatello, for example, the owners required that the rectors hire three or four priests and clerics and pay them with both money salaries and a fixed amount of wine.[28] The owners of San Matteo in Salerno stipulated that the rectors give land in benefice to support eight clerics and priests.[29] Prince Guaimarius III and his brother Count John, when investing a new priest in Santa Maria de Domno in 1022, declared that the rector could give lands in benefice to other priests and clerics, although they did not require any specific number.[30]

Generally the clerics appointed to administer ecclesiastical foundations were priests, who then administered the church and religious life of their foundations personally. Out of the 31 rectors appointed between 971 and 1070, 25 were priests. As a rule, they took the title of "abbot" or "rector" in recognition of their position as head of the foundation. Sometimes the priests were also monks, reflecting the tradition of mixing monastic and secular clerical duties.[31] However, not all rectors were priests. In two instances deacons became church rectors and twice simple clerics took over the administration of ecclesiastical foundations.[32] On at least one occasion, in 1043, a layperson named Stephen became rector of SS Maria and Nicola in Mercatello.[33]

Although non-priests could become rectors, the documents required them to appoint priests to carry out the religious services. In the 1022 appointment of a deacon to head Santa Maria and the 1050 appointment of a cleric to San Matteo, the owners stipulated that the rectors provide

---

[28] CDC 6: 282–84, no. 1052; CDC 7: 111–13, no. 1121.

[29] CDC 7: 191–93, no. 1174.

[30] CDC 5: 51–52, no. 738.

[31] Six examples exist: in 974 for the church of San Giovanni in Vietri, in 1047 for the church of Sant'Andrea in Arcelle, in 1049 for the church of SS Maria and Nicola in Mercatello, in 1052 for the monastery of San Venero in Corneto, in 1058 for the church of San Nicola in Gallocanta, and in 1063 for the church of SS Michele Arcangelo and Martino in Passiano. CDC 2: 81–2, no. 276; CDC 7: 33–34, no. 1077; CDC 7: 111–13, no. 1121; CDC 7: 191–93, no. 1174; CDC 8: 38–40, no. 1258 (Cherubini, 197–200, no. 77); CDC 8: 208–12, no. 1345.

[32] In 1022, the deacon Ferus, son of Ferus, was appointed as rector to Santa Maria de Domno, while in 1046 the deacon Peter, son of John, became rector of San Nicola in Priato. CDC 5: 51–52, no. 738; CDC 7: 22–23, no. 1070. In 1045, the cleric Lazzarus, son of Peter a cleric, became rector of SS Maria and Nicola, while in 1050 the cleric John, son of Leo, became rector of San Matteo in Salerno. CDC 6: 282–84, no. 1052; CDC 7: 126–28, no. 1131. Also Stephen a cleric was appointed as co-rector to the church of Sant'Adiutore in 1024, along with Maurus a priest. CDC 5: 82–84, no. 757.

[33] CDC 6: 225–27, no. 1016.

benefices to priests who would perform the office in the churches.[34] Similarly, the layman appointed in 1043 and the cleric appointed in 1045 to the church of SS Maria and Nicola had to provide salaries, food, and clothing for priests who would celebrate the religious office.[35] The only exception to this occurs in 1047, when a deacon named Peter, appointed as rector of the church of San Nicola in Priato, is not specifically instructed to appoint a priest. However, in the document, Peter speaks in the first person plural, suggesting that he did not administer the church alone.[36] In two cases monks who were not priests were appointed to run religious foundations, and in one case a nun, but these were foundations which did not exercise secular clerical duties.[37] Thus, certain religious duties only could be performed by priests, although the secular clergy shared their pastoral duties with both the regular clergy and the laity.

Apart from these examples, the church owners did not stipulate how the rectors were to pay for other priests or clerics, how they should administer the ecclesiastical patrimonies, or how they had to fulfill their other obligations. Instead the owners of churches and monasteries placed the administration of the houses into the hands of the clergy they appointed. The clerics were responsible both for the religious duties attached to the churches and for the management of the church's patrimony. They received usufruct rights over church lands, meaning the right to keep the produce from the lands and the authority to lease property out for either money or a share of the produce. The church rectors generally did not need to seek the owners' permission when leasing or buying lands, and the church owners rarely participated in legal transactions or disputes involving their foundations. The investiture charters themselves set down only broad requirements for the rectors, and for most religious houses the only connection between clerics and owners after an appointment was the annual or bi-annual payment given to the owners by the rectors. Moreover, most of the time family members received no special treatment, and the ecclesiastical foundations themselves were rarely used to bolster family power.[38]

[34] CDC 5: 51–52, no. 738; CDC 7: 126–28, no. 1131.

[35] CDC 6: 225–27, no. 1016; CDC 6: 282–84, no. 1052.

[36] CDC 7: 22–23, no. 1070.

[37] In 979, the bishop of Salerno gave permission to a nun, Sosanna, to found and head a new convent. CDC 2: 137–38, no. 317. In 1025, Alferius became abbot of the newly founded abbey of the Holy Trinity at Cava, while in 1035 Luca became abbot of the monastery of Santa Barbara in Lucania. CDC 5: 93–95, no. 764; CDC 6: 38, no. 896, with date corrected by Galante, *La Datazione*, 55, no. 34.

[38] In only one instance did a rector have special duties vis-à-vis the church owners, being required to visit them if they were ill and to bury them in the church free of charge. CDC 7: 126–28, no. 1131.

Investitures of priests provide a precise inventory of the churches' possessions for thirteen religious foundations in the Principality of Salerno. All the foundations contained books, at the very least an antiphonary and a "liber comitem" (containing gospels and epistles). Most also had other works, such as homilies, saints' lives, or psalters. The church of San Giovanni in Vietri, for example, contained ten books, including a homily, four Gospels, antiphonaries, sacramentaries, and the Acts of the Apostles, all written in Greek. Santa Maria in Vietri had forty-one "Gestae" in addition to a "liber comitem," a homily, an antiphonary, and a Psalter. The churches of San Nicola in Gallocanta and SS Maria and Nicola in Mercatello both possessed over ten books, including prayer books, penitential books, sacramentaries, and psalters. The foundations possessed a wide variety of liturgical attire, generally chasubles, amices, and orariums. They also had icons, chalices, incense burners, candle-holders, curtains, hangings, and other religious artifacts and church ornaments. The churches of San Giovanni di Staffilo in Vietri and SS Maria and Nicola in Mercatello contained over fifty such items, while San Nicola in Gallocanta had hundreds of ornaments, vestments, and decorations. Many of these items were quite costly, made of gold, silver, or silk, and some were specified as coming from far away. San Giovanni di Staffilo in Vietri, for example, had a candelabra from Constantinople, San Felice in Felline and SS Maria and Nicola in Mercatello had ecclesiastical robes made of African silk, and San Nicola of Gallocanta had icons and glass candelabras from Constantinople. Many churches also possessed farming implements or animals for agricultural activities, as well as stalls and barns. The priests of the church of San Giovanni in Tresino, for example, had plows and other farming implements, in addition to numerous animals. The church of SS Maria and Nicola in Mercatello possessed a large variety of farm animals, including pigs, goats, chickens, cows, lambs, and oxen. San Venero in Corneto had sheep, pigs, and a pair of oxen, while San Giovanni in Vietri had plows. San Nicola in Gallocanta had mules, goats, chickens, and oxen, as well as barns and casks of wine stored in a cellar in Salitto.[39] Thus, although churches tended to be modest structures, they

[39] San Giovanni in Vietri: CDC 2: 81–2, no. 276; CDC 2: 145–46, no. 323; and CDC 2: 233–34, no. 382; Santa Maria in Vietri: CDC 4: 71–73, no. 582; Sant'Adiutore in Nocera: CDC 5: 82–84, no. 757; SS Maria and Nicola in Mercatello: CDC 5: 170–72, no. 812; CDC 6: 225–27, no. 1016; CDC 6: 282–84, no. 1052; CDC 7: 111–13, no. 1121; and CDC 7: 254–56, no. 1205; San Giovanni in Tresino: CDC 6: 182–83, no. 990; San Nicola in Priato: CDC 7: 22–23, no. 1070 and CDC 7: 275–76, no. 1220; Sant'Andrea in Arcelle: CDC 7: 33–34, no. 1077; San Venero in Corneto: CDC 7: 191–93, no. 1174; Sant'Angelo in Velanzanu: CDC 7: 198–200, no. 1178; San Felice in Felline: CDC 8: 25–27, no. 1252; San Nicola in Gallocanta: CDC 8: 38–40, no. 1258 (Cherubini, 197–200, no. 77); CDC 8: 66–68, no. 1270 (Cherubini, 193–96, no. 76);

often possessed expensive books, garments, and decorations, as well as animals and farming utensils.

Two documents mention the existence of *chartae fraternitatis* in some religious houses, although they give precise information neither on the function of these documents nor on the exact type of organization religious confraternities assumed in the region.[40] Most likely confraternities in Salerno were simple prayer unions, in the sense that people gave money for prayers, both during life and after death, as well as funeral ceremonies and burials.[41] A charter for the church of San Massimo dated 902, for example, specifically mentioned that the religious community would say prayers and give masses for a donor.[42] Moreover, a late medieval manuscript found in the cathedral church of Salerno, the "Liber Confratrum" of San Matteo, contains death notices of various people dating back to the Lombard and Norman period.[43] Obviously the clergy in the church of San Matteo were meant to say prayers for the people listed on the anniversary of their deaths, and the *chartae fraternitatis* found in other churches might have served the same function. As a result, confraternities in the Principality of Salerno do not seem to have referred to the well-organized associations familiar to scholars of northern and central Italy, in which members participated in a variety of religious and social activities throughout they year.[44] Nonetheless, they did create communities of prayer centered on specific religious foundations, most likely for the people living nearby.

San Nicola of Gallocanta provides a good example of a community house

---

and CDC 9: 3–9 no. 1 (Cherubini, 219–23, no. 88); San Michele Arcangelo in Passiano: CDC 8: 208–12, no. 1345; San Giovanni di Staffilo in Vietri: CDC 9: 107–11, no. 32. In addition, a 904 document for San Massimo mentions gold and silver objects, books, and slaves belonging to the church. CDC 1: 150–51, no. 119.

[40] CDC 7: 22–23, no. 1070; CDC 7: 275–76, no. 1220.

[41] Giovanni Vitolo, "Istituzioni ecclesiastiche e pietà dei laici nella Campania medievale: la confraternità di S. Maria di Montefusco (secc. X–XV)," *Campania Sacra* 8/9 (1977/78): 39.

[42] CDC 1: 143–44, no. 114.

[43] An edition of the manuscript can be found in C. A. Garufi, *Necrologio del Liber confratrum di S. Matteo di Salerno*, vol. 56 of *Fonti per la storia d'Italia* (Rome: Istituto Storico Italiano per il Medio Evo, 1922).

[44] According to historians such as Vitolo and Houben, Garufi's study brought preconceptions based on research in northern and central Italy to southern Italy and, as a result, they have rejected his characterization of southern Italian confraternities as similar to those in the north. For a good summary of the debate, see Hubert Houben, "Confraternite e religiosità dei laici nel Mezzogiorno medievale (sec. XII–XV)," in *Mezzogiorno Normanno-Svevo: Monasteri e castelli, ebrei e musulmani* (Naples: Liguori, 1996), 355–62. Also see Thomas Frank, *Studien zu italienischen Memorialzeugnissen des XI. und XII. Jahrhunderts* (Berlin/New York: de Gruyter, 1991).

built by a local family. The church was founded sometime around 979 by a smith named Marinus in a place just outside of Vietri on a hill overlooking Salerno, on some property Marinus had recently purchased. Originally dedicated to San Felice and San Nicola, the church was sold to Count Adelbertus in 996 by Marinus' son Ursus "Caballario," who claimed that he was forced to sell the property and church because of debts owed to creditors, as well as his obligation to return a dowry to his mother Blacta, who had remarried a man named Constantinus after Marinus' death.[45] After the sale, the church, dedicated now only to Saint Nicholas, remained in the hands of Count Adelbertus' family for over one hundred years. (See figure 2.)

Under Adelbertus and his descendants, the church became an important property-holder in the region and a central part of the family's patrimony, which was split in two lines by the two sons of Count Adelbertus: Landoarius and Lambertus. Count Adelbertus' descendants took a keen interest in the church's activities, donating lands to the foundation and helping the abbot defend its rights. San Nicola housed a community of Greek monks and priests who leased out lands locally and built up an extensive patrimony of books, gowns, church utensils, and decorations. Up until the end of the eleventh century, the church's lands and interests were completely local, focused in and around Vietri. This area contained many immigrants from Greek areas, whose religious needs were obviously served by the church, although interestingly the owners themselves were Lombard.

Count Adelbertus and his family provided well for the church and its rectors in the eleventh century, donating lands, houses, and churches in towns in and around San Nicola. Although not all of the donation charters survive—perhaps in some cases donations were made without written documentation—the surviving evidence clearly demonstrates the family's generosity to the church. Count Adelbertus himself donated all his property to the rectors of San Nicola upon his death.[46] His sister-in-law Countess

---

[45] Ursus brought along with him three charters that documented his father's purchase of the property in 979 from a certain Blacta, his subsequent construction of the church shortly thereafter, and an emancipation charter issued to the church by John bishop of Salerno in 981. After showing the charters, Ursus then proceeded to sell the lands and the church to Count Adelbertus for 20 *tarì*, with the permission of Prince John and according to Roman law. CDC 3: 50–54, no. 494 (Cherubini, 126–29, no. 30). For more information on the church of San Nicola of Gallocanta, see the introduction to Cherubini, *Le Pergamene di S. Nicola di Gallucanta*, 1–92 and Giovanni Vitolo, "La Latinizzazione dei monasteri Italo-Greci del Mezzogiorno medievale. L'Esempio di S. Nicola di Gallocanta Presso Salerno," in *Minima Cavensis. Studi in margine al IX volume del Codex Diplomaticus Cavensis*, ed. Simeone Leone and Giovanni Vitolo (Salerno: P. Laveglia, 1983), 75–90.

[46] Cava XII, 37–38 (Cherubini, no. 92, 230–34).

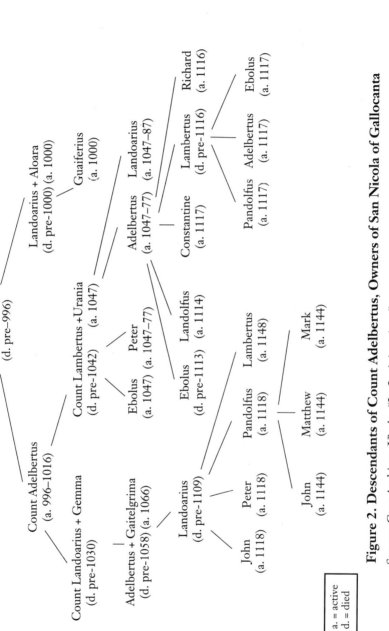

Figure 2. Descendants of Count Adelbertus, Owners of San Nicola of Gallocanta

Source: Cava Archives; Vitolo, "La Latinizzazione"

Aloara, the widow of his brother Count Landoarius, and her son Guaiferius donated lands to the church in Priato, Albori, and Vietri in May of 1000.[47] In 1066 Counts Peter, Lambertus, and Landoarius, sons of Count Lambertus, along with Count Landoarius, son of Count Adelbertus and his mother Gaitelgrima, confirmed a donation that Count Adelbertus had made to the church years before.[48] In 1089 this same Landoarius, son of Count Adelbertus, donated two pieces of land in Gualdu and Passiano; additionally, in 1093 he donated lands in Balnearia along with Lambertus son of Count Peter.[49] In the same year, Landoarius also donated his portion of the church of Sant'Angelo in Aurole with some additional land.[50] Four years later Landoarius donated some property and then entered the religious community of San Nicola.[51]

By the mid-eleventh century, the church was a large landholder in the region. It had houses, cells, lands, and mills in Priato, Albori, Vietri, Salitto, Bosanola, and Balnearia, all in the area surrounding the church. San Nicola's movable wealth, listed in three documents dated between 1058–1065, included over ten books, numerous robes, chalices, crosses, icons, candelabras, and other ornaments.[52] It also had oxen, a mule, seven cows, fourteen goats, and casks of wines stored in Salitto, Priato, and in the church itself. Beginning sometime before 1012, San Nicola began to lease out lands for cultivation. Only seven land leases survive, although a 1058 document mentions that eight "cartulae pastenationis" existed in the church at that time.[53] By 1065 it also had a dependent church nearby in Albori dedicated to Sant'Andrea.[54]

The rectors of San Nicola initiated a number of disputes before judges in the mid-eleventh century in order to defend the church's property rights in the region. In 1065, 1066, 1067, and 1070, Abbot Theophilus brought prop-

47 CDC 3: 107–08, no. 534 (Galante, *La Datazione*, 207–10, no. 24 and Cherubini, 132–35, no. 34).

48 CDC 9: 68–75, no. 19 (Cherubini, 230–34, no. 92).

49 Cava XIV, 116 (Cherubini, 277–79, no. 108); Cava XV, 72 (Cherbuini, 290–91, no. 116).

50 Cava C, 41 (Cherbuini, 296–97, no. 119).

51 Cava XVI, 70 (Cherubini, 305–7, no. 123).

52 CDC 8: 38–40, no. 1258 (Cherubini, 197–200, no. 77); CDC 8: 66–68, no. 1270 (Cherubini, 193–96, no. 76); CDC 9: 3–9, no. 1 (Cherubini, 219–23, no. 88).

53 CDC 4: 203, no. 656 (Cherubini, 166–72, no. 62 and Galante, *La Datazione*, 95–96, no. 68), CDC 4: 264–67, no. 692 (Cherubini, 141–45, no. 40), CDC 5: 10–11, no. 714 (Cherubini, 145–47, no. 41), CDC 5: 294, no. 715 (Cherubini, 147–51, no. 42), CDC 5: 187–89, no. 824 (Cherubini, 154–57, no. 48), CDC 6: 233–35, no. 1021 (Cherubini, 172–75, no. 63), CDC 8: 38–40, no. 1258 (Cherubini, 197–200, no. 77).

54 CDC 9: 27–28, no. 9 (Cherubini, 224–25, no. 89).

erty holders in areas where the church held lands before judges and accused them of trespassing on San Nicola's lands.[55] In all four cases the defendants pleaded ignorance, claiming they did not know which lands belonged to the church and which to them, and in all four cases the disputes ended with a clarification of borders. Theophilus was obviously interested in defining borders in order to lease the lands and keep their fruits in the church's power. In fact, the church leased out a number of lands in the area over the course of the eleventh century, and thus helped initiate the agricultural expansion that was characteristic of the Principality of Salerno in the eleventh century.[56]

The two priests who served as abbots of San Nicola in the eleventh century, Praxis and Theophilus, both signed their names in Greek on documents. Although it is not clear whether they came from Byzantine territories or whether they were born locally, the religious community which they headed included mostly if not all Greek monks, and the abbots themselves were required to officiate in the church according to Greek traditions.[57] Three investiture charters survive from the mid-eleventh century, in which the abbot's duties were specifically spelled out. In 1058, Counts Adelbertus and Landoarius sons of Count Lambertus, along with Count Landoarius son of Count Adelbertus and his mother Gaitelgrima appointed Theophilus, a monk and priest, church rector. The first charter, issued in January, came from Adelbertus, son of Count Peter, and Gaitelgrima, daughter of Count Landolfus and widow of Count Adelbertus, along with her son Landoarius. The second, from June, was by Count Adelbertus, son of Count Lambertus, and his brother Count Landoarius.[58] Theophilus was required to hold the divine office daily, "as was right for Greek priests" ("sicut decet presbiteris grecis"), keep the church lit and in good condition, and keep the lands under cultivation. The priest kept all donations to the church and profits from the mill and in return brought wax and other unspecified dona-

[55] CDC 9: 27–28, no. 9 (Cherubini, 224–25, no. 89); CDC 9: 38–56, no. 13 (Cherubini, 225–29, no. 90); CDC 9: 118–21, no. 36 (Cherubini, 234–36, no. 93); CDC 9: 271–90, no. 94 (Cherubini, 241–45, no. 96).

[56] CDC 4: 203, no. 656 (Cherubini, 166–72, no. 62; Galante, *La Datazione*, 95–96, no. 68), CDC 4: 264–67. no. 692 (Cherubini, 141–45, no. 40), CDC 5: 10–11, no. 714 (Cherubini, 145–47, no. 41), CDC 5: 294, no. 715 (Cherubini, 147–51, no. 42), CDC 5: 187–89, no. 824 (Cherubini, 154–57, no. 48), CDC 6: 233–35, no. 1021 (Cherubini, 172–75, no. 63), CDC 8: 38–40, no. 1258 (Cherubini, 197–200, no. 77).

[57] A charter from 1092 specifically referred to the community as an "order of Greek monks" ("ordo grecorum monachorum") Cava XV, 48 (Cherubini, 286–87, no. 114).

[58] CDC 8: 38–40, no. 1258 (Cherubini, 197–200, no. 77); CDC 8: 66–68, no. 1270 (Cherubini, 193–96, no. 76).

tions to the owners' houses three times a year: on Christmas, Easter, and the feast of Saint Nicholas. In addition, Theophilus was to give three of the owners twenty-four gold *tarì* of Amalfian money the first year, and then thirty gold *tarì* of Salernitan money for six years after. To the other two he gave thirty-four *solidi* for the first six years and then five *solidi* for the six years after that. Finally Theophilus pledged that during his lifetime he "would not go under the authority of other lords" ("non habeam potestatem alios dominos habere").[59]

The owners of San Nicola participated actively in the church's activities. In addition to appointing priests to serve in the church, they also took part in disputes and supervised land exchanges and leases. During three of the four disputes mentioned above, the owners appeared with the abbot to uphold the church's rights.[60] In a 1012 charter that documented the end of a sharecropping agreement, the abbot of San Nicola, Praxis, specifically stated that he acted with the permission of the church's owners.[61] When the abbot of San Nicola exchanged some church lands with the vicecount Vivus, son of Peter in 1077, the four owners appeared to oversee the transaction.[62] Moreover, all the charters specifically mentioned San Nicola's owners, demonstrating the strong connection between the family and the church.

The documents also paid close attention to what percentage of the church each owner possessed. In a 1058 charter, for example, Gaitelgrima, the widow of Adelbertus, owned one-eighth, Count Landoarius, son of Adelbertus, owned three-eighths, and the grandsons of Adelbertus—Peter, son of Count Lambertus, Adelbertus, son of Count Lambertus, and Landoarius, son of Count Lambertus—owned one-sixth each.[63] In charters from the late eleventh and early twelfth centuries, most of which documented the donation of San Nicola to the abbey of Cava, each owner's percentage of the church was specified exactly.[64] Thus the descendants of Count Adelbertus, who bought San Nicola in 996, remained active partici-

[59] CDC 8: 38–40, no. 1258 (Cherubini, 197–200, no. 77).

[60] CDC 9: 27–28, no. 9 (Cherubini, 224–25, no. 89); CDC 9: 38–56, no. 13 (Cherubini, 225–29, no. 90); CDC 9: 118–21, no. 36 (Cherubini, 234–36, no. 93).

[61] CDC 4: 203, no. 656 (Cherubini, 166–72, no. 62; Galante, *La Datazione*, 95–96, no. 68.)

[62] CDC 10: 224–28, no. 92 (Cherubini, 250–55, no. 99).

[63] CDC 8: 66–68, no. 1270 (Cherubini, 193–96, no. 76).

[64] Cava XIV, 78 (Cherubini, 264–65, no. 104); Cava XIX, 31 (Cherubini, 315–17, no. 128); Cava XIX, 52 (Cherubini, 317–18, no. 129); Cava XIX, 90 (Cherubini, 319–20, no. 130); Cava E, 37 (Cherubini, 321–22, no. 132); Cava XX, 34 (Cherubini, 323–34, no. 133); Cava XX, 38 (Cherubini, 324–26, no. 134; Cava XX, 59 (Cherubini, 326–28, no. 135).

pants in the church's administration and well-being for over one hundred years, until the church passed into the hands of the abbey of Cava at the beginning of the twelfth century.

In addition to being an important part of the life of Count Adelbertus' descendants, San Nicola was also a powerful force in the community. It received donations not only from the owners, but also from the local population, particularly from families who had immigrated from Greek territories or from the town of Atrani, located nearby on the Amalfi Coast.[65] For example, a Greek named Policarpus, son of Constantine, donated some lands in Bosanola in 1069.[66] In 1073, Mansus Atranese, son of Peter Atranese, gave the church some empty lands in Vietri.[67] Lupenus Atranese, son of John Atranese, donated lands in Salitto in 1084.[68] None of these donors appeared with titles and were most likely small landholders in the region. Some of them also sought to become part of the religious community of San Nicola, such as Policarpus, son of Constantine, who was assured entry into the monastery without any payment after he donated the above-mentioned lands in Bosanola.[69] Similarly, Constantine who donated lands in 1088 was allowed to become a monk.[70]

San Nicola was clearly an important religious and economic center for the area of Vietri. Although a dynastic foundation, it responded to the religious needs of the local population. Its lands and influence lay near to the church, and in all its activities, it was closely linked to the community it served. The donors and sharecroppers all lived in the vicinity and the clerics were recruited locally. It leased out lands to the neighboring population and was a catalyst for the expansion of agriculture in the region. It also served the religious needs of Greek Christians who had immigrated to the region in the tenth and eleventh century; the priest investitures specifically mentioned that the priests serving in San Nicola were to perform the divine office in the manner of other Greek priests.[71]

The administration of religious houses in other regions in southern Italy

---

[65] For information on the immigrants from Atrani, see Bruno Figliuolo, "Gli Amalfitani a Cetara: vicende patrimoniali e attività economiche (secc. X–XI)," *Annali dell'Istituto Italiano per gli Studi Storici* 6 (1979/80): 30–82 and Taviani-Carozzi, *La Principauté*, 800–833.

[66] CDC 9: 238–41, no. 82 (Cherubini, 238–41, no. 95).

[67] CDC 10: 35–36, no. 10 (Cherubini, 249–50, no. 98).

[68] Cava XIV, 14 (Cherubini, 260–62, no. 102).

[69] CDC 9: 238–41, no. 82 (Cherubini, 238–41, no. 95).

[70] XIV, 92 & 93 (Cherubini, 266–68, no. 105).

[71] CDC 8: 38–40, no. 1258 (Cherubini, 197–200, no. 77); CDC 8: 66–68, no. 1270 (Cherubini, 193–96, no. 76); CDC 9: 3–9, no. 1 (Cherubini, 219–23, no. 88).

similarly relied upon local custom rather than written law. The dispute between Prince Sicard and the bishop of Benevento in 839, discussed briefly in the last chapter, reflects well this tradition.[72] The point of contention related to the baptismal church of San Felice, which a Beneventan nobleman had founded some years prior and had left to the prince upon his death. The prince, in turn, donated it to the monastery of Santa Maria di Luogosano shortly thereafter. The bishop brought forward a lawsuit, claiming that, as a baptismal church, San Felice by law belonged to him, since church councils had legislated that all baptismal churches in a diocese were under the authority of a bishop. In the end, however, custom trumped canon law when Prince Sicard decided that the church would remain a dependency of Santa Maria because the princes and other leading men had always relied on local usage in these matters rather than upon the canons or laws of the Lombard people.[73] Thus custom and the force of community guided practices, rather than conciliar legislation or regulations issued by ecclesiastical hierarchies.

Greek Foundations

The existence of Greek foundations also shows the importance of local custom, as well as the problems inherent in defining categories of religious life in Lombard southern Italy in terms of ideas from other times and places. Throughout the region, both "Eastern" and "Western" practices were found, as well as a merging of the two traditions. Calendars and liturgies that survive from Benevento, Calabria, and Naples, for example, contain both Greek and Latin elements, as well as bi-lingual hymns.[74] A study of the few liturgical books that survive from Benevento in the early medieval period reveal many divergences from Roman traditions, including an *oratio post evangelium*, an *oratio super populum*, and additional lessons taken from the Book of Prophets for Sunday Mass, all characteristic of Byzantine re-

---

[72] *Chronicon Vultunense del monaco Giovanni*, ed. Vincenzo Federici, vol. 58 of *Fonti per la Storia d'Italia* (Rome: Istituto Storico Italiano per il Medio Evo, 1925), 297–302, doc. 61. Martin, *La Pouille*, 241–43; Vitolo, "Vescovi e Diocesi," 103; Fonseca, "Particolarismo," 1163–65, 1174.

[73] ". . . quia semper principes et antistites, ponentes in oblivionem canones et edicta gentis nostre Langobardorum, semper usus huius nostrę provincie sic est iudicaturi" *Chronicon Vultunense*, 300.

[74] Vitolo, "Vescovi e Diocesi," 91; Taviani-Carozzi, *La Principauté*, 815–16; Enrica Follieri, "Il culto dei santi nell'Italia greca," in *La Chiesa Greca in Italia dall'VIII al XVI secolo. Atti del Convegno storico interecclesiale, Bari, 30 April–4 May 1969* (Padua: Edictrice Antenore, 1973), 553–77.

gions.[75] The feast days of both Greek-speaking saints from the East and Latin-speaking ones from the West were celebrated.[76] In Salerno, Greek and Latin clerics often served in the same religious houses, and some churches even switched between Latin and Greek rectors.[77] Moreover, some practices now identified as Greek or Eastern were, in fact, indigenous to southern Italy. Clerical marriage, baptism by priests as well as bishops, and the performance of baptisms on the Epiphany, Easter, and the Pentecost were all common practices dating back to the earliest days of Christianity.[78] Two councils held in the ninth century even suggest that Christians in southern Italy, laypeople as well as clerics, had adopted Jewish and Muslim practices, celebrating Jewish holidays, adhering to Jewish religious beliefs, taking Saturday rather than Sunday as a day of rest, and applying Muslim laws with regard to slavery.[79] Ibn Hawqal, a tenth-century Muslim visitor to Fatimid Sicily, complained about the widespread intermarriage between Muslims and Christians, as well as the uncanonical religious practices of the Muslims on the island that once again suggest a mixing of the two religious traditions. The writer was so shocked by the hybrid form of Islam practiced on the island that he declared it to be a corruption of true religion and a sect unique in the Muslim world.[80]

The first documentary evidence for Greek-speaking clerics in Salerno dates from 970, when a monk from the monastery of San Lorenzo signed his name in Greek. After this, a number of documents attest to Greek-speaking clerics in the religious houses in both Salerno and surrounding areas, with a particularly strong concentration in the southern regions of Capaccio and Cilento. Archaeological, hagiographical, and toponymic

---

[75] Klaus Gamber, "La liturgia delle diocesi dell'Italia centro-meridionale dal IX all'XI secolo," in *Vescovi e Diocesi in Italia nel Medioevo (sec. IX–XIII). Atti del II Convegno di storia della chiesa in Italia, Rome, 5–9 September, 1961* (Padua: Antenore, 1964), 145–56.

[76] Follieri, "Il culto dei santi," 553–58.

[77] This is the case for San Giovanni in Vietri, Santa Sofia in Salerno, and San Benedetto in Salerno. For San Giovanni, see CDC 2: 81–2, no. 276; CDC 2: 145–46, no. 323; CDC 2: 233–34, no. 382. For Santa Sofia, see CDC 6: 159–61, no. 977; CDC 7: 150–51, no. 1147. For San Benedetto, see Acocella, "La figura e l'opera di Alfano I," 20.

[78] Silvano Borsari, *Il monachesimo bizantino nella Sicilia e nell'Italia meridionale prenormanne* (Naples: Istituto italiano per gli studi storici, 1963), 18–19.

[79] "Un concile inédit," ed. Morin, 146–47, no. 9 and Amelli, "Acta Synodi," 390, no. 9. Vitolo, "Vescovi e Diocesi," 99.

[80] Ibn Hawqal, *Configuration de la Terre*, trans. J.H. Kraemers and G. Wiet (Paris: G.-P. Maisonneuve, 1964), 128–30; Francesco Gabrieli, "Ibn Hawqal e gli Arabi di Sicilia," *Rivista degli Studi Orientali* 36 (1961): 249.

sources provide evidence for even more Greek monasteries and churches in both the Lombard and Norman periods.[81] In other regions of southern Italy, such as Calabria and the Basilicata, Greek monks and clerics also appear in large numbers in the early medieval period, and in Calabria, Greek eventually became the primary liturgical language of Christianity.[82]

There has been much discussion surrounding the origins of these Greek immigrants, as well as their reasons for immigrating.[83] Hagiographical

[81] San Lorenzo in Salerno, San Giovanni in Vietri, San Nicola in Gallocanta, and Santa Sofia in Salerno contained Greek priests, clerics, or monks. CDC 2: 126–27, no. 309; CDC 2: 233–34, no. 382; CDC 6: 159–61, no. 977; CDC 8: 38–40, no. 1258 (Cherubini, 197–200, no. 77); CDC 8: 66–68, no. 1270 (Cherubini, 193–96, no. 76); CDC 9: 3–9, no. 1 (Cherubini, 219–23, no. 88). The monastery of San Benedetto in Salerno had a Greek rector appointed in 1043. Cherubini, 14–15. Charter evidence survives at the abbey of Cava for numerous Greek foundations in Lucania, and other evidence, written as well as archaeological and toponymic, indicates the existence of an even greater number of Greek-speaking or Greek-inspired foundations in the area. See Pietro Ebner, "I monasteri bizantini nel Cilento: I Monasteri di S. Barbara, S. Mauro et S. Marina," *Rassegna Storica Salernitana* 28 (1967): 77–142; Peduto, "Insediamenti altomedievali," 464.

[82] Borsari, *Il monachesimo bizantino*, 22.

[83] The bibliography on Greek foundations and the "hellenization" of southern Italy and Sicily is long. The important works include François Lenormant, vol. 2 of *La Grande-Grèce. Paysage et histoire* (Paris: A. Levy, 1883); Pierre Batiffol, *L'abbaye di Rossano. Contribution à l'Histoire de la Vaticane* (Paris: Picard, 1891); Kirsopp Lake, "The Greek Monasteries in South Italy," *The Journal of Theological Studies* 4 (1903): 345–68, 517–542 and 5 (1904): 22–41; Alberto Vaccari, *La Grecia nell'Italia meridionale: Studi letterari e bibliografici*, vol. 13 of *Orientalia Christiana* (Rome: Pontificio istituto orientale, 1925); Peter Charanis, "On the question of the Hellenization of Sicily and Southern Italy during the Middle Ages," *The American Historical Review* 52 (1946): 74–86; Mario Scaduto, *Il monachesimo basiliano nella Sicilia medievale* (Rome: Edizioni di storia e letteratura, 1947); Léon-Robert Ménager, "La 'byzantinisation' religieuse de l'Italie méridionale (IXe–XIIe siècles) et la politique monastique des Normands d'Italie," *Revue d'Histoire Ecclésiastique* 53 (1958): 747–774; Biagio Cappelli, *Il monaschesimo basiliano ai confini calabro-lucani* (Naples: F. Fiorentini, 1963); Borsari, *Il monachesimo bizantino*; Agostino Pertusi, "Aspetti organizzativi e culturali dell'ambiente monacale greco dell'Italia meridionale" and André Guillou, "Il monachesimo greco in Italia meridionale e in Sicilia nel medioevo," in *L'eremitismo in Occidente nei secoli XI e XI: Atti della seconda Settimana internazionale di studio, Mendola, 30 August-6 September 1962* (Milan: Società Editrice Vita e Pensiero, 1965), 382–426 and 355–426; *La Chiesa Greca in Italia dall'VII al XVI secolo. Atti del Convegno storico interecclesiale, Bari, 30 April–4 May 1969* (Padua: Editrice Antenore, 1973); Enrico Morini, "Eremo e cenobio nel monachesimo greco dell'Italia meridionale nei secoli IX e X," *Rivista di storia della Chiesa in Italia* 31 (1977): 1–39, 354–90; Vera von Falkenhausen, "I monasteri greci dell'Italia meridionale e della Sicilia dopo l'avvento dei Normanni: continuità e mutamenti," in *Il passaggio dal dominio bizantino allo stato normanno nell'Italia meridionale: Atti del II Convegno internazionale di studi sulla Civiltà rupestre medioevale*

sources often speak of Muslim invasions as the impetus behind the movement, and many historians have adhered to this explanation. Some have also
postulated that theological debates, such as the Monophysite controversy,
caused orthodox clerics to flee to Rome and Italy. However, other documents suggest that the flow of people in the eastern Mediterranean was constant, and although moments of crisis most likely did increase the number of
immigrants to Italy, movement was not an unusual phenomenon from both
Greek- and Latin-speaking areas.[84] Most of the Greek immigrants in the
Principality of Salerno came from Sicily and Apulia, and they were no more
foreign, and no more noteworthy in the sources, than immigrants from
Naples, Benevento, Capua, or even Amalfi. Place of origin was a common
means of identifying individuals in charters and there is no evidence that
people from outside of the Principality of Salerno, be it from other Lombard territories, from Frankish territories, or from Greek lands, were
treated any differently from a legal standpoint. Moreover, no moment in
particular seems to stand out as a period of massive immigration. It is important not to exaggerate the crisis element in what seems to be a normal
flow of people and families.

Equally difficult to ascertain is the exact meaning of "Greek" Christianity and "Greek" foundations in the early medieval period. Historians and archaeologists classify religious foundations as Greek based on purely linguis-
tic evidence. If liturgical books, inscriptions, charters, or even signatures
were written in Greek, then the church or monastery is characterized as
"Greek." No specific form of architecture or religious life distinguished
Greek churches and monasteries from Latin ones.[85] Thus the question
arises of how precisely these ecclesiastical foundations and their clerics differed from their Latin counterparts. Was language the only distinguishing
characteristic, or did liturgy and practices also set them apart?

The popes in Rome clearly distinguished between Latin (i.e. Roman) and
Eastern practices, and at times they condemned non-Roman ones as im-

---

nel Mezzogiorno d'Italia. Taranto-Mottola, 31 October–4 November 1973 (Taranto: Am-
ministrazione proviniciale, 1977), 197–229, "Il Monachesimo italo-greco," and "Pat-
rimonio e politica patrimoniale dei monasteri greci nella Sicilia normanno-sveva," in
*Basilio di Cesarea: la sua età e il Basilianesimo in Sicilia: Atti del Congresso Internazionale,
Messina, 3–6 December 1979* (Messina: Centro di Studi Umanistici, 1983), 777–90;
Loud, *The Age of Robert Guiscard*, 54–59.

[84] For an in-depth look at the movement of people in the early medieval Mediterranean, see McCormick, *Origins of the European Economy*, pt. 2, 123–277.

[85] Peduto, for example, comments on how it is impossible to distinguish between
Lombard and Byzantine settlements in southern provinces. Peduto, "Insediamenti
altomedievali," 454.

proper. From an early date, western and eastern territories had different traditions regarding the date for celebrating Easter and other religious holidays, when and how to perform the eucharist and baptism, and which saints were worthy of veneration. During the first 1000 years of Christianity, such differences did not lead to schism. Although popes at times complained of Eastern practices that had entered the Roman church, at the same time they embraced and integrated certain rituals imported from Constantinople. In the seventh century, for example, the Roman church adopted the *Theophania*, the Exaltation of the True Cross, and the Annunciation, Dormition, and Nativity of the Virgin Mary. Greek hymns and chants imported from Constantinople were also introduced at this time. Moreover, Greek religious houses were founded in Rome, and there is no evidence of conflict between Greek and Latin clerics in the city. In the case of at least one house, the church of SS. Alexius and Boniface, Greek and Latin clerics served side by side.[86]

In addition, monks seemed to have been aware of divergent monastic traditions in Greek-speaking and Latin-speaking areas, although they did not condemn such variations as invalid. An interesting exchange between Latin- and Greek-speaking monks can be found in the Life of St. Nilos, a Greek-speaking monk born in Calabria who traveled to central Italy at the end of the tenth century and founded the famous Greek monastery of Grottaferrata not far from Rome. During his travels, Nilos stayed at Montecassino and the monks there were curious about his views on the issue of fasting on Holy Saturday during Lent, a tradition found in western but not eastern territories. Nilos explained how he followed the practice established by saints such as Athanasius, Gregory, Basil, and John Chrysostom and upheld by church councils. However, in a rare moment of tolerance and open-mindedness, he conceded that the Western tradition was not prohibited, since God is always pleased with sacrifice. Both practices, he said, were equally valid since both were done for the glory of God.[87] The monks of Montecassino also found Eastern and Western traditions equally acceptable; they asked St. Nilos to comment on the Holy Scriptures, to perform the

---

[86] Richards, *The Popes and the Papacy*, 278–80.

[87] *De S. Nilos Abbate, Acta Sanctorum*, September VII, 302–5, chaps. 73–78. Βίος καὶ πολιτεία ὅς Πάτρος ἡμῶν Νείλος τοῦ νεοῦ, ed. Germano Giovanelli (Grottaferrata: Badia di Grottaferrata, 1972), 112–17, chaps. 73–78. Also see discussions in Borsari, *Il monachesimo bizantino*, 111–15; Olivier Rousseau, "La Visite de Nil di Rossano au Mont-Cassin," in *La Chiesa Greca in Italia dall'VIII al XVI secolo. Atti del Convegno storico interecclesiale, Bari, 30 April–4 May 1969* (Padua: Edictrice Antenore, 1973), 1111–37; Jean-Marie Sansterre, "Saint Nil de Rossano et le monachisme latin," *Bollettino della Badia greca di Grottaferrata* 45 (1991): 339–86.

holy office, and to compose a number of hymns in Greek in honor of Montecassino's founder, St. Benedict, whom Nilos depicted as an heir to St. Anthony and other desert fathers from the eastern Mediterranean. It is interesting to note that the modern-day Italian translator of the Life described St. Nilos as performing the divine office "according to the Greek rite"; however, the Greek text clearly states that he did so "in the Greek language" (τῇ ἑλλάδι φωνῇ) without any hint that the liturgy was somehow seen as different.[88] Thus, while the monks noted some divergence in their traditions and practices, they accepted them as equally legitimate.

The church of San Giovanni in Vietri is a good example of the way in which Greek clerics and Greek Christians fit into the religious life of the Principality of Salerno. Our information for this church comes from three charters, redacted between 974 and 986, in which the families of two brothers appointed priests to serve in the church, which they owned in the town of Vietri and dedicated to St. John.[89] In the first charter, dated January of 974, they appointed a monk and priest from Naples named Guaimarius, in March of 980 they appointed Leo son of Leo from Amalfi, and in January of 986 they appointed two new priests: Sabas referred to as a priest and abbot and Cosmas referred to simply as a priest. The requirements in all three investiture charters were more or less the same: the priests were required to officiate in the church day and night along with other clerics of their own choosing. They were required to live in a house attached to the church and to keep the church's lands under cultivation. They were allowed to keep all offerings and burial fees collected by the church, but were required to give the owners a donation on the feast day of St. John, as well as a portion of the citrus fruit from the church's orchard. However, while the first two priests were told simply to officiate in the church "as was right for a peasant church" ("sicut decet ecclesia billana"), Sabas and Cosmas were told to officiate in the church "as was right for Greek peasant priests" ("sicut decet sacerdos grecos villanus"). Moreover, Sabas and Cosmas were referred to as being "of the Greek race" ("ex genere grecorum") and both signed the 986 charter in Greek. In addition, the 986 charter mentioned that the church now contained a number of books and decorations not mentioned in the previous two investiture charters, including a homily, four Gospels, antiphonaries, and sacramentaries all written in Greek, as well as icons, chalices, incense burners, candle-holders, and other church ornaments, some of which were specified as coming from Constantinople.

---

[88] Germano Govinelli, trans., *Vita di S. Nilo* (Grottaferrata: Badia di Grottaferrata, 1966), 90, chap. 73.

[89] CDC 2: 81–2, no. 276; CDC 2: 145–46, no. 323; CDC 2: 233–34, no. 382.

These charters point to a number of interesting overlaps between "Greek" and "Latin." First of all, the owners alternated between appointing Latin and Greek priests, as occurred in other churches in the area.[90] Second, the owners themselves were not Greek, even though they appointed clerics who were. Sabas and Cosmas, as other Greek priests in the area, were allowed to officiate according to their own traditions, even though the church owners did not necessarily adhere to these traditions themselves. Finally, the church contained both Greek- and Latin-speaking clerics, which was another common feature of the area.[91] Thus, Greek and Latin practices were clearly not seen as antithetical and the documents even suggest that for the local population one set of practices was as valid as another.

Overall the evidence suggests that Greek Christianity in Salerno and southern Italy was not a distinct entity characterized by a unique liturgy and practiced by a specific group of foreigners living in the region. First of all, many practices identified as Greek or Eastern could be found in the region from the earliest days of Christianity, and the constant flow of Greek-speaking immigrants into the region meant that "Eastern" traditions remained alive. Second, Lombard southern Italy was not part of any larger ecclesiastical hierarchy, neither a Latin church centered on the pope in Rome nor a Greek Church centered on the patriarch of Constantinople. What is more, the Principality of Salerno itself lacked a centralized ecclesiastical system, which meant that the region contained a great deal of diversity with regard to religious practices. Third, the distinction between Latin and Greek practices was not as clear cut in the early Middle Ages as it would become later on. The real period of differentiation between the two forms of Christianity occurred in the High Middle Ages, as the result of renewed contact between popes and patriarchs. Finally, the issue of perspective comes into play. Literate and well-educated prelates, such as popes and patriarchs, were much more concerned about deviations in liturgical formulae or religious practices than the average Christian. Moreover, religious issues of vital importance in Rome were often of little interest in other areas. Documents from Salerno suggest that priests, monks, and holy men and women were judged not based on their geographical origin or language of worship but rather on their abilities or background, be it piety of lifestyle, the capacity to perform miracles, administrative skills, or a family

[90] See, for example, the investiture charters for the church of Santa Sofia in Salerno, in which sometimes a Latin-speaking and sometimes a Greek-speaking rector was appointed. CDC 6: no. 159–61, no. 977; CDC 7: 150–51, no. 1147.

[91] See, for example, charters for the monastery of San Lorenzo in Salerno, which contained both Latin and Greek signatures. CDC 2: 126–27, no. 309; CDC 2: 81–2, no. 276.

tradition of entering the clergy. In many ways language appears to have been the main, or perhaps only distinguishing characteristic. Both Greek-speaking clergy and so-called Eastern practices were accepted as part of the religious environment in southern Italy, and there is no sign of friction between Greek and Latin clergy. It is anachronistic to view the Catholic and Greek Orthodox Churches in the early medieval period as two separate institutions each with their own unique brand of Christianity. It is even difficult to know how far local Christians could distinguish between Greek and Latin practices, and if they could, whether or not it would have mattered. Councils held in southern Italy in the ninth century suggest that the local population even had trouble differentiating between Christian, Jewish, and Muslim laws and rituals.[92]

The Lifestyle of the Secular Clergy

In the same way that Greek and Latin Christianity were not two distinct entities existing side-by-side, lifestyle did not separate the clergy from the laity in early medieval Salerno, as Roman and Frankish councils of the period advocated.[93] Priests, for example, married, produced offspring, and lived with their families. They often lived far away from the religious houses in which they served, taking lands in benefice or living on private property with their wives and children. They appear in the documents in all capacities and did not have any legal limitations placed on them. They also did not exercise unique legal functions or monopolize administrative offices that required education and literacy.

Both priests and monks held property just as other citizens did. In Salerno, all the investiture charters made a distinction between the church's possessions and those of the foundation's rector. The property belonging to a church when a priest or cleric took over remained part of the church's patrimony; the priest merely exercised usufruct rights over it. Also books, objects, and other movables donated to the church during a rector's tenure remained part of the church's patrimony, with the exception of animals of which the priests generally received a portion.[94] The goods that a priest or

---

[92] "Un concile inédit," ed. Morin, 146–47, no. 9 and Amelli, "Acta Synodi," 390, no. 9. Vitolo, "Vescovi e Diocesi," 99.

[93] Maureen Miller has noted a similar situation in Verona. Miller, *The Formation*, 46.

[94] The priests appointed to SS Maria and Nicola in Mercatello, for example, kept one-third of all the offspring of the church's animals. CDC 5: 170–72, no. 812, CDC 6: 282–84, no.1052, CDC 7: 111–13, no. 1121.

cleric brought with him remained his own, and on his death he could appoint an heir. However, a rector was also often required to donate a portion of his individual wealth, either one-third or one-half, to the foundation upon his death.

Clerics bought, sold, and leased lands in their capacity as private citizens, and when doing so, they acted independently of the religious houses in which they served. For the period before 1070, more than 10 percent of the parties involved in land sales carried an ecclesiastical title. Similarly, priests and clerics leased out private property to tenants, divided inheritances with siblings and other family members, participated in land disputes involving family property, and passed on their property to heirs in the same manner as laypeople.[95] They also appeared as lessors and sharecroppers, living on and directly working the lands they rented.[96] Finally, clerics served as guarantors and witnesses for transactions, appeared as advocates, and exercised guardianship ("mundium") over women, and no evidence of special legal rules applying to them appears in the documents.

Clerics also owned slaves and servants. The church of San Massimo in Salerno received a donation of a family of slaves in 899, while other documents from the tenth and eleventh century spelled out the rights of free women marrying slaves belonging to the church.[97] A nun named Imelsenda freed her slave, John, when she fell ill in 940, while in 981 a nun named Alferada did the same.[98] A priest named Bernard, who was appointed to

---

[95] For leases of personal property, see CDC 4: 130–32, no. 613; CDC 4: 171–73, no. 636; CDC 5: 230–32, no. 851; CDC 6: 258–59, no. 1037; CDC 8: 179–81, no. 1328. For land divisions with family members, see CDC 4: 132–35, no. 614; CDC 5: 14–16, no. 716; CDC 5: 139–41, no. 796. For disputes involving clerics and their personal property, see CDC 2: 51–52, no. 253; CDC 2: 276–77, no. 415. For inheritances given to children, see CDC 9: 171–74, no. 56.

[96] CDC 1: 236–37, no. 183; CDC 2: 46–47, no. 249; CDC 2: 105–6, no. 295; CDC 2: 318–19, 440; CDC 2: 66–67, no. 264; CDC 3: 17–18, no. 471; CDC 4: 1–2, no. 537; CDC 4: 4, no. 539; CDC 4: 23–25, no. 553; CDC 4: 30–31, no. 557; CDC 4: 77–79, no. 585; CDC 4: 95–96, no. 597; CDC 4: 126–28, no. 610; CDC 4: 142–43, no. 620; CDC 4: 200–202, no. 654; CDC 5: 58–60, no. 742; CDC 5: 70–71, no. 750; CDC 5: 135–77, no. 794; CDC 5: 204–5, no. 836; CDC 6: 34–36, no. 894; CDC 6: 95–96, no. 935; CDC 6: 162–64, no. 979; CDC 6: 262–63, no. 1040; CDC 7: 52–56, no. 1089; CDC 7: 139–40, no. 1141; CDC 7: 188, no. 1171; CDC 7: 261–62, no. 1209; CDC 8: 132–34, no. 1303.

[97] CDC 1: 139–40, no. 111. For example, in 981 the abbot of San Massimo promised not to place into servitude a woman, named Maria, who was marrying one of the church's slaves ("famulus"), named Andrea. Similarly in 1004, the abbot agreed not to place in servitude a woman, named Lieta, who was marrying a slave belonging to the church named Martinus. CDC 2: 235, no. 383; CDC 4: 47–48, no. 568.

[98] CDC 1: 192, no. 149; CDC 2: 159–60, no. 334.

head the church of San Giovanni in Tresino in 986, entered into service with an unspecified number of male and female servants ("servi et ancillae"), over whom Bernard had complete possession. Upon his death, Bernard was able to dispose of these servants freely, bequeathing them to whomever he pleased.[99]

Priests and clerics in the Principality of Salerno did not occupy any special place in governmental administration or the legal system. As discussed above, lay gastalds and counts were the main officials used by princes to administer their realm. In addition, the majority of notaries in the region were lay. In the city of Salerno itself, only one example of an ecclesiastical notary is documented before the late eleventh century.[100] Moreover, in Salerno disputes and trials were almost always conducted in the prince's palace in front of lay judges and gastalds. In fact, for the pre-1070 period, no disputes took place in ecclesiastical foundations in Salerno. Although in other regions, in particular, Lombard Lucania, ecclesiastical notaries were common, the judges and gastalds who decided disputes and oversaw other legal transactions were lay.[101] Thus, clerics did not occupy a special place in the government, as they did in many Frankish regions.

It is unknown how priests were educated or whether they underwent similar training. Most likely clerical education was based on a sort of apprenticeship program, with clerics serving in a religious house for a while under a priest before taking over the administration of a church themselves. Sons of priests who themselves became priests quite likely received their training at the hands of their father. It is also unknown how and by whom priests were ordained. Given the limited authority of the bishop, it is unlikely that he personally ordained all the priests in his diocese. Unfortunately, the documents do not allow us to draw any solid conclusions about the type and manner of religious education received by the clergy of early medieval Salerno.

Clerical marriage, common throughout southern Italy, occurred frequently in Salerno, and the wives and children of priests had the same legal rights as those of laypeople. In the pre-1070 Cava documents, countless people are identified as the sons and daughters of priests, deacons, and clerics. A marriage contract and Morgengabe concession even survives for a cleric from Avellino, while other wives appear in documents alienating the

---

[99] CDC 2: 241–42, no. 388.

[100] Taviani-Carozzi, *La Principauté*, 542–43.

[101] See, for example, CDC 5: 16–19, no. 717; CDC 5: 197–98, no. 829; CDC 6: 17–20, no. 881; CDC 6: 89–90, no. 931; CDC 8: 32–33, no. 1255; CDC 8: 148–49, no. 1315.

one-quarter Morgengabe they received upon marriage.[102] In 1041, for example, Sichelgaita wife of a cleric named Peter gave permission for him to sell her one-fourth of lands in Nocera.[103] In fact, it is not infrequent to see the wives and children of clerics show up in legal actions alongside their clerical husbands and fathers, giving permission to sell or lease their portion. In 1037, for example, a cleric, Peter, son of a cleric named Peter, with his wife Grifa, sold lands they owned jointly as husband and wife.[104] In 1040, Stephen a priest and cardinal of the church of SS Matteo and Tomaso in Salerno appeared with his wife Marenda donating lands to his church. The same Stephen actually held his ecclesiastical benefice along with his son, John.[105]

Children of clerics inherited property just as the offspring of laypeople did, and priest investitures specifically stated that priests had the right to keep and then pass on their private property. Moreover, the practice of providing benefices gave priests the liberty to live separately on church property along with their wives and children. In some cases, benefice-holders received lands in Salerno to live on, while in other cases they were given property outside the city, which they could then lease out and profit from. Sons could inherit the benefices if they, too, became clerics and were willing to officiate in the same church, and at times fathers and sons actually received benefices together.[106]

The clerical calling in early medieval Salerno seems almost a hereditary one, with many sons of priests, clerics, and deacons following in their fathers' footsteps and becoming, themselves, clerics.[107] Some of the sons even inherited their fathers' offices, taking over as priests and clerics in the same ecclesiastical foundations when their fathers died. For example, in the 1047

---

[102] CDC 2: 77–8, no. 272.

[103] CDC 6: 168–70, no. 984.

[104] CDC 6: 111–13, no. 948.

[105] CDC 6: 127–31, no. 958. Also see CDC 9: 271–90, no. 94; CDC 3: 5–6, no. 462; CDC 6: 117–19, no. 951; CDC 8: 306–7, no. 1378; CDC 9: 259–63, no. 89.

[106] For the most detailed descriptions of clerical benefices, see CDC 1: 141–43, no. 113, with date corrected by Galante, *La Datazione*, 79–81, no. 55; CDC 2: 339, no. 454; CDC 4: 97–98, no. 598; CDC 6: 127–31, no. 958.

[107] See, for example, CDC 2: 42–43, no. 245; CDC 2: 103–4, no. 293; CDC 4: 49–50, no. 571; CDC 5: 70–71, no. 750; CDC 5: 113–14, no. 778; CDC 6: 2–3, no. 871; CDC 6: 134–36, no. 894; CDC 6: 95–96, no. 935; CDC 6: 117–19, no. 951; CDC 6: 158–59, no. 976; CDC 6: 165–66, no. 981; CDC 6: 219–21, no. 1013; CDC 6: 236–38, no. 1023; CDC 6: 258–59, no. 1037; CDC 6: 262–63, no. 1040; CDC 7: 139–40, no. 1141, with date corrected by Galante, *La Datazione*, 123–24, no. 86; CDC 7: 188, no. 1171; CDC 7: 203–5, no. 1181; CDC 7: 195–97, no. 1176; CDC 7: 208–9, no. 1184; CDC 8: 132–34, no. 1303; CDC 9: 76–79, no. 21.

charter of investiture for Peter, a priest in San Nicola in Priato, the church owner stated that the sons of Peter could follow him as priest under the same conditions.[108] In 1052 Muscatus the priest and abbot of the church of Santa Sofia in Salerno handed over one of its dependent houses, the monastery of San Venero in Corneto, to a father-son team. According to the document, Nicolas, a priest and monk along with his son Leo, were to administer the monastery jointly in the same manner as other rural monasteries inhabited by Greek monks. Upon the father's death, the son would pay eighty gold *tarì* and then continue to run the monastery on his own under the same conditions.[109] In 1053 an investiture charter for the church of Sant'Angelo in Velanzano stipulated that at the death of the new rector, John, his sons had a right to take over the church, as long as they, too, were priests.[110]

The lifestyles of clerics thus differed little from those of laypeople.[111] They held private property, married and produced heirs, and occupied no special position because of their education or calling. They operated independently of the bishop, and no ecclesiastical authority set rules for their behavior or for correct religious usages. Also the foundation owners participated minimally in the day-to-day life of their houses, leaving the clergy they appointed free to decide how best to administer the foundation and its property. In effect, the clergy who administered the ecclesiastical foundations operated autonomously, answerable only to local custom.

Anchorites and Monks

Although the line separating the laity from the clergy could often be blurred because secular clerics were fully integrated into lay society and the communities in which they served, the distinction between a religious life and a secular one was more clearly defined. Men and women who turned their backs on the world in order to lead an ascetic existence devoted completely to God were the true "religious" in society. Nonetheless, as in the case of the secular clergy, the lifestyle of monks and nuns was based more on custom than rules set down by an ecclesiastical authority. Southern Italian bishops made little effort to standardize monastic lifestyles, as their counterparts in Carolingian territories attempted to do, and both hagiography and

---

[108] CDC 7: 275–76, no. 1220.
[109] CDC 7: 191–93, no. 1174.
[110] CDC 7: 198–200, no. 1178.
[111] This is a point also made by Miller in her study of Verona. Miller, *The Formation*, 96–97.

charter evidence from early medieval southern Italy depict a wide variety of monastic lifestyles that generally diverge from the rules set down in papal documents and at Carolingian councils.[112] Although some of the holy men and women in southern Italy and Salerno resided in cloisters and followed a rule, most of them lived as hermits, wandering ascetics, or household religious.[113] In many ways the term "regular clergy" is not an apt category for describing them, since they did not live a cloistered life, follow a rule, or pledge obedience to an abbot. Many changed from one lifestyle to another, and family ties remained strong even after conversion. Families of monks not only embarked upon a religious life simultaneously, but traveled and lived together either in monasteries or at home. Moreover, many monks and nuns did not lead the type of ascetic lifestyle exalted in hagiography but, like members of the secular clergy, remained a part of lay society. They owned property, inherited lands, and participated in legal proceedings in the same manner as lay people.

---

[112] The following section is based on a study of nine saints' lives: Leo-Luke (810–910), *De S. Leone Luca Carolionionesi, Abbate Mulensi in Calabria, Acta Sanctorum* March I, 97–102; Elia the Younger (823–903), *Vita di Sant'Elia il Giovane,* ed./trans. Giuseppe Rossi Taibbi (Palermo: Istituto siciliano di studi bizantini e neoellenici, 1962); Elia the Speleote (860/70–960), *Vita Sancti Eliae Spelaeote Abbate, Acta Sanctorum* September III, 848–88; Vital (d. 990), *De S Vitale Siculo Abbate ordinis S Basilii Armenti et Rapollae in Italia, Acta Sanctorum* March II, 26–36; Sabas the Younger (d 989–91), *Vita et Conversatio Sancti Patris Nostri Sabae Iunioris,* ed./trans. Giuseppe Cozza-Luzi, vol. 12 of *Studi e Documenti di Storia e Diritto* (Rome: Tipografia poliglotta, 1891), 37–56, 135–68, 311–23; Christopher and Macaire (10th century), *Vita et Conversatio Sanctorum Patrum Nostrorum Christophori et Macarii,* ed./trans. Giuseppe Cozza-Luzi, vol. 13 of *Studi e Documenti di Storia e Diritto* (Rome: Tipografia poliglotta, 1892), 375–400; Luke of Armento (d. 993), *De S. Luca Abbate Confessore, Acta Sanctorum* October VI, 332–42; Nilos of Calabria (910–1005), *De S. Nilos Abbate, Acta Sanctorum* September VII, 259–320; Fantino the Younger, *La Vita di San Fantino il Giovane: Introduzione, Testo Greco, Traduzione, Commentario e Indici,* ed./trans. Enrica Follieri (Brussels: Société des Bollandistes, 1993). These hagiographical sources, dating from the ninth and tenth centuries, were composed shortly after the saints' deaths in various monasteries in southern Italy, Sicily, and Greece. They were originally written in Greek, although in some cases only survive in later Latin translations found elsewhere in Italy or Europe. Although most of the lives are anonymous, historians and paleographers believe them to have been written by disciples or acquaintances of the monks who actually witnessed at least some of the events described. For summaries of many of these saints' lives, as well as important information about the texts, see G. Da Costa-Louillet, "Saints de Sicile et d'Italie méridionale aux VIIIe, IXe e Xe siècles," *Byzantion* 29–30 (1959–60): 89–173 and Borsari, *Il monachesimo bizantino,* 38–65.

[113] A good recent study on ascetics in late antique Italy is found in Georg Jenal, *Italia ascetica atque monastica: das Asketen- und Mönchtum in Italien von den Anfängen bis zur Zeit der Langobarden (ca. 150/250–604)* (Stuttgart: Hiersemann, 1995).

Southern Italian hagiography contains a clear bias toward the anchoritic lifestyle, depicting the monks able to live in the wilderness, surrounded by various temptations, as superior to their brethren who remained in a community. Even saints who started their careers in monasteries almost inevitably ended their lives in isolation, with the initial period of communal life serving merely as preparation for the more rigorous but more fulfilling experience of an anchoritic existence. Although most extant hagiography from early medieval southern Italy originated in Byzantine territories, both the saints and saints' lives traveled north into Lombard areas. In fact, most hagiographical texts produced in Lombard southern Italy had Byzantine origins.[114] Moreover, archaeological evidence confirms the popularity of the anchoritic lifestyle throughout Campania and the Principality of Salerno in the early Middle Ages. Excavations have revealed a large number of hermitages in the region, generally located in cliffs or caves.[115] In the province of Salerno, traces of hermit dwellings still exist in the mountains of Serino, Calvanico, Nocera, Cava, and Dragonea (Transboneia). The Amalfi coast, in fact, had one of the highest concentrations of cliff hermitages found in southern Italy, while the famous ascetic retreat found on top of Mt. Erasmo near Olevano sul Tusciano was the largest in Campania.[116] Hermitages most likely outnumbered monasteries in early medieval southern Italy, including Salerno. These hermitages, moreover, were not necessarily humble affairs, but could encompass numerous dwellings and multiple chapels with expensive decorations and sophisticated architecture and artwork. The *grotta* above Olevana sul Tusciano, for example, contains the remains of a highly complex cult center decorated with beautiful ninth- and tenth-century frescoes depicting various religious scenes from the Bible and the lives of saints. It clearly served as a major religious center for the local population in the Lombard period, as well as a site of pilgrimage for Christians throughout southern Italy. The hermitage was even visited by a Frankish monk who traveled to the region sometime between 867–70.[117]

In addition to cave monasticism, the wandering ascetic was an extremely popular figure in southern Italian hagiography. In fact, all the saints found

[114] Vuolo, "Agriografia beneventana," 202–4.

[115] Gino Kalby, "Gli Insediamenti rupestri della Campania," in *La civiltà rupestre medioevale nel Mezzogiorno d'Italia. Ricerche e Problemi: Atti del primo convegno internazionale di studi, Mottola-Casalrotta, 29 September–3 October, 1971*, ed. Cosimo Damiano Fonseca (Genoa: Edizioni dell'Istituto Grafico S. Basile, 1975), 153–72.

[116] Giovanni Vitolo, *Caratteri del Monachesimo nel Mezzogiorno Altomedievale (secc. VI–IX)* (Salerno: P. Laveglia, 1984), 15; Kalby, "Gli Insediamenti," 168.

[117] François Avril and Jean-René Gaborit, "Itinerarium Bernardi monachi et les pélégrinages d'Italie du Sud pendant le Haut-Moyen-Age," *Mélanges d'archéologie et d'histoire* 79 (1967): 269–98.

in southern Italian hagiography traveled extensively throughout their life-times, some on pilgrimages to visit the tombs of famous martyrs, some to find wilderness where they could lead solitary lives, some to search out famous ascetics who could further their religious education, and some to found new monasteries. In a few cases they journeyed their whole lives without ever entering a monastic community of any sort. Saint Elia the Younger, for example, born in Sicily, captured by Muslims, and then tonsured by the patriarch of Jerusalem as a young man, spent his whole existence traveling throughout the eastern Mediterranean.[118] He began his career in the Holy Land, moving around for a couple of years before finally settling on Mt. Sinai for three years, where he received instruction from various fathers. Next he went to Alexandria, Persia, Antioch, Africa, and then Sicily to visit his mother. While in Taormina he received Daniel as a disciple and the pair continued to travel. They journeyed to Greece, Rome, and then down to Calabria where Elia evidently founded some sort of community before leaving once again for Rome.[119] In Rome, the pair stayed with Pope Stephen V, then went back to Calabria where they resided again in the monastery they had founded.[120] Afterward they traveled briefly to both Patras and Taormina, then returned to Italy and headed north to Amalfi to cure the niece of an important official there. Toward the end of Elia's life, the pair went back to Greece at the behest of Emperor Leo VI who wished to meet the saint.[121] Elia, however, died on his journey to Constantinople.[122]

Household religious also appear in documents from Salerno. A monk named Anastasius, for example, who appears in a text describing the translation of the relics of Saint Matthew, inhabited a cell next to his mother's house.[123] A monk in Salerno named Iohannelgarus made a donation of some lands to the church of San Massimo in 923, along with his former wife Ermengarda and his son John, who was a cleric; he does not appear to have been attached to any ecclesiastical foundation.[124] For women, the choice of remaining at home after converting to a religious life was quite common.[125]

---

[118] *Vita di Sant'Elia il Giovane*, 10–15, 26–29, chaps. 6–9 and 18.

[119] Ibid., 28–47, chaps. 19–30.

[120] Ibid., 54–61, 74–77, chaps. 36–39 and 49.

[121] Ibid., 82–85, chap. 54.

[122] Ibid., 104–7, 112–15, chaps. 66 and 70.

[123] *In Translatione Sancti Matthaei Apostoli et Evangelistae*, ed./trans. Giuseppe Talamo Atenolfi, *I Testi medioevali degli Atti di S. Matteo l'Evangelista* (Rome: C. Bestetti, 1958), 100–101.

[124] CDC 1: 179–81, nos. 140 and 141.

[125] For a discussion of the phenomenon of uncloistered nuns in medieval southern Italy, see Patricia Skinner, *Women in Medieval Italian Society, 500–1200* (Harlow: Pearson, 2001), 151–52.

Many nuns found in the Cava charters were widows who assumed the monastic habit after their husbands' death, but continued to live at home and hold property. For example, a certain Teoperga, daughter of Ermerisus and widow of Ragemprandus, took up a religious life in 899 while remaining in her house.[126] In 999 a widow named Iaquinta entered the monastic life.[127] She was to continue to live at home and she gave her Morgengabe to her sons, with the stipulation that they would provide her with food and wine for the rest of her life.[128] Thus entry into a religious life did not always mean a physical departure from home into a monastery or wilderness.

Although archaeological evidence suggests that most of the monasteries founded in southern Italy in the early medieval period were hermitages, three important Benedictine monasteries arose in southern Lombard territories in the early medieval period. The monastery of Montecassino, which the Lombards had destroyed in 580–81, was rebuilt in 717–720 by a monk from Brescia named Petronax, along with the aid of the Lombard prince Gisolf II. At around the same time, three Beneventan nobles founded the first Benedictine monastery in Lombard territories at Volturno, dedicated to San Vincenzo.[129] Over a century later in 873, Emperor Louis II founded the abbey of San Clemente of Casauria in the Abruzzi as a new center of imperial power after his defeats in the south.[130] All three of these monasteries, built in regions of weak episcopal power, grew to become preeminent religious, political, and economic forces. However, they were always much more closely linked to Rome and the Frankish world than Lombard southern Italy.[131]

Other smaller cenobite monasteries also appeared in southern Italy at this time. Naples, for example, had a number of small monasteries in which monks led a communal life.[132] Also in Salerno some examples of monastic-type communities are found in the documents. San Massimo and Santa Maria de Domno, although churches, both had communities of monks at-

---

[126] According to the document, she "dressed herself in a religious habit and lived at home" ("religionis habitum super me induta sum et in domum meam habito"). CDC 1: 124–26, no. 98, with date corrected by Galante, *La Datazione*, 23–24, no. 4.

[127] CDC 3: 91–93, no. 524.

[128] Also see the following Cava documents: CDC 1: 61–2, no. 49; CDC 1: 102–3, no. 79, with date corrected by Galante, *La Datazione*, 19–20, no. 1; CDC 1: 137–38, no. 109; CDC 2: 159–60, no. 334; CDC 6: 1–2, no. 870; CDC 6: 221–23, no. 1014.

[129] On the foundations of Montecassino and San Vincenzo, see von Falkenhausen, "I longobardi meridionali," 316–18; Vitolo, *Caratteri*, 19–20; Cowdrey, *The Age of Abbot Desiderius*, 2–3 and Hodges, *Light in the Dark Ages*, 23–29.

[130] Feller, *Les Abruzzes*, 167–79.

[131] Martin, "L'ambiente," 229.

[132] See Vitolo, *Caratteri*, 16–19, for more specific information.

tached to them.[133] San Lorenzo and SS Maria and Benedetto in Salerno contained communities of monks, as did the monastery of San Pietro in Erecka.[134] Monks connected to San Lorenzo and SS Maria and Benedetto appear to have led a common life, and they had to seek their abbot's permission before carrying out any legal activities.[135] Finally, three convents for nuns appear in the documents: one founded by Sosanna on a hill just outside Salerno, another dedicated to San Michele within the city's walls, and a third dedicated to San Giorgio found in the territory of Giffoni.[136]

Hagiographical sources demonstrate that monasteries in southern Italy and Sicily varied widely in terms of size and organization. Only a very few of the monasteries were large, permanent structures organized around a rule. Leo-Luke, for example, who became abbot of the monastery at Mt. Mula, presided over a community of over one hundred monks who owned and managed a large number of fields and vineyards in the area.[137] The abbots of this community named successors on their deathbeds, thus assuring the monastery's continuity.[138] Saint Fantino's experience in Elia's monastery reflects closely the type of lifestyle found in the Rule of Saint Benedict. When Fantino first arrived at the monastery's gate and knocked on the door, he was forced to remain outside for a while and then was thoroughly interro-

---

[133] For San Massimo, a document from 895 describes a certain Peter's entrance into the monastic community: "(He) desired to enter our monastery and take the monastic habit and live out his days here in the service of God" ("querebant introire in prefato nostro monasterio ad monachilem habitum recipiendum super se, et ut in servitium dei in eodem monasterio diebus vite sue commorarent"). CDC 1: 136–37, no. 108. For Santa Maria, a 1063 document describes a certain monk named Amatus who was "part of the congregation of monks in that monastery" ("ex congregatione monachorum ipsius monasterii"). CDC 8: 256–58, no. 1359.

[134] For San Lorenzo, see CDC 2: 126–27, no. 309. For SS Maria and Benedetto, see CDC 2: 331–32, no. 450 and CDC 5: 217–19, no. 845. For San Pietro, see CDC 4: 152–54, no. 625. Documents for ecclesiastical foundations in Cilento suggest that these, too, contained communities of monks.

[135] In 979, for example, Adelferius donated lands, along with his mother, with the permission of Abbot Nichodemus. CDC 2: 126–27, no. 309. In 992 John, a monk in SS Maria and Benedetto in Salerno, donated lands to Santa Maria de Domno with the permission of the abbot, while in 1032 John, a monk of the same foundation, sold lands with the abbot's permission. In the document, John claimed to be under the authority ("dominium") of the abbot. CDC 2: 331–32, no. 450; CDC 5: 217–19, no. 845.

[136] CDC 2: 137–38, no. 317; CDC 4: 139, no. 618; CDC 2: 31, no. 237.

[137] *De S. Leone Luca*, 101, chap. 14.

[138] Christopher named Leo-Luke as a successor while Leo-Luke similarly designated one of the monks to succeed him shortly before he died. *De S. Leone Luca*, 100–101, chap. 13.

gated by the abbot, who demanded to know why he desired to become a monk. The abbot warned Saint Fantino about the difficulties of the monastic life and after the saint was finally allowed to enter the community, he became a cook for the other monks as part of his initiation.[139]

Most of the monastic communities found in the hagiography, however, were based on an anchoritic rather than a communal lifestyle. A famous ascetic abode ("ascetica palestra") mentioned in the Life of Saint Elia the Younger, for example, housed a permanent community of hermits who lived in separate cells and had little or no contact with one another. This community, located in Calabria two kilometers northeast of Seminera, survived up into the eighteenth century.[140] The Life of Saint Sabas talks about the variety of monastic lifestyles in the forest of Mercourion, where some monks lived alone in caves, some in small groups of two or three, and some in large communities headed by an abbot.[141] Most of the hermetical retreats contained men and women living side-by-side. The life of Saints Christopher and Macaire, for example, describes how Christopher was surrounded by a multitude of men and women, including his wife, who desired to emulate his holy life.[142] The *vita* also mentions that the forest on Mt. Mercourion contained many hermitages where both men and women lived together.[143]

Most of the monasteries found in the hagiography were ad hoc structures that grew up around a holy man and his disciples and generally did not survive the founder's death. In fact, the saints, once their reputations had been established, spent the better part of their later lives setting up small, ephemeral monasteries throughout southern Italy and Sicily.[144] Similarly, in the charters from the abbey of Cava, most monasteries appear only once or twice in the documents, and then disappear. Monks and monastic lifestyles in early medieval Salerno thus differed noticeably from Benedictine abbeys such as Montecassino and Cluny, which had large communities of monks, vast landed estates, and historical continuity spanning centuries.

[139] *La Vita di San Fantino*, 404–9, chaps. 4–6.

[140] *Vita di Sant'Elia il Giovane*, 44–47, chap. 30.

[141] *Vita et Conversatio Sancti Sabae*, 46–47, chap. 7.

[142] *Vita et Converstio Sanctorum Chritophori et Macarii*, 384, chap. 7.

[143] *Vita et Converstio Sanctorum Chritophori et Macarii*, 386–87, chap. 9. The monastery founded by Luke of Armento also accepted monks of both sexes into its community. *De S. Luca*, 341, chap. 14.

[144] *De S. Leone Luca*, 100, chap. 9; *Vita di Sant'Elia il Giovane*, 32–33, 44–47, chaps. 22, 30; *Vita Sancti Eliae Spelaeote*, 863–65, chaps. 39–42, ; *De S. Vitale Siculo*, 30–32, chaps. 12, 16; *Vita et Converstio Sanctorum Chritophori et Macarii*, 382–84, 387, 391–92, chaps. 6, 10, 15; *Vita et Conversatio Sancti Sabae*, 46–47, 49–51, chaps. 7, 9; *De S. Luca*, 340, chaps. 8–9; *De S. Nilos*, 283, 302–3, 312, chaps. 38, 72–73, 87; *La Vita di San Fantino*, 420–25, chaps. 17–19.

The charters from Cava contain little evidence for monastic rules for the early medieval period. Before the 1070s, only two documents mention a rule for religious houses within the Principality of Salerno: the first in 979, when a monk named Adelferius claimed to be under the rule of the monastery of San Lorenzo, and the second in 1063 when the text of a monastic rule appeared in the inventory of the church of SS Michele Arcangelo and Martino in Passiano.[145] It has been suggested that for the early medieval period, a rule did not necessarily mean a written text, but rather an attitude or lifestyle, and thus one should not assume that the lack of a written rule means that no rule at all was followed.[146] Nonetheless, the cenobitic monasteries which did exist did not necessarily follow the Benedictine rule.[147] For many regions in southern Italy no evidence for Benedictine monasteries exists at all before the Norman period.[148] For Salerno, the Benedictine rule had limited, if any, success in Salerno before the foundation of the abbey of Cava in around 1020.

Despite the emphasis in the hagiography on the transformative nature of a conversion from a lay to a religious life, many monks and nuns in southern Italy and Salerno did not cut themselves completely off from the outside world, and both family and community ties remained important for them. Family members of ascetics often abandoned lay lives and themselves became monks or nuns, and frequently the saints founded monasteries alongside parents or siblings or accepted family members into their communities. Saint Fantino the younger, for example, convinced his parents to give away all their worldly possessions and spend their remaining years

[145] CDC 2: 126–27, no. 309. According to the 979 document, Adelferius completed a transaction "with permission of the venerable lord Nichodemus, abbot of the monastery of S. Lorenzo, under whose rule I live" ("per absolutione domni nichodemi venerabilis abbatis monasterii sancti laurentii, sub cuius regula permaneo"). CDC 8: 208–12, no. 1345. The monastery of Santa Maria in Elce was also observing the Benedictine rule by the mid-eleventh century, but it was located in Conza, effectively outside the Principality of Salerno. G. A. Loud, "The Monastic Economy of the Principality of Salerno during the Eleventh and Twelfth Centuries," *Papers of the British School at Rome* 71 (2003): 144.

[146] Charles Dereine, "Vie commune, règle de Saint Augustin et chanoines réguliers au XIe siècle," *Revue d'histoire ecclésiastique* 41 (1946): 395. Also see Toubert, "La vie commune," 18.

[147] Vitolo, *Caratteri*, 19.

[148] In Apulia, Benedictine abbeys appeared a bit earlier, beginning in the late tenth century. Martin, *La Pouille*, 665. The renewal of Montecassino under the auspices of Abbot Algernus (949–86) similarly caused the spread of the rule to nearby monasteries and dependent houses before the Norman period. However, no documentation from the pre-Norman period speaks of the Benedictine rule in Calabria. Von Falkenhausen, "Il Monachesimo italo-greco," 126–27.

leading a monastic existence. He then built two monasteries, one for his mother and sister and another for his father and two brothers.[149] Saint Nilos, the famous Calabrian abbot who founded the abbey of Grottaferrata in central Italy, had a disciple named Stephan who entered into a monastery with his mother and sister. Saint Luke of Armento, a Sicilian ascetic who spent time in Calabria as well as Sicily, took his widowed sister and her two children into his monastic community, with all three eventually accepting the monastic habit.[150] All the members of Saint Sabas' family eventually took up a religious life, traveling together and residing in the same monasteries.[151]

Even family members who did not enter into the monastic life continued to have contact with the saints after they had embraced a monastic life. Saint Elia the Younger, for example, visited his mother in Palermo, and the saint even predicted her death after receiving a vision of it while living in isolation.[152] Saint Fantino's parents sought contact with their son while he was living in solitude in the mountains of Lucania, although they had no plans to make him abandon his eremitical life.[153] The monk from Salerno named Iohannelgarus, mentioned above, donated lands to the church of San Massimo in 923 along with his wife and son John, with the stipulation that the church would give food and wine every year to support the family.[154] Sometimes family members reunited on holidays or when danger arose. Christopher, for example, left his life of solitude in order to escort his family to safety in Calabria during a Muslim attack, while Sabas came out of isolation to celebrate Easter with his family.[155] Thus the hagiographical sources did not advocate a renunciation of family ties and affections after entry into the monastic life.

Like members of the secular clergy, many monks and nuns appear in documents from the Principality of Salerno with all the same legal rights as laypeople. They held private property, bought and sold land, participated in disputes, and bequeathed and inherited property, generally without the per-

---

[149] *La Vita di San Fantino*, 420–23, chaps. 16–18.

[150] *De S. Luca*, 341, chap. 14.

[151] According to the life of Saint Christopher, after the fame of the saint had spread far and wide, his wife and children rushed to Ctisma, the region where he was leading a hermitical life, and also took up religious lives. *Vita et Converstio Sanctorum Chritophori et Macarii*, 381–82, chap. 5.

[152] *Vita di Sant'Elia il Giovane*, 36–39, 58–61, chaps. 25, 39.

[153] *La Vita di San Fantino*, 418–21, chaps. 15–16.

[154] CDC 1: 179–81, nos. 140 and 141.

[155] *Vita et Converstio Sanctorum Chritophori et Macarii*, 384–87, chaps. 8–10; *Vita et Conversatio Sancti Sabae*, 49–51, chap. 9.

mission of an abbot. In 980, for example, a monk from Sorrento named John bought some property from two brothers, Mansus and Leo.[156] John had, in fact, formerly leased this land from the brothers in exchange for a share of the produce. Similarly, a monk named Peter leased lands in Cetara in 991, promising to give the owners a portion of the crop.[157] A monk named Sellictus was the plaintiff in a dispute over large tracts of land in Balnearia in 1030, contending with his brother-in-law Machenolfus over property that had belonged to his father.[158] In all these cases, the monks conducted the legal activities on their own, without the permission of an abbot or community.

Conclusions

The wide variety of monastic lifestyles makes it difficult to generalize about the monastic experience in Salerno and southern Italy, and in some ways it is even difficult to define precisely what it meant to be a monk or nun, or how someone entered into a religious life. In the hagiographical sources initiation into the monastic life generally occurred at the hands of an older, venerated monk, who either tonsured the initiate or dressed him in monastic garb, often giving him a new name as well.[159] Nonetheless, nuns and monks who lived at home may have had no such initiation. Moreover, the lifestyles of monks took on a range of forms. Although the monastic ideal in early medieval southern Italy, including the Principality of Salerno,

---

[156] CDC 2: 155–56, no. 330.

[157] CDC 2: 322. no. 443.

[158] CDC 5: 189–94, no. 825.

[159] Saint Leo-Luke, for example, was tonsured by an old monk who lived in solitude in Calabria, although he received his monastic habit and new name later on from Christopher the abbot of a monastery on Mt. Mula in Calabria. *De S. Leone Luca*, 99–100, chaps. 4, 8. Saint Elia the Younger received his habit and new name from the patriarch of Jerusalem and Saint Elia the Speleote took his habit in the Church of Sant'Ausiliatrice in Sicily. *Vita di Sant'Elia il Giovane*, 26–29, chap. 18; *Vitae Sancti Eliae Spelaeote*, 850, chap. 7. The abbot of the monastery of San Philipe in Agira initiated Saint Vital and Saint Luke of Armento into the monastic life, while Nicephrous the "praepositus" of the same monastery gave the monastic habit to both Christopher and his son Saint Sabas the Younger. *De S. Vitale Siculo*, 27, chap. 2; *De S. Luca*, 337, chap. 3; *Vita et Converstio Sanctorum Chritophori et Macarii*, 378–80, chap. 3; *Vita et Conversatio Sancti Sabae*, 39–40, chap. 2. Saint Fantino received his tonsure and habit from the abbot Elia. *La Vita di San Fantino*, 406–9, chap. 6. Saint Nilos was converted by a monk from Mercourion but accepted the monastic habit in the monastery of San Nazario in Cilento. *De S. Nilos*, pp. 263–64, chaps. 5–7.

was based more on an anchoritic and peripatetic lifestyle than a cloistered existence, regular monasteries under the authority of an abbot were not despised but rather seen as one of many options available to the men and women who chose to lead a religious life. Most ascetics, in fact, alternated between wandering, cloistered, and isolated existences. As a result, in the same way that the line between secular and regular clergy was not always well pronounced, the anchorite/cenobite dichotomy was not an important distinction. Even more surprising was the ability given to monks and nuns to maintain close ties with family members, to live at home with children, and even to switch between a secular and monastic existence. The only criteria for becoming a religious appear to have been the desire to dedicate oneself to God and to lead a life centered on religious devotion and prayer. Such a life could be carried out in a variety of environments, either alone, in small groups, in large monasteries, or even with family members.

Similarly, it is hard to generalize about the ecclesiastical foundations of early medieval Salerno, since they exhibited such a great deal of variety with regard to size and wealth, mode of administration, and area and degree of influence. However, the majority of religious houses in the Principality of Salerno were the product of local communities, founded and controlled either by a well-off family from the community or by groups of individuals combining their resources together. They were administered on the basis of local custom, received donations from the neighboring population, and admitted local citizens into their religious communities. Although small, many houses were quite wealthy, possessing expensive furnishings, ecclesiastical robes, and books, as well as animals and agricultural implements. They leased out lands to sharecroppers, rented houses to local residents, and had wine cellars and stalls for animals. Their clergy performed a wide range of religious and economic functions. Thus, whether small or large, these local churches served as centers for the religious, social, and economic life of their communities.

Clearly the religious landscape of the Principality of Salerno in the early Middle Ages differed noticeably from the situation in the Carolingian empire. No episcopal hierarchy ever developed to oversee religious life and organization. It contained no large Benedictine-style abbeys with members focused on prayer and religious services for the noble families who built and maintained them. Bishops and abbots were not used as instruments of government, and Christianity never served as an important unifying factor for the princes of Salerno. No attempt was ever made to institutionalize or standardize Christianity, and religion remained community based, with a large amount of variety seen in both organization and practice. As a result, early medieval Salerno exhibited much continuity with the past, because in the early centuries of Christianity religious life was based primarily on custom and communities of believers without a well-organized ecclesiastical hierarchy as an intermediary.

The religious landscape of Francia, by contrast, underwent many far-reaching changes as kings and prelates introduced new liturgical practices and churchmen were given new administrative roles. Both Merovingian and Carolingian rulers used bishops and abbots as integral parts of their administrative system, bestowing on them wide authority over both the religious and political lives of their dioceses. Church councils issued rules not only on religious matters and ecclesiastical organization, but on a wide range of topics including economic policy, lay morality, and the judicial rights of bishops.[160] Moreover, bishops in Frankish territories developed a group identity and began to act as a unity during the Carolingian era.[161] Large monastic orders based on the Benedictine rule also developed over the course of the ninth and tenth centuries, and, like bishops, abbots became powerful forces in the political and religious structures of Francia.[162] In addition, the Christianization of political identity in the Carolingian era further transformed the role of religion as kings used liturgy as a means of propagating royal ideology and strengthening the links between themselves and their subjects.[163] At the same time, the reinforcement of the metropolitan structure challenged the traditional autonomy of bishops. Although diversity in practice and liturgy continued to be the norm in Frankish territories throughout the early Middle Ages, an ecclesiastical hierarchy closely linked to political power developed and took the place of the smaller Christian communities characteristic of the early Church.

Although the religious landscapes of the Principality of Salerno and the Carolingian empire diverged noticeably during the early Middle Ages, many of the features characteristic of Salerno were commonplace not only in other parts of southern Italy but in other areas of the Mediterranean world as well. First of all, ecclesiastical hierarchies were the exception and

---

[160] See examples given in Emile Amann, *L'époque carolingienne. Histoire de l'Eglise,* 6:75.

[161] Wallace-Hadrill, *The Frankish Church,* 176.

[162] For discussions of large Benedictine abbeys in Carolingian territories, see Southern, *Western Society and the Church,* 223–30; Barbara H. Rosenwein, chap. 1 in *To Be the Neighbor of Saint Peter: The Social Meaning of Cluny's Property, 909–1049* (Ithaca: Cornell University Press, 1989); Stephen D. White, chap. 2 in *Custom, Kinship, and Gifts to Saints: The Laudatio Parentum in Western France, 1050–1150* (Chapel Hill: University of North Carolina Press), 1988.

[163] Hen, *The Royal Patronage,* 86–95; McCormick, *Eternal Victory,* 342–77.

not the norm throughout southern Italy and the Byzantine empire before the eleventh century. Bishops in the eastern territories of the Roman empire never developed into the powerful charismatic figures characteristic of Gaul, and in the early Middle Ages not much changed. Throughout the eastern Mediterranean, bishops tended to be humble officials with little political clout and limited authority over the ecclesiastical foundations of their dioceses.[164] The office of the bishop itself was not as venerated in southern Italy or the Byzantine empire as in Frankish territories. Holy ascetics rather than pious bishops were the saints *par excellence*, and there was little separation between secular clerics and laypeople. The dichotomy between desert and world, that is, between regular and secular clergy, was the more significant distinction.[165]

In addition, proprietary religious foundations served as a major source for pastoral care throughout the eastern Mediterranean in the early medieval period, and both lay rulers and prelates encouraged and relied on private patronage, especially in rural areas.[166] The responsibility for building religious institutions was a joint one shared by lay rulers, bishops, and private patrons, and despite periodic attempts in councils held in Byzantine territories to place private religious houses under episcopal supervision, in general the only concern was that orthodox creeds be preached in these private churches.[167] Proprietary foundations in the Byzantine empire operated virtually autonomously, and the owners had the power to sell, bequeath, and donate their foundations, the right to nominate clerics serving in the foundations, and the authority to manage and exploit the foundations' properties.[168] Evidence even suggests that in some places proprietary churches provided pastoral care for the majority of the population. For example, papyri evidence from Egypt in the early Byzantine period suggests that the patriarchs of Alexandria generally only founded churches in the city of Alexandria itself, leaving the vast majority of church building in the hands of the laity.[169] In one case a cathedral church, in the town of Hermapolis, was under lay direction, and in the seventh through tenth century it was not uncommon for episcopal churches in many regions of the Byzantine empire to rely on local magnates to manage their properties and handle relations with the peasants who provided their endowments.[170] In the late ninth and tenth

---

[164] Brown, *The Rise of Western Christendom*, 113–14; Martin, "L'ambiente," 218–19.

[165] Ibid., 117–19.

[166] Martin, "L'ambiente," 224; Thomas, *Private Religious Foundations*, 5, 17–18.

[167] Thomas, *Private Religious Foundations*, 17–19; Brown, *The Rise of Western Christendom*, 114.

[168] Thomas, *Private Religious Foundations*, 71.

[169] Ibid., 61.

[170] Ibid., 65, 112.

centuries the rights and privileges of private foundations even increased such that they took over all of the duties of parish churches, including baptism, making private foundations more important than public ones.[171]

In the same way that the Principality of Salerno contained numerous small, ephemeral religious houses, other areas of the eastern Mediterranean were dotted with small private churches and monasteries, many of which were humble affairs, and many of which did not survive the demise of the founder or founders. In the Byzantine empire, for example, small communal religious houses were often constructed by villagers, and it was not uncommon after the death of the patrons for a religious community to leave the foundation and for the foundation itself to cease to exist.[172] Both the disappearance and secularization of religious houses were common features of Byzantium. Cities in the Byzantine empire, as well as in places like Egypt under Arab rule, contained numerous small religious houses that took on a variety of forms.[173] For example, a tenth-century document from Constantinople lists over 150 religious houses in the capital city itself, the majority of which were founded by laypeople.[174] The Arab geographer Ibn Hawqal, who traveled around the Mediterranean in the tenth century, remarked that the Christians in Egypt owned a vast number of churches.[175] Moreover, the organization of Muslim communities in the Mediterranean could at times be remarkably similar. When Ibn Hawqal visited Sicily, he was amazed at the large number of small mosques that dotted the city of Palermo—more than three hundred, according to his calculations.[176] As in the case of Christian territories, the majority of these religious houses were owned and managed by individuals and families. Thus throughout the Mediterranean in the early Middle Ages, Christians and non-Christians alike tended to worship in small, private religious foundations.

Finally the distinction between the laity and the clergy, and between a secular and a religious life, was not well pronounced. In the Byzantine empire, both laymen and clerics pursued careers that mixed state service, private estate administration, and the management of ecclesiastical institutions, and the distinction between an ecclesiastical career and a secular one was not clear cut.[177] Patrons of private foundations were often prominent participants in the political and military affairs of the empire, and some-

---

171 Ibid., 143.
172 Ibid., 20–25; 160–61.
173 Ibid., 97.
174 Ibid., 5–6.
175 Ibn Hawqal, *Configuration de la Terre*, 159.
176 Ibid., 119.
177 Thomas, *Private Religious Foundations*, 73.

times they would even alternate between a religious and secular life.[178] Evidence from Egypt shows clerics and monks working for great property owners in a number of different capacities, and in some cases rural clerics farmed lands to earn a living in the same manner as ordinary parishioners.[179] Thus the experience of Salerno not only represents continuity with the early period of Christianity but also fits into a larger Mediterranean tradition of an ecclesiastical system based on small religious houses built and administered by both the laity and the clergy outside any well-organized ecclesiastical hierarchy.

[178] Ibid., 116.
[179] Ibid., 69–70.

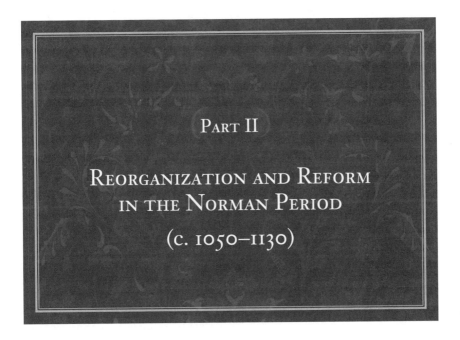

PART II

REORGANIZATION AND REFORM IN THE NORMAN PERIOD

(c. 1050–1130)

The archbishop of Salerno and the abbey of Cava transformed the religious landscape of the Principality of Salerno in the eleventh century through the creation of ecclesiastical networks with territorial rights and centralized administrations. Many religious houses in the region, along with their lands and revenues, slowly came under the power of one of these two organizations. The clerics administering the ecclesiastical foundations, in turn, became part of their hierarchies under the direct authority of the archbishops or abbots. The duties of clerics became better defined and clerical orders more differentiated. By the twelfth century, both the cathedral church of Salerno and the abbey of Cava oversaw ecclesiastical hierarchies that extended throughout the Principality of Salerno and, in the case of Cava, beyond.[1]

The archbishops of Salerno and the abbots of Cava also constructed territorial lordships, where they not only administered religious houses but exercised political and economic power over the rural inhabitants as well. They collected dues on a wide array of activities, including food cultivation, animal pasturing, wood-gathering, and fishing. They controlled and taxed

---

[1] For another discussion of church reform in the Principality of Salerno, see Taviani-Carozzi, *La Principauté*, 980–1020 and 1036–65.

commerce and received profits from mills. They judged disputes which arose among the rural population, and required landholders and tenants alike to seek permission before leaving their lands or alienating them to others. Thus, the archbishops and abbots developed religious, political, and economic power simultaneously.[2]

Traditionally, scholars of medieval southern Italy and Sicily attributed church reform solely to the efforts of the pope, the Norman conquerors, or a papal-Norman alliance. They studied the phenomenon either as part of the papal reform program or as a component of Norman state building, largely ignoring the local element.[3] More recently, however, historians have begun to stress the local nature of church reform, in particular, the important role that monasteries in the region played in reorganization.[4] Not just

---

[2] For a discussion of the development of the lordships of both the archbishop of Salerno and the abbey of Cava, see Taviani-Carozzi, *La Principauté*, 956–980, 1020–36, and 1066–86. For the lordship of Cava, also see Loud, "The Monastic Economy."

[3] See, for example, Chalandon, *Histoire*; Erich Caspar, *Roger II und die Gründung der normannisch-sizilischen Monarchie* (Innsbruck: Wagner, 1904); Emile Amann and Auguste Dumas, *L'Eglise au pouvoir des laïques (888–1057)*, vol. 7 of *Histoire de l'Eglise depuis les origines jusqu'à nos jours* (Paris: Bloud and Gay, 1942); Augustin Fliche, *La réforme grégorien et la reconquête chrétienne (1057–1125)*, vol. 8 of *Histoire de l'Eglise* (Paris: Bloud and Gay, 1940). Even historians such as Kamp and Klewitz, who have acknowledged the importance of the activities of local reformers, have still preferred to view the situation from the top down. Hans-Walter Klewitz, "Studien über die Wiederherstellung der Römischen Kirche in Süditalien durch das Reformpapsttum," in *Reformpapsttum und Kardinalkolleg* (Darmstadt: Wissenschaftliche Buchgesellschaft, 1957), 137–205. Kamp, "Vescovi e diocesi," and "The Bishops of Southern Italy in the Norman and Staufen Periods," trans. G. A. Loud and Diane Milburn, in *The Society of Norman Italy*, 185–209. Also see C. D. Fonseca, "Particolarismo" and "L'organizzazione ecclesiastica dell'Italia normanna tra l'XI e il XII secolo: i nuovi assetti istituzionali," in *Le Istituzioni ecclesiastiche della 'societas christiana' dei secoli XI-XII: diocesi, pievi, e parrocchie: Atti della Sesta Settimana della Mendola, Milan, 1–7 September 1974* (Milan: Vita e Pensiero, 1977), 2:327–52 and Raoul Manselli, "Roberto il Guiscardo e il Papato," in *Roberto il Guiscardo e il suo tempo: Atti delle prime giornate normanno-sveve, Bari, 28–29 May 1973*, 183–201 (Rome: 1975; reprint, Bari: Edizioni Dedalo, 1991). These historians, similar to Klewitz and Kamp, also view church reorganization in terms of papal and ducal policies.

[4] Cowdrey's study of Montecassino has elucidated the abbey's role in both local reform and papal politics, while Loud's monograph focuses on ecclesiastical reorganization in Capua. Cowdrey, *The Age of Abbot Desiderius*; Loud, *Church and Society*. Loud has also studied the role of the abbey of Santa Sofia in church reform in Benevento. G. A. Loud, "A Lombard Abbey." Taviani-Carozzi has stressed the importance of the abbey of Cava for reorganization in the Principality of Salerno, while Martin's study of Apulia similarly emphasizes the local nature of reform, although in this region smaller monasteries were the norm. Taviani-Carozzi, *La Principauté*, 954–55; Martin, *La Pouille*, 659–91. Also see Nicola Cilento, "La politica 'merid-

in southern Italy, but also in places like Verona and the Abruzzi the local element has been highlighted.[5] Southern Italian historians have also noticed continuity between the pre-Norman and Norman periods, and in most places ecclesiastical reorganization started well before the Norman conquest. Although the new Norman rulers continued and at times accelerated the process, they did not as a rule initiate it.[6] In the end, ecclesiastical reform in southern Italy was a complex and heterogeneous process that grew out of a web of interested parties, found both inside and outside the region, including popes, lay rulers, bishops, abbots, and the local clergy and laity.

Historians have also begun to recognize that church reform was never a unified program. Even within the city of Rome itself, the specific goals of various reformers could differ. Although reformers could agree upon general principles, such as the need to reorganize society in order to create a more Christian world or the desire to reform the church in order to administer pastoral duties more capably, they disagreed both on the concrete form that this new society was to take, as well as the specific methods of achieving such lofty goals.[7] In southern Italy, local reform programs often did not mesh with some of the primary objectives of papal reforms, since people were loathe to give up certain customary practices condemned by eleventh-century popes. For example, in Salerno the tradition of clerical marriage continued undisturbed, as did the participation of the laity in both founding and administering religious houses. Moreover, many disputes took place over suffragan bishops in the eleventh century, with the popes, the Normans, and local ecclesiastics all taking different positions. The archbishop of Salerno and the papacy, for example, had a number of disputes in the eleventh century when the popes reshuffled Salerno's dependencies and

---

ionale' di Gregorio VII nel Contesto della riforma della Chiesa," *Rassegna Storica Salernitana*, n.s. 3 (June 1985): 123–36, and Vitolo, "Vescovi e Diocesi," 122.

[5] Feller has looked at the role of the abbey of Casauria in the reform movement in the Abruzzi, while Howe has not only examined the role of the Benedictine foundations of Dominic of Sora in the same region, but also has underscored the importance of local charismatic figures, outside the orbit of Rome, in the reform of the Italian countryside in general. Feller, *Les Abruzzes*, 840–48; John Howe, *Church Reform and Social Change in Eleventh-Century Italy: Dominic of Sora and His Patrons* (Philadelphia: University of Pennsylvania Press, 1997), 79–96. Miller, in her study on church reform in Verona, has shown that the activities of local churchmen were far more decisive for church reform in the city than Roman prelates. Miller, *The Formation*, 53–54.

[6] Loud, *The Age of Robert Guiscard*, 263.

[7] Gilchrist has even questioned whether or not there was such a thing as a "programme of reform." John Gilchrist, "Was There a Gregorian Reform Movement in the Eleventh Century?" *The Canadian Catholic Historical Association, Study Sessions* 37 (1970): 1–10.

subtracted bishoprics from the cathedral church's power. However, this did not mean that reformers were split into hostile camps at odds with one another. As Cowdrey has shown in the case of Cluny, the perceived antagonism between Pope Gregory VII and Abbot Hugh over whether the truer service of St. Peter was to be performed in the cloister or in the world did not mean that the two men never worked together or that they had wildly differing philosophies. Rather, Gregory and Hugh could respect the choice of one another and see the two approaches as equally valid means of achieving reform.[8] Similarly in Salerno prelates such as Archbishop Alfanus I (1058–85) and Abbot Peter (1070–1123) had good relations with the papacy and with each other, and disputes more often than not represented a means of achieving a compromise suitable to all parties.

As earlier historians noted, both the Norman conquest of Salerno and the papal reform program emanating from Rome were key elements in ecclesiastical reorganization in Salerno. Papal and ducal privileges supported the development of the archbishop's and Cava's power by allowing them to create independent ecclesiastical networks and to exercise autonomous authority over dependent religious foundations and clerics. They also granted them privileges which allowed them to collect dues, demand services, and administer justice for the lay population living on their lands. In addition, both the archbishops and the abbots espoused the ideology of the Roman reformers, calling for the rehabilitation of clerical behavior and the development of an ecclesiastical system independent of the laity. Finally, the Norman dukes donated lands and granted commercial privileges to the archbishops and abbots which permitted them to grow into important political and economic forces in the region.

Despite the participation of the popes and Norman dukes, ecclesiastical reorganization in Salerno grew out of local initiative and responded to local society. Reform in Salerno started well before the Norman conquest, and the Lombard princes of Salerno gave both the archbishop and the monks of Cava their most important privileges. Although the Norman rulers did increase the economic power of both the abbey of Cava and the cathedral church, in general they merely confirmed, rather than created privileges. Papal privileges, moreover, often did not hold force in the region. The vast privileges and authority granted to the archbishops were never realized, while the abbey of Cava, which became the largest ecclesiastical power in the region, created and developed its religious empire autonomously, receiving papal and ducal privileges only after the abbots and monks were al-

---

[8] H. E. J. Cowdrey, *The Cluniacs and the Gregorian Reform* (Oxford: Clarendon Press, 1970), 141–56.

ready exercising control. Thus for the Principality of Salerno, the activities of both the cathedral church and the abbey of Cava proved far more decisive for ecclesiastical reform in the region than either the papacy or the Norman dukes, even if the relationships that the abbots and archbishops formed with popes and dukes had important implications. Religious reform in Salerno was not a foreign import bringing completely alien forms of religious life and organization to the region. Instead local reformers appropriated and assimilated the ideas of churchmen in faraway places such as Rome and Cluny, while at the same time maintaining some of their own customs. The new religious landscape created over the course of the twelfth century was certainly more familiar to other regions of Latin Christendom, but at the same time it retained a distinctly local flavor.

As church reform gradually transformed the religious landscape of Salerno, the political and economic structures of the Principality also underwent radical change in the eleventh century as a result of both internal and external forces. The Norman conquest of southern Italy, the establishment of territorial lordships, and *incastellamento* all led to a reorganization of government and economy. By the early twelfth century, the region was controlled by a small group of lay families and ecclesiastical institutions who over the course of the eleventh century had built up territorial lordships centered on fortresses and fortified cities. These lords exercised a much more pervasive control over rural and urban inhabitants than had previously been the case. They collected revenues on all the properties within defined territories, demanded labor services from the local population, and restricted the movement and activities of the inhabitants living within the borders of their lordships. They asserted authority over uncultivated lands, such as forests, rivers, and pastures, which formerly had been considered communal property. They began to exercise judicial power in their territories and to develop rudimentary administrative apparatus, which included notaries, judges, and viscounts who worked exclusively for them. In addition, they had armed retinues under their command. In documents, the lords referred to themselves as either "dominus" or "senior" of a specific place, generally the *castrum* which served as their power base, and called the inhabitants of their territories "our men."[9] Some documents even give the

---

[9] For more detailed descriptions of *incastellamento* and the emergence of territorial lordships in Salerno and southern Italy, see Ramseyer, "Territorial Lordships"; Bruno Figliuolo, "Morfologia" and "Longobardi e Normanni," in *Storia e civiltà della Campania: il medioevo*, ed. Giovanni Pugliese Carratelli (Naples: Electa Napoli, 1992), 67–74; Taviani-Carozzi, *La Principauté*, 839–947; Vitolo, "Da Apudmontem"; G. A. Loud, "The Monastic Economy" and "Continuity and Change in Norman Italy: The Campania during the Eleventh and Twelfth Centuries," *Journal of Me-*

precise geographical boundaries of a particular lordship.[10] Although such a system of government is familiar to scholars of other regions of Europe, it was a truly novel development for Salerno.

One of the first lordships in the Principality of Salerno was constructed in Capaccio by Pandolfus, brother of Prince Guaimarius IV.[11] He began building his power in 1047 when the princely fisc in the southern part of the Principality was divided between himself and his two brothers, Prince Guaimarius IV and Guido.[12] Between 1048 and his death in 1052, he appeared in documents with the title of lord ("dominus") and in possession not only of numerous lands but also a number of churches in and around Capaccio.[13] Although Pandolfus never appeared in the documents as "domi-

---

dieval History 22 (1996): 313–43; Del Treppo, "La vita economica"; Cilento, *Le origini*, 22–44; Martin, *La Pouille*, 255–328; Raffaele Licinio, *Castelli medievali: Puglia e Basilicata dai Normanni a Federico II e Carlo I d'Angio* (Bari: Dedalo, 1994); Hubert Houben, "I castelli del Mezzogiorno normanno-svevo nelle fonti scritte," in *Mezzogiorno Normanno-Svevo*, 159–76; Feller, *Les Abruzzes*, 211–303. Also important for any study of *incastellamento* in Italy is Pierre Toubert's classic work, *Les Structures du Latium Médiéval*, 305–549. More recently, Martin has produced an excellent comparison of the process of *incastellamento* in the various areas of southern Italy. Martin, "Settlement," 18–36.

[10] See, for example, the privilege of Nicolas count of the Principate issued to the inhabitants of his lordship in 1128, an edition of which is found in Leon-Robert Ménager, "Les foundations monastiques de Robert Guiscard," *Quellen und Forschungen aus italienischen Archiven und Bibliotheken* 39 (1959): 105–7.

[11] For a detailed study of Pandolfus' creation of a lordship, see Taviani-Carozzi, *La Principauté*, 869–97.

[12] CDC 7: 43, no. 1083, and Cava XVIII, 88. The princely fisc in areas of the northern part of the Principality were also divided at this time. CDC 7: 94, no. 1115; CDC 7: 102, no. 1116. For more details on the divisions, see Taviani-Carozzi, *La Principauté*, 857–65.

[13] In July 1047, the bishop of Paestum consecrated a church built by Pandolfus, giving him complete power over it. CDC 7: 49–50, no. 1086. In December of 1048, a sharecropping agreement from the monasteries of Sant'Angelo and Santa Sofia of Salerno mentioned Pandolfus as the owner. CDC 7: 80–82, no. 1107. In February 1052, shortly before his death, Pandolfus bought 1/3 of the church of Sant'Eustasio inside the walls of Capaccio, along with other lands and houses in the city and nearby. CDC 7: 179–81, no. 1166. A document from December 1052 mentioned that Pandolfus had previously donated San Venero in Corneto to the monastery of Santa Sofia in Salerno. CDC 7: 191–93, no. 1174. In March 1053, after Pandolfus's death, his widow Teodora and four sons showed up as owners of Sant'Angelo, appointing a priest to head it. CDC 7: 198–200, no. 1178. Pandolfus also participated in the economic activities of Santa Sofia: CDC 7: 77–78, no. 1104; CDC 7: 80–82, no. 1107; CDC 7: 120–21, no. 1127. Finally, he purchased two pieces of land in the region of Capaccio: CDC 7: 90, no. 1112; CDC 7: 179–81, no. 1166. A division among his sons after his death showed that his heirs owned eighteen ecclesiastical foundations and vast

nus" of a specific place, after his death both his widow Teodora and his sons were referred to as "domini nostri" or "seniori nostri" by sharecroppers, priests, notaries, and other officials.[14] This is the first time that such language is found in the region, and by the twelfth century such terms had become commonplace.[15] Although no documents give specific information about the rights exercised by Pandolfus and his widow Teodora, their sons and grandsons appear in documents as lords of specific *castra* with the right to collect revenues and control the economic activities within their territories.[16] (See figure 3.)

Pandolfus and his descendants owned a number of religious houses which they used to administer their lordships and supervise the local population. Unlike other lay-owned churches in the region, Pandolfus and his family took a direct interest in the administration of their churches and placed the clergy serving in them directly under their power. The 1053 priest investiture for the church of Sant'Angelo in Velanzanu demonstrates this unique relationship between the clergy and family members.[17] In it, the priest appointed referred to Teodora and her sons as his lords ("domni" and "seniori") and stated that he and his heirs would forever remain under their authority. Although the document specified that John remained free, it also stipulated that he was to provide certain payments and services because of his subordinate position. In other charters, John reiterated that Teodora and her sons were his lords.[18] Although this 1053 investiture alone describes a cleric actually subordinating himself to Pandolfus' family, the document suggests that he was not the only priest to have this type of relationship; when John placed himself under the family's power, he stated that he and his heirs "would remain under the authority of our lords and their heirs in the same manner as other free abbots in the region of Capaccio" ("siant in dominio supradicti domni nostri seniori, vel de illorum eredibus, sicut et alii

---

properties in the region. Cava D, 28 (edition in Fedele, "I Conti del Tusculo," 19–21).

[14] For example, in 1053, a viscount named Guidelmarus leased out a church in Teodora's name, referring to her and her sons as "our lords" ("seniori nostri"), suggesting that he took his title for services rendered to them. CDC 7: 198–200, no. 1178. Similarly, a priest and notary named John, who carried out a number of transactions for Teodora and her sons, called Pandolfus's widow his "senior." CDC 7: 189–90, no. 1172; CDC 7: 208–9, no. 1184; CDC 7: 246–48, no. 1199; CDC 7: 300–301, no. 1232; CDC 8: 25–27, no. 1252.

[15] Ramseyer, "Territorial Lordships," 85–86.

[16] Cava C, 10; Cava XXIII, 82; Cava G, 12.

[17] CDC 7: 198–200, no. 1178.

[18] CDC 7: 189–90, no. 1172; CDC 7: 246–48, no. 1199.

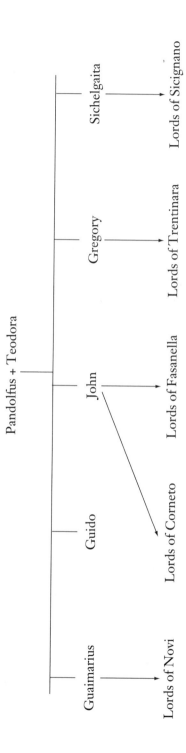

Figure 3. Descendants of Pandolfus and Teodora, Lords of Capaccio

Sources: Cava Archives; *Catalogus Baronum*; Loud, *Age of Robert Guiscard*; Drell, *Kinship and Conquest*

liveri abbati de ecclesie abbatie uic terre caput aquis faciunt sui seniori"). Moreover, in other documents, a different cleric named John referred to Teodora and her sons as his lords when he oversaw transactions for them.[19] Although not all clerics serving in the family foundations placed themselves under the family's authority, the majority seem to have.[20] Thus, the clergy serving in the religious houses of Pandolfus and his family did not administer their church autonomously, as the vast majority of rectors in the region did. Instead, they had a unique relationship with the owners that stressed their subordinate position vis-à-vis the family.

The dynastic foundations belonging to Pandolfus' family also developed a unique relationship to the rural population beginning in the 1050s when numerous small landholders in the region began to donate lands to their religious houses and go under the protection ("sub defensione") of the rectors. For example, in 1053 a certain Peter son of Rackisus donated all his lands, cultivated and uncultivated, to the church of Sant'Angelo in Ulmo, reserving the usufruct for himself, but not his heirs. He was to continue to cultivate the land, giving an annual rent of oil worth four *follari*.[21] At his death, the land with its usufruct was to go to the church, along with one-third of his movable wealth.[22] Similarly in July 1068 a family went under the protection ("sub defensione") of the church of San Michele Arcangelo in Velanzanu. Ursus and Peter, sons of Alfanus, along with their wives, Fresa, daughter of John, and Laita, daughter of Marconus, donated to the church all their property with houses located in Lauri and Murtitu, agreeing to continue cultivating the lands in return for an annual rent of eight *tarì*. The four also promised one-third of their movable wealth to the church upon their deaths, although they reserved the right for their heirs to continue to cultivate the land under the same conditions.[23]

The church of San Nicola, belonging to Pandolfus' son Gregory, absorbed numerous properties in this manner. Fourteen such donations occurred between 1073 and 1118, and although the terms differed in some de-

---

[19] In a 1053 sharecropping agreement, Teodora is John's "senior," while in another one she is his "domina." CDC 7: 189–90, no. 1172, no. 208–9, no. 1184.

[20] In 1057, for example, when Teodora and her sons appointed Romoaldus a priest along with his son Romoaldus, also a priest, to administer the church of San Felice in Felline near Capaccio, they gave the two priests complete autonomy to administer the foundation, and the document mentions nothing about the priests' status vis-à-vis the owners. CDC 8: 25–27, no. 1252.

[21] *Follari* were copper coins in use in southern Italy at this time. For information on them, see Travaini, *La Monetazione*, 235–340.

[22] CDC 7: 212–13, no. 1187.

[23] CDC 9: 191–95, no. 59. Also see CDC 7: 128–29, no. 1132.

tails, the basic provisions were the same. A family would give property to the church that they agreed to continue cultivating. They then placed themselves and their legitimate heirs under the protection of the church ("sub dominio et defensione") and promised to make an annual payment, in money, services, or both. In addition, they gave the church the right to inherit the property in the case that there were no legitimate heirs or if the family left the land.[24]

The motivations behind such donations are multifold, and it is unfair to ignore the religious element of placing oneself under the protection of a powerful religious house and the saint connected to it. Nonetheless, military activities also affected the decision. In both the 1050s and the 1070s, the two decades during which such donations were most common, Norman soldiers were consolidating power in southern regions of the Principality. In the 1050s, the two Norman leaders William and Humphrey were campaigning heavily in the area, and one chronicler even remarked that inhabitants here began to fortify their cities as a result.[25] In the 1070s, Robert Guiscard was completing his conquest of the Principality of Salerno, and evidence suggests that heavy fighting occurred in Cilento when Prince Gisolf sent his brother, Guido, there to halt Robert's expansion from Calabria northward into his lands.[26] Charters from the late eleventh century show Duke Robert and Duke Roger giving away confiscated lands in the regions, suggesting that life in the southern part of the Principality was more greatly affected by the Norman conquest than northern regions where Duke Robert avoided change and disruption as much as possible.[27] Seeking the protection of a powerful religious house, often linked to a more powerful lay family or ecclesiastical order, may very well have been one way for landholders to avoid confiscations. Historians of other regions of southern Italy have similarly noted the imposition of seigneurial regimes during the political upheaval caused by the Norman conquest.[28]

By the early twelfth century documents show that this new type of landlord-tenant relationship had become normalized and even expanded upon as a handful of powerful lay families and ecclesiastical foundations, whose authority was linked to *castra* and fortified centers, established far-

---

[24] CDC 10: 79–81, no. 23; CDC 10: 81–82, no. 24; CDC 10: 82–85, no. 25; CDC 10: 85–88, no. 26; CDC 10: 94–97, no. 30; CDC 10: 132–34, no. 48; CDC 10: 137–40, no. 51; CDC 10: 275–77, no. 115; Cava XIV, 66; Cava XIV, 71; Cava XV, 110; Cava XVI, 16; Cava XVI, 74; Cava XVI, 80.

[25] Amatus, 161–62, bk. 3, chap. 45.

[26] Amatus, 371, bk. 8, chap. 30; Alfanus, *Carmi*, 150–52, no. 20.

[27] Cava C, 22; Cava D, 1; Cava C, 30; Cava XVII, 13.

[28] Martin, "Settlement," 31.

reaching authority over the lands and inhabitants of specific territories.[29] Although information on both the creation and administration of these lordships is sparse, new language that appears in charters at this time reflects the changed relationship: inhabitants were said to be under the power and jurisdiction of their lords and they were bought, sold, donated, and traded along with the lands they lived on. The lords became both tax collectors and judges, as they began to levy dues on all of the various economic activities of the inhabitants, as well as judge disputes that arose among them. *Incastellamento* thus had both an economic and political significance in the region, connected to the expansion of agriculture and the establishment of new centers of power.[30]

The process of *incastellamento* and the formation of territorial lordships should not be viewed as a wholly predatory process in which powerful military leaders imposed new and heavy burdens on the rural population. A document from 1138, for example, demonstrates that the population of Castellabate, the Cava lordship in Cilento, only had to give one-tenth of their wine production to the abbey, a much lower percentage than the usual one-third or one-half specified in sharecropping agreements.[31] In addition, privileges issued by the new lords demonstrate that they respected local custom and limited the authority of both themselves and their followers.[32] For example, Nicolas, count of the Principate, issued a pledge in 1128 to the inhabitants of his lordship in the territory of Eboli in which he promised to uphold local customs and to protect the lives and properties of the population, punishing anyone who did them harm, even if the perpetrator was one of his own soldiers.[33] As a result, local custom still held force even as lords established a much more localized and pervasive form of power.

Unlike other areas of Europe, *incastellamento* and the emergence of territorial lordships in the Principality of Salerno represented not a fragmenta-

---

[29] For a fuller description of this, see Ramseyer, "Territorial Lordships," 86–92. Also see Loud's study of this process, in which he traces its development up through the end of the twelfth century. Loud, "The Monastic Economy."

[30] The process of *incastellamento*, although it changed the political and economic structures of the region, did not, in most cases, result in a movement of population since *castra* were built in or near existing settlements. Moreover, open villages, referred to as *casales* in the documents, characteristic of the Lombard period in Campania, persisted into the Norman period. Ramseyer, "Territorial Lordships," 94; Figliuolo, "Longobardi e Normanni," 62–66; Loud, "Continuity and Change," 322–23.

[31] Cava XXIV, 61.

[32] Loud, "The Monastic Economy," 157–58; Donald Matthew, *The Norman Kingdom of Sicily* (Cambridge: Cambridge University Press, 1992), 24–25.

[33] Ménager, "Les fondations monastiques," 105–7.

tion or devolution of power but a means for centralizing authority and gaining greater control over the economic activities of the local population. Both the Lombard princes, and the Norman dukes who followed, encouraged the construction of lordships in order both to increase their authority over the activities and lives of the inhabitants residing in their realms and to aid them in protecting their lands. Territorial lordships offered an efficient means of supervising and managing local matters more closely, and in the Principality of Salerno rulers established careful oversight over the local lords.[34] Conflicts between the Norman dukes and local lords did at times take place, but overall the dukes retained authority over the lordships in the Principality.

In other regions of the Norman Duchy of Apulia, ducal control was more tenuous and some lords exercised autonomous authority within their lordships. This was mainly a consequence of the fragmented nature of the Norman takeover of southern Italy, which was carried out by a number of fortune seekers who arrived from Normandy and other areas of Francia over the course of the eleventh century.[35] Unlike the Norman conquest of England, the Normans of southern Italy did not constitute a single force undertaking a unified conquest. Instead various groups of Norman soldiers lived, traveled, and fought together, and their leaders established separate political units over the course of the eleventh century.[36] Rainolf, for example, one of the earliest Norman leaders, fought for rulers around Capua,

[34] Loud, *The Age of Robert Guiscard*, 259.

[35] The fundamental book on the Norman conquest of southern Italy remains Ferdinand Chalandon, *Histoire de la domination normande en Italie méridionale et en Sicile*. More recently in English Loud has produced a monograph on the conquests destined to become a standard textbook on the subject. Loud, *The Age of Robert Guiscard*. In addition to Loud's book, two other monographs on Robert Guiscard have recently appeared: Huguette Taviani-Carozzi, *La Terreur du Monde. Robert Guiscard et la conquête normande en Italie* (Paris: Fayard, 1996) and Richard Bünemann, *Robert Guiskard 1015–1085. Eine Normanner erobert Süditalien* (Cologne: Böhlau, 1997). Also see Jean-Marie Martin, *Italies Normandes XIe–XIIe siècles* (Paris: Hachette, 1994); Ernesto Pontieri, *I normanni nell'Italia meridionale* (Naples: Libreria Scientifica Editrice, 1948); Salvatore Tramontana, *Mezzogiorno normanno e svevo* (Messina: Peloritana Editore, 1972) and "La monarchia normanna e sveva," in *Storia d'Italia: Il Mezzogiorno dai Bizantini a Federico II*, ed. André Guillou, 3:437–810 (Turin: UTET, 1983); Errico Cuozzo, "L'unificazione normanna e il regno normanno-svevo," in *Storia del Mezzogiorno*, ed. Giuseppe Galasso (Naples: Edizione del Sole, 1986), 2/2: 593–825 (Naples: Edizione del Sole, 1990).

[36] Chalandon, chap. 2 in *Histoire*; Loud, *The Age of Robert Guiscard*, 67–80, 291–92. I have trouble accepting Taviani-Carozzi's thesis that the Norman conquest of southern Italy was part of an ambitious papal project to pull southern Italy into the western sphere. Taviani-Carozzi, *La Terreur Du Monde*, 134.

Naples, and Benevento before establishing his power in Aversa. His nephew, Richard, carried out campaigns in the county of Capua and points north, while two Hauteville brothers, William and Drogo, concentrated most of their energy in Apulia. Another Hauteville brother, Robert Guiscard, spent many years subjugating Calabria, before assuming the title of duke of Apulia and uniting Apulia, Calabria, and southern Campania under one leader. Still another Hauteville brother, Roger, led the conquest of Sicily, establishing a county on the island separate from Robert Guiscard's sphere of power.[37] Other smaller realms of power were also created by Norman soldiers, although by the time of Robert Guiscard's death, three main political units had emerged: the Principality of Capua, the County of Sicily, and the Duchy of Apulia, whose capital was Salerno.

When Robert Guiscard captured Salerno in 1077, and became ruler of former Byzantine and Lombard territories encompassing Apulia, Calabria, and the southern regions of Campania, he did as little as possible to disrupt life. He relied on the local nobility to administer his duchy, which meant that indigenous Lombard families, such as the descendants of Prince Guaimarius III, continued to hold power. Moreover, the Normans arrived in small numbers, most of whom were soldiers and many of whom married native women. Robert Guiscard himself was married to Prince Gisolf II's sister, Sichelgaita, while Count William of the Principate married a daughter of Gisolf's uncle, Guido, and Roger of Sanseverino married a daughter of Gisolf's brother, Pandolfus.[38] In addition, Robert continued to patronize local religious foundations, such as the cathedral church of Salerno and the abbey of Cava, and even furthered the consolidation trend that led to the creation of ecclesiastical hierarchies in the area. As one historian has aptly observed, the Normans did not conquer southern Italy as much as they infiltrated it.[39] The establishment of Norman power in the region relied on military activity as well as the formation of alliances with the various local ruling families.

Despite the continuity, the Norman conquest of southern Italy did result in some important changes. For one, the Normans united under one leader lands that had formerly been held by many different rulers, and they extinguished forever both Byzantine and Muslim political power. In addition, the Norman conquest of southern Italy resulted in an expansion of papal influ-

---

[37] For detailed information on the military and political activity of all these Norman leaders, see Loud, chaps. 2–4 in *The Age of Robert Guiscard*.

[38] For a detailed discussion of intermarriage between Norman and Lombard noble families in the Principality of Salerno, see Drell, *Kinship and Conquest*.

[39] *The Age of Robert Guiscard*, 1.

ence in the region, both in the political and the religious realms. At the Council of Melfi in 1059, Robert swore fealty to Pope Nicholas II and received the ducal title as well as his lands from the pope. He became a vassal of the Holy See and promised to render military aid to the papacy, thus setting himself up as protector of the pope, as Frankish and Ottonian emperors before him had done.[40] Local church reformers, including the archbishops of Salerno and abbots of Cava, created new ecclesiastical hierarchies directly dependent on the papacy, and even if lay rulers never completely relinquished their ability to supervise religious organization in their territories, popes began to participate actively in the activities of local prelates. Furthermore, similar ideas began to emerge regarding lordship, the exercise of political and economic power, and warfare, and from the eleventh century forward both the religious and political structures of the principality began to develop in a manner similar to other areas of the Latin West. Even if the Normans themselves hastened rather than initiated many of these changes, and even if local customs continued to hold force, creating a kingdom with noticeable diversity with regard to political, judicial, and economic structures, the Norman takeover nonetheless marks a point in time when southern Italy and the Principality of Salerno were becoming increasingly integrated not only into a larger southern Italian kingdom, but also into an expanding Latin Christian world.[41]

[40] Ibid., 188–94.
[41] This point is also made by Loud. Ibid., 291.

CHAPTER 4

The New Archbishopric of Salerno

The archbishops of Salerno embarked upon a slow reorganization of their archdiocese beginning in the late tenth century, constructing an autonomous ecclesiastical system based on parish rights, papal overlordship, and Roman canon law. They gradually built up a separate hierarchy in their archdiocese, composed of bishops and archpriests, with the archbishop himself exercising control at the top. They began to claim authority over a system of churches within their diocese, including the right to appoint priests, discipline clergy, and control ecclesiastical revenues. They sought to limit lay power over the ecclesiastical system and began to turn more and more to the papacy, rather than the prince, for privileges, support, and aid. Finally, they endeavored to reform the clergy based on Roman models by setting rules for the education and conduct of priests and monks and assuring that simony played no role in their promotion.[1]

The goals of diocesan reform in Salerno echoed those of ecclesiastical re-

---

[1] For the history of the reorganization of Salerno's archdiocese, see Ruggiero, " 'Parrochia' e 'Plebs' "; Taviani-Carozzi, *La Principauté*, 949–1036; Klewitz, "Zur Geschichte," 16–18; and Vitolo, "Vescovi e Diocesi," 116–41. For the reordering of the ecclesiastical system in medieval Apulia, see Martin, *La Pouille*, 563–91, for the Abruzzi, see Feller, *Les Abruzzes*, 785–850, and for Lazio, see Toubert, *Les Structures*, 789–933. More generally on church reform in southern Italy, see G. A. Loud, "Churches and Churchmen in an Age of Conquest: Southern Italy, 1030–1130," *Haskins Society Journal* 4: 37–53 and *The Age of Robert Guiscard*, 260–78; Giovanni Spinelli, "Il papato e la riorganizzazione ecclesiastica della Longobardia meridionale," in *Longobardia e longobardi nell'Italia meridionale*, 19–42; Fonseca, "L'organizzazione"; and Kamp, "Vescovi e diocesi" and "The Bishops of Southern Italy."

formers in Rome who took control of the papacy in the mid-eleventh century. The desire to set up an ecclesiastical hierarchy separate from lay power and to standardize clerical behavior were two central features of the Roman reformers' program, and the popes themselves actively supported the archbishops in Salerno as they endeavored to reorganize their archdiocese. However, the goals of the papacy at times conflicted with the aims of the archbishops. The popes, who sought to create a new ecclesiastical hierarchy throughout southern Italy and Sicily in which the papacy exercised power at the top, reshuffled dependencies and granted exemptions that would benefit papal power in the region. As a result, the pope subtracted six bishoprics formerly dependent on the cathedral church of Salerno and exempted from archiepiscopal authority the abbey of Cava, which possessed numerous dependent houses throughout the dioceses of Salerno and Paestum. In addition, not all aspects of clerical reform promoted in Rome received support from the archbishops, and non-Roman practices, such as clerical marriage, continued unabated in the principality.

Local lay rulers in Salerno, both the Lombard princes and the Norman dukes after them, played a vital role in church reform. The Lombard princes, in particular, granted the archbishops some of their most important privileges, including authority over all the clerics in their archdiocese. In addition, both Lombard and Norman rulers granted the archbishops important new economic powers, such as control over the dues and services owed on archiepiscopal lands, which formerly had belonged to the prince, and the ability to engage in commerce free of taxation. Moreover, they added to the patrimony of the cathedral church by donating additional lands and ecclesiastical foundations. They also gave the archbishops a place in the new political system that emerged in the Principality of Salerno in the eleventh century by allowing them to construct one of the earliest territorial lordships based on the *castrum* of Olevano sul Tusciano. In the end, lay privileges did more for the archbishops than papal ones, by increasing their authority over the ecclesiastical system, augmenting their political power, and enhancing their economic base.

By 1100 both lay and papal privileges conferred on the archbishops vast powers within their archdiocese. Moreover, the boundaries of the archdiocese of Salerno were quite large, encompassing dependencies in Basilicata and Calabria as far away as Acerenza and Cosenza. These privileges, however, existed only on paper, and the archbishops proved incapable both of asserting their newly granted powers and holding onto old privileges. Although they set in place a centralized, hierarchical system of bishops and archpriests, they never managed to assert hegemony over the religious houses, clerics, and ecclesiastical revenues of their archdiocese. The majority of clerics and religious houses remained outside of their control.

The Return of the Pope

Beginning in the second half of the tenth century, the papacy began to play a more visible role in church organization in southern Italy, reorganizing bishoprics, granting monastic exemptions, and participating in ecclesiastical appointments and disputes. The first sign of renewed papal interest occurred between 966 and 989, when popes raised the bishoprics of Benevento, Capua, and Salerno to the status of metropolitans and granted the three new archbishops privileges that clarified their dependencies.[2] From this time on, southern Italian archbishops began to travel to Rome on a consistent basis for consecration by the popes, who issued written documents conferring their offices on them for the first time in centuries. During the eleventh century, the papacy's activities in southern Italy increased even further as they partnered with the new Norman conquerors to create a more centralized and standardized ecclesiastical system in the region. As the Normans conquered Apulia and Sicily, new bishops and metropolitans were established in areas formerly under Byzantine and Muslim control, while in Lombard territories, bishoprics and archdioceses continued to be reorganized and centralized for both political and religious reasons.

Both the motives for and consequences of the creation of the new metropolitans in southern Italy differed from region to region, and from one pope to another. Many historians have explained the promotion of the three Lombard capitals in the second half of the tenth century as the consequence of competition between the pope and the patriarch of Constantinople, and to a certain extent this is true.[3] As Byzantine armies successfully extended imperial power in southern Italy in the tenth century, the patriarchs of Constantinople created new metropolitans in Bari, Taranto, and Brindisi, and placed bishoprics under them in Acerenza, Matera, Tursi, Gravina, and Tricarico. The tenth-century Byzantine reorganization was thus part of

---

[2] John XIII made Benevento and Capua metropolitans, while twenty years later, sometime between 983 and 989, Pope Benedict VII or John XV did the same for Salerno. Spinelli, "Il papato," 27–34; Loud, "Southern Italy in the Tenth Century," 630–31.

[3] Klewitz, "Zur Geschichte," 4–18; Kamp, "Vescovi e diocesi," 167–68; Loud, "Southern Italy in the Tenth Century," 630–31 and "Churches and Churchmen," 40; Spinelli, "Il papato," 19–42.

the empire's political expansion into former Muslim and Lombard territories that had begun in the late ninth century. The Byzantine rulers not only created new themes to administer their territories, in Apulia (called the theme of Longobardia and later the Catepan of Italy), Calabria, and, most likely, Lucania, but they also created new Greek bishoprics as a means of consolidating their power.[4] The pope, in response, placed churches and bishoprics in Byzantine territories under the authority of the three newly created metropolitans in Lombard areas. As a result, the archbishop of Salerno received Acerenza, Malvito, Bisignano, and Cosenza as suffragans at the end of the tenth century, while about fifty years later, the archbishop of Benevento was granted a number of suffragans on the border between Beneventan and Byzantine territory, including Troia, Dragonara, Civitate, Montecorvino, and Fiorentino, which the Byzantine catepan Basil Boiannes had established after he had successfully quelled the Apulian uprising led by Melus in 1017–18.[5]

Byzantine-Lombard conflict was not the only reason the three bishops residing in Lombard capitals were raised to the rank of archbishop. In fact, their promotions had much more to do with the exile of Pope John XIII, who had been handpicked by Emperor Otto I in 965 to occupy the papal throne. In 966 John was imprisoned and then chased out of Rome by rival families hostile to his elevation. He found refuge in Capua where he remained for a year, and most historians believe it was out of gratitude for the protection given him by Prince Pandolfus I that he made Capua a metropolitan. Later on, John and one of his successors did the same for the bishops of Benevento and Salerno, perhaps because the bishops there felt slighted and worried that the new archbishop of Capua would insist on making Benevento and Salerno suffragans, or perhaps due to the growing fear that Pandolfus was becoming too powerful. It could very well have been the case that Pandolfus planned on using ecclesiastical foundations to expand his kingdom, which at the time of Capua's promotion included both the county of Capua and the Principality of

---

[4] On the ecclesiastical organization of Byzantine southern Italy in the ninth and tenth centuries, see von Falkenhausen, *La dominazione bizantina*, 161–72 and Martin, *La Pouille*, 258–72, 695–715. On the strong possibility of the existence of a Byzantine theme in Lucania, see André Guillou, "La Lucanie byzantine: Etude de géographie historique," *Byzantion* 35 (1965): 119–49. Greek bishops may even have served in the church of San Michele Arcangelo on Mt. Aureo, in the southern region of the Principality of Salerno, in the first half of the eleventh century. Martin, "Cennamus episcopus," 91–95. It is interesting to note, too, that Stephen IX's privilege issued to Alfanus I expressly forbade the archbishop from placing a bishop in the church of San Michele. Pflugk-Harttung, 2: 82–84.

[5] Spinelli, "Il papato," 39–40; Loud, *The Age of Robert Guiscard*, 67–68.

Benevento and soon after would encompass the territories of Spoleto, Camerino, and Salerno. As for the popes, the promotions put them in a position to control religious life and organization in southern Italy more closely. But whatever the specific motivations of the various individuals, the promotion of the three capitals represented a reorganization of the ecclesiastical system, rather than a simple reconstitution of ancient Sees, and all parties involved, including the popes, princes, and archbishops, had political as well as religious goals in mind, some short term and some long term in nature.[6]

No papal privilege survives for the elevation of Salerno to the status of metropolitan. Up until June 983, documents still refer to the head of the Salernitan Church as "bishop."[7] Many historians have set the date of Salerno's elevation at 983, based on information from the forged "Chronicon Cavense."[8] In fact, no documents mention the bishop or archbishop of Salerno between the June 983 charter from Cava and the July 989 papal privilege from John XV, in which Amatus is called archbishop. Thus, the elevation must have occurred between these two dates.

The first surviving papal privilege for the archbishop of Salerno dates from 12 July 989 issued by Pope John XV.[9] The first half of the document is damaged and illegible, but in the second half the pope conferred on the archbishop the authority to appoint and consecrate the bishops dependent on him in Paestum, Conza, Acerenza, Nola, Bisignano, Malvito, and Cosenza. From this time on, the newly elected archbishops from Salerno began to travel regularly to Rome for investiture. In the 994 privilege from John XV to the newly elected archbishop Grimoaldus (994–1012), the pope specifically stated that Grimoaldus' successors were to come to Rome for proper consecration, receiving the pallium directly from the pope.[10] Thus, in 1012 Sergius IV invested Michael (1012–1016), in 1016 Benedict VIII invested Benedict (1016–1019), in 1019 he invested Amatus II (1019–1036?), in

---

  [6] Spinelli, "Il papato," 27–37; Vitolo, "Vescovi e Diocesi," 116–17, 122.

  [7] CDC 2: 185–86, no. 352 for April 983 and CDC 2: 188–89, no. 355 for June 983 both refer to Amatus as "bishop" of Salerno. Also Otto II's privileges, issued on 18 April and 2 November 982, called John "bishop" of Salerno. MGH, *Diplomata*, 2/1: 317–18, no. 273, and 332–33, no. 285.

  [8] Ventimiglia and Ughelli both included editions of the chronicle's excerpt, and Kehr in *Italia Pontificia* followed their conclusions. See Ughelli 7: 363, Domenico Ventimiglia, *Notizie storiche del Castello dell'Abbate e de' suoi casali nella Lucania* (Naples: Reale, 1827), 188, and IP, 8: 340. Klewitz hypothesized a date between November 982 and October 983, although he gives no reason for it. Klewitz, "Zur Geschichte," 16. Vitolo put the date at 974–81, although he, too, does not say why. Vitolo, "Vescovi e Diocesi," 116.

  [9] IP, 8: 340 and 346, no. 11; Pflugk-Harttung 2: 52, no. 87.

  [10] Ughelli, 7: 376–77.

1036 Benedict IX invested Amatus III (1036?-1046), in 1047 Clement II invested John (1047–58), in 1051 Leo IX invested John again, and in 1058 Stephen IX invested Alfanus I (1058–85).[11] The formula remained more or less the same, with the archbishop given the Church of Salerno to possess and take care of ("possedere," "custodire"), as well as the right to ordain bishops in its dependencies. Between 989 and 1047 these dependencies remained basically the same, encompassing the bishoprics of Paestum, Conza, Acerenza, Nola, Bisignano, Malvito, and Cosenza.[12] However, with the exception of Paestum, the cathedral church of Salerno never exercised any real control over these bishoprics.

In the mid-eleventh century, papal influence in the region increased even more as the Norman conquests in southern Italy and Sicily opened the way to the creation of new bishoprics and archbishoprics, as well as Benedictine-style abbeys, directly dependent on the papacy. Clement II, Leo IX, and the popes who followed all actively promoted the Roman reform program throughout southern Italy and indeed all of Christendom. They pushed for clerical reform, censuring simony and nicolaitism. They sought to end the practice of lay-owned foundations and interference on the part of lay rulers in ecclesiastical matters. They even required the new Norman rulers, in the oaths of fidelity they received from them, to place all churches within their territories under papal authority.[13] Finally, they sought to extend the

[11] See Kehr, IP, 8: 346–50 and Galante, "La documentazione vescovile," 239 and 247–49. For editions, see Ughelli, 7: 377 (for 1012 investiture); Pflugk-Harttung, 2: 61–63, nos. 95 and 97 (for the 1016 and 1019 investitures); Ughelli, 7: 378–80 (for the 1047 and 1051 investitures); and Pflugk-Harttung, 2: 82–84, no. 116 (for the 1058 investiture). The investiture of Amatus III exists only as a seventeenth-century copy found in the archiepiscopal archives in Salerno, and dating problems make it impossible to be certain to which Benedict and to which Amatus the document refers. Kehr and Pflugk-Harttung dated the document to 1021, claiming that it was a second investiture of Amatus II by Pope Benedict VIII. IP, 8: 348, no. 9; Pflugk-Harttung, 2: 64–65, no. 99. Crisci and Campagna dated it to March 1032, suggesting that it was Benedict IX investing Amatus III. Generoso Crisci and Angelo Campagna, *Salerno sacra: Ricerche storiche* (Salerno: Edizioni della Cura arcivescovile, 1962), 68. However, Galante has pointed to a May 1032 document in which Amatus II is still bishop. In addition, the investiture is dated fourth indiction, and the only year of Benedict IX's papacy which corresponds to the fourth indiction is 1036. Thus, although Galante does not exclude the possibility that Amatus III became bishop sometime in 1032, she believes the investiture charter was most likely written in 1036. For more details, see Galante, "La documentazione vescovile," 230–32.

[12] The bulls did not always consistently list all seven dependencies. For example, Conza is not mentioned in the 994 confirmation, while Nola is missing from the 1012 and 1036 bulls.

[13] "And I will relinquish all churches in my realm, along with their possessions, and place them under your authority" ("Omnes quoque ecclesias que in mea consis-

church's power through the creation of a single ecclesiastical hierarchy that was controlled by the papacy and supported by a universal payment of a tithe. To this end, they held councils, visited dioceses, issued privileges, and wrote letters, directly participating in the elections and activities of archbishops and abbots.[14]

When Pope Clement II traveled to Salerno in 1047 to invest the new archbishop John, the bull that was redacted stands in stark contrast to the ones issued between 989 and 1032. The pope did not merely confer the office on the new archbishop, but also investigated his election and scrutinized his moral character. First Clement determined that the election had followed proper procedure, and that the new archbishop had been accepted and then elected unanimously by the clergy, the *populus* of Salerno, and Prince Guaimarius IV. Then he certified that John had not been elected out of ambition, to serve some specific purpose, or through the simoniac heresy. Only after the pope was assured that John had, in fact, been chosen because of his merits did he proceed to confer on him the office of archbishop.[15]

Three years later, Pope Leo IX traveled to Salerno to hold a synod. Amatus of Montecassino gives a dramatic description of how the pope came south in order to do battle against the perversity of Simon, who had tried to purchase the grace of the Holy Spirit from the apostle Peter. When Leo arrived in Salerno, he discovered, much to his chagrin, that the church there was rife with simony, as well as perjury and adultery. The pope was at a loss at what to do in front of such rampant sin. After seeking advice from Saints Paul and Peter, he meted out the proper punishments: excommunication for some, penance for others. He also instructed the people present at the synod to recognize the church's primacy and to pay the tithe.[16]

---

tunt dominatione cum earum possessionibus dimittam in tuam potestam"), according to the oath sworn by Robert Guiscard in 1059. *Liber Censuum de l'église romaine*, ed. Louis Duchesne and Paul Fabre (Paris: A. Fontemoing, 1889), 1: 422. Similar oaths were sworn by Richard I of Capua in 1061 and again by Robert Guiscard in 1080. Loud, "Churches and Churchmen," 46.

[14] For information on eleventh-century papal reform, see Colin Morris, *The Papal Monarchy: The Western Church from 1050 to 1250* (Oxford: Clarendon, 1989); Uta-Renate Blumenthal, *The Investiture Controversy: Church and Monarchy from the Ninth to the Twelfth Century* (Philadelphia: University of Pennsylvania Press, 1988); H. E. J. Cowdrey, *Pope Gregory VII, 1073–1085* (Oxford: Clarendon Press, 1998); Gerd Tellenbach, *The Church in Western Europe from the Tenth to the Early Twelfth Century*, trans. Timothy Reuter (Cambridge: Cambridge University Press, 1993); Walter Ullmann, *The Growth of Papal Government in the Middle Ages*, 2nd ed. (London: Methuen, 1962); and, of course, the classic work by Augustin Fliche, *La réforme grégorienne*.

[15] IP, 8: 349, no. 18; Ughelli, 7: 378–79.

[16] Amatus, 128–30, bk. 3, chap. 15.

Leo IX and the popes who followed closely monitored the archiepiscopal elections in Salerno, placing a special emphasis on the pastoral responsibilities of both archbishops and bishops.[17] Like Clement II, they tested the moral character of the archbishops and ascertained that the new archbishops had followed correct election procedures, and that their promotion was not the result of simony. However, the bulls also began to stress the importance and difficulty of the office's pastoral duties. According to Leo IX's re-confirmation of John in 1051, the archbishop no longer advanced merely "in ordine Archiepsicopatus," but rather "entered into the realm of pastoral care" ("ad hoc pastoralis regiminis curam aggreditur"). Stephen IX in his 1058 confirmation of Alfanus I called on the archbishop to monitor the bishops under him, assuring that they executed their pastoral duties properly and that they had the correct moral character. Alexander II's 1067 bull claimed that the pope had issued the re-confirmation of Alfanus I out of consideration for pastoral care.

Leo IX, Stephen IX, and Alexander II also set down guidelines for the archbishops on how to administer their archdiocese, based on rules issued in Rome. Leo IX, for example, required the archbishop to ordain dependent bishops "according to the rules of the Holy Fathers" ("secundum regulam SS Patrum").[18] Similarly Stephen IX and Alexander II gave the archbishop the ability to elect and ordain bishops dependent on the cathedral church of Salerno, but warned that he must do so "according to the laws of the holy canons" ("sanctorum canonum statuta").[19] For the first time Roman standards were being actively promoted in the region.

In addition to their program of moral and clerical reform, popes also took an active interest in the reorganization of dioceses in southern Italy in the eleventh century, creating new metropolitans and bishops, reshuffling dependencies, issuing new privileges, and granting exemptions. The popes sought to create an ecclesiastical system free from lay interference that was based on a single church hierarchy centered in Rome. They also promoted the idea that prelates should rely on Rome and the pope for support, rather than local secular rulers. Finally, they set out to rationalize the rather chaotic religious landscape that had arisen in the previous centuries, which was characterized by overlapping claims and contradictory privileges, as well as an almost complete lack of parish churches or episcopal hierarchies

---

[17] For Leo IX's 1051 privilege, see IP, 8: 349–50, no. 19 and Ughelli, 7: 379–80. For Stephen IX's 1058 privilege, see Pflugk-Harttung, 2: 82–84, no. 116. For Alexander II's 1067 privilege, see Ughelli, 7: 382–83.

[18] Ughelli, 7: 379–80.

[19] Ughelli, 7: 382–83, and Pflugk-Harttung, 2: 82–84, no. 116.

and, in some areas, cathedral churches placed in remote villages rather than major population centers.[20]

Stephen IX was the first pope to introduce the idea of parish rights in documents relating to Salerno. In his confirmation bull from 1058 for the new archbishop Alfanus I, he forbade under threat of anathema any cleric or layperson who dared to profit off the lands or possessions of any churches that made up part of Salerno's archdiocese without the permission of the archbishop.[21] Alexander II claimed that the archbishops alone could appoint and ordain clerics and abbots for the religious houses that pertained to the cathedral church, based on "both hereditary and parish rights" ("tam haereditario, quam parochiali jure").[22] Urban II asserted that "all churches in the parish of Salerno should be remitted to the power of the archbishop" ("omnes ecclesias Salernitane parrochie remitteret in potestate archiepiscopi").[23] In addition, Leo IX, Stephen IX, and Alexander II conceded privileges that had previously been granted by lay rulers alone.[24] In this way the popes hoped that the archbishops of Salerno would no longer look to local lay rulers for their power and privileges, but to the papacy in Rome.

Papal support existed not only on paper but in action, too. Pope Alexander II twice supported the archbishop of Salerno in disputes with lay rulers over ecclesiastical lands, punishing Norman leaders who had "usurped" property from the cathedral church. The first time, at the Council of Melfi in 1067, he anathematized William, son of Tancred, brother of Robert Guiscard and count of the Principate, along with his knight Guimond de Moulins, for having invaded the patrimony of the archbishop in the region of the Tusciano river, which included the *curtes* of San Pietro da Toro and of San Vito al Sele, the church of San Michele Arcangelo on Mt. Aureo, and the *castrum* of Olevano.[25] Evidently the two perpetrators quickly gave back the property, for a papal document from the same year announced the restitution of the lands, which the pope then conferred on the archbishop in a ceremony in Salerno, attended by both Norman and Lombard leaders.[26] In the same year, Alexander II excommunicated Turgisius de Rota, the founder

---

[20] Loud, "Churches and Churchmen," 47; Martin, "L'ambiente," 211–13; Feller, *Les Abruzzes*, 785–86, 792–95.

[21] Pflugk-Harttung, 2: 82–84, no. 116.

[22] Ughelli, 7: 382–83.

[23] Pflugk-Harttung, 2: 149–50, no. 184.

[24] According to the bulls, all three popes confirmed everything that emperors, kings, and princes had bestowed on the archbishops and bishops of Salerno in the past. Ughelli, 7: 379–80; Pflugk-Harttung, 2: 82–84, no. 116; Ughelli, 7: 382–83.

[25] IP, 8: 351, no. 23.

[26] IP, 8: 351, no. 25. Taviani-Carozzi, *La Principauté*, 982–83.

of the powerful Sanseverino family, for having usurped some lands and *curtes* of the archbishop.[27] The outcome of this request is unknown, although in the same year the pope conferred the usurped lands on the archbishop, along with other possessions.[28] It is interesting to note that in both cases the pope, not the Lombard prince, restored the lands to Alfanus, demonstrating once again how the idea of papal overlordship over ecclesiastical lands and revenues was taking hold in the region.[29] It most likely also reflects the growing powerlessness of Prince Gisolf II at this time.

Pope Urban II aided Alfanus II in 1092 in an investiture dispute with Duke Roger Borsa.[30] Archbishop Alfanus had complained to the pope that the duke had unjustly dismissed an archpriest whom Alfanus had appointed to the church of Santa Maria de Domno, replacing him with one of his own choice. Urban II immediately issued a bull condemning the lay-appointed priest Lanzarius. He then traveled to Salerno to clear up the matter. After Archbishop Alfanus II had presented his case, Duke Roger replied that he had appointed Lanzarius according to the ancient custom of the Lombard princes of the region. Urban II, in turn, declared this custom to be evil and unjust, asserting that "no layman should administer churches or have them under his control because they should all be under archiepiscopal power" ("nullus laycus debet ecclesias ordinare vel sub sua potestate habere, set omnes sub potestate episcoporum esse"). Once again the pope and archbishop were pushing to establish new traditions based on a Roman model.

The papacy also supported Archbishop Alfanus I in a dispute against the archbishop of Benevento. The case was brought before the papal legate Desiderius, abbot of Montecassino, sometime between 1075 and 1085 and the point of contention was authority over lands, churches, and *castra* in the area of Forino, on the border between the two archdioceses.[31] Roffrid the archbishop of Benevento argued his side based on custom, claiming that since he had exercised authority in the area for over thirty years, he had the right to continue to do so. Alfanus I, however, cited a canon from the 633 Council of Toledo stating that the borders of dioceses were always to be respected. Next he showed the 849 division of the Lombard Principality of Salerno, which included Forino within Salerno's diocese. Desiderius decided in Alfanus' favor, demonstrating the importance of territorial integrity

---

[27] IP, 8: 351, no. 24.

[28] IP, 8: 351–52, no. 25; Ughelli, 7: 382–84.

[29] Taviani-Carozzi, *La Principauté*, 983–90.

[30] Cava C, 40; IP, 8: 353–54, nos. 31–32; Pflugk-Harttung, 2: 149–50, no. 184.

[31] Hartmut Hoffmann, "Die Älteren Abtslistern von Montecassino," *Quellen und Forschungen aus Italienischen Archiven und Bibliotheken* 47 (1967): 352–54. Taviani-Carozzi, *La Principauté*, 993–96.

for dioceses and showing how arguments based on universal canon law emanating from Rome held more force than customary practice.[32]

Thus the period between 950 and 1050 represented a major shift in the relationship between the papacy and southern Italian prelates. For the first time in centuries, papal activity became a consistent and significant force in the region's church organization. Popes began to personally invest archbishops, insisting they come to Rome to receive the pallium directly from them. They traveled to the region to hold synods and intervene in local disputes. They introduced new rules, based on Roman customs, for the administration of pastoral care. They started to issue bulls to bishoprics and abbeys, in some cases granting new privileges and in other cases confirming rights that previously had been bestowed on prelates by lay rulers, insisting in such a way that church organization be under papal and not lay authority. In the late eleventh and early twelfth centuries, popes such as Urban II and Paschal II increased papal activity even further. They traveled frequently to southern Italy to hold councils and consecrate new churches. They took part in the elections of important church officials, at times handpicking their own nominees who, in some cases, were not local men but cardinals from Rome.[33] They granted exemptions to local abbeys and sent a papal legate to Sicily.[34] Although their power over clerics and church organization in southern Italy was far from absolute, and they tended to exercise influence rather than outright authority, nonetheless over the course of the eleventh century the popes became active participants once again in the religious and political landscape of southern Italy.

Lay Privileges and Diocesan Reorganization

Lay rulers also played an important role in the growth of archiepiscopal power in the tenth and eleventh centuries. As early as 946, Prince Gisolf I conceded to Bishop Peter the mortuary tax ("ex res mortuorum") on episcopal lands, as well as all the goods pertaining to priests, deacons, subdeacons, and clerics in the principality who died without heirs.[35] In addition, the

[32] Also see the abbey of Cava's use of Roman law in 1089 to argue the legitimacy of a donation made to the monastery by a fourteen-year-old boy. Taviani-Carozzi, *La Principauté*, 974–77.

[33] Kamp, "The Bishops of Southern Italy," 195–96.

[34] Hurbert Houben, "Urbano II e i Normanni (con un'appendice sull'itinerario del papa nel Sud)," in *Mezzogiorno Normanno-Svevo*, 132.

[35] Although the original charter is now lost, it was edited in the nineteenth century by the authors of the *Regii Neapolitani Archivi Monumenta*. RNAM, I: 160–65,

prince granted the bishop everything given by priests and clerics to women with whom they committed adultery. He confirmed episcopal authority over all the slaves ("servi") who belonged to the bishop along with their wives and exempted the bishop's *censiles* men from paying dues to the prince. Finally, he conceded to the bishop the port tax ("portaticum") owed either at the port of Salerno itself or in other places subject to the prince.

Two important imperial privileges were also granted to the cathedral church of Salerno, the first by Emperor Otto II during his southern Italian campaigns in 982. The emperor, in fact, issued two privileges, one in Taranto on April 18 and the other in Capaccio on November 2.[36] In the first, he granted to Bishop John all the ancient privileges conceded to him by the princes of Salerno. He reconfirmed his authority over episcopal lands between the Tusciano and Sele rivers, including dues ("angaria" and "cens"), fishing, hunting, waterways, and mills. In the second, he conceded the bishop all the monasteries, both male and female, within the diocese, as well as some property confiscated from a certain Landolfus son of Landolfus.

On 31 May 1022, Emperor Henry II granted the archbishop of Salerno a privilege during his campaigns in southern Italy.[37] In it, he not only conceded the privileges issued by his predecessor, such as authority over all the lands from the Tusciano to the Sele rivers, including the *castrum* of Olevano, but he also established important parish rights for the archbishop within the diocese. The emperor asserted that all *censiles* men belonging to churches were to be under the authority of the archbishop alone, just as in ancient times. Moreover, he placed all priests and clerics within the diocese, along with their families, under the archbishop's authority, including power over the dues and services owed by them. Finally, Henry gave the archbishop additional economic privileges, including permission to build three butcher shops in Salerno and power over the lands and goods of those who died without heirs. Thus, long before Pope Alexander II issued his bull, the Saxon emperor Henry granted the archbishop of Salerno parish rights in his diocese.

---

no. 45. A similar document issued by the prince of Salerno to the bishop of Benevento in 953 (Ughelli, 8: 55–56) still survives and Taviani-Carozzi has argued convincingly that similarities between the 946 and 953 privileges provide evidence for the validity of the now lost 946 privilege. Taviani-Carozzi, *La Principauté*, 616.

[36] MGH, Diplomata, 2/1, 317–18, no. 273, and 332–33, no. 284.

[37] MGH, Diplomata, 3: 601–2, no. 472. It is possible that these imperial privileges are forgeries, although princely privileges issued in 1023 and 1058, as well as papal bulls from the eleventh century, acknowledge that emperors had formerly granted privileges to the cathedral church of Salerno. Carmine Carlone, *Documenti per la Storia di Eboli (799–1264)* (Salerno: Carlone Editore, 1998), 7.

The 1023 privilege issued by Princes Guaimarius III and IV followed Emperor Henry's privilege closely, granting some additional economic rights and establishing in more specific terms the archbishop's control over the ecclesiastical system in the archdiocese.[38] First, the princes reiterated the cathedral church's authority over the lands and goods of men living on church lands who died without heirs, both within and outside episcopal lands. In addition, they gave the archbishops power over all the streets, alleys, and staircases adjoining episcopal lands in Salerno, the fortifications above the lands, the rivers and waterways flowing through episcopal lands, and finally the various dues and services ("angaria," "servitio," "cens," "datio") owed from freemen ("liberi") living on episcopal property. Similarly, the *censiles* men living on episcopal lands were to pay dues and perform services for the archbishop alone, and they had to get his permission before alienating their property. The princes placed all priests, deacons, subdeacons, and clerics under the judicial power of the archbishop, asserting that he alone had the right to judge them "just as the holy canons set forth" ("qualiter sancti canones docent"). Moreover, the archbishop was no longer required to take an oath when involved in a dispute, but could have representatives ("scariones") do it in his place.

Later privileges from Prince Guaimarius IV in 1032 and Gisolf II in 1058 reconfirmed these rights, again stressing the archbishop's immunity from dues and services.[39] They continued to promote a territorial concept of episcopal power, as well as to expand the cathedral church's base by granting additional economic concessions. Gisolf II, for example, gave the archbishop permission to build new stores and send men there to sell meat and other merchandise, without having to pay any dues on these commercial activities. Thus lay rulers proved to be allies as valuable as the papacy during the period of the cathedral church's reorganization and expansion.

Based on privileges issued by popes and lay rulers, archbishops in the eleventh century set in place an ecclesiastical hierarchy to oversee religious life and organization in their archdiocese. They created new bishoprics and established a system of archpriests located in important rural villages. They also personally participated in the activities of their bishops and archpriests, setting norms for their behavior, standardizing their duties and religious practices, and specifying how they were to administer their lands and spend ecclesiastical revenues. The first evidence for this new metropolitan hierarchy comes from the bull issued by Stephen IX in 1058, which mentioned four new bishops dependent on the Church of Salerno, in Policastro, Mar-

---

[38] API XV, vol. 62, no. 12–13; Muratori, 1: 187–88; Paesano, 1: 99–101.
[39] Muratori, 1: 189–92; Paesano, 1: 101–2, 115–17.

sico, Martirano, and Cassano.[40] The pope also gave Archbishop Alfanus I permission to create new bishops in other places, which he did soon after in Sarno, Nusco, and possibly, Acerno.[41] Later popes reconfirmed this privilege, and although Martirano and Cassano, both in Calabria, remained suffragans for only a brief time, the other five survived as dependencies of the cathedral church of Salerno up through modern times. The appearance during this period of new titles for clerics dependent on the bishop, including cardinal and "primicerius," also reflects the new hierarchical system put in place.[42]

A 1066 document from Sarno gives direct evidence for the administration of the new metropolitan hierarchy. According to the document, addressed to the clergy and people of Sarno, Archbishop Alfanus I traveled to Sarno in order to invest and advise the newly elected bishop, Risus.[43] First Alfanus set down rules for ordaining new clerics. He told Risus to make sure they had not committed any illicit actions that would bar them from holding office, such as engaging in bigamy or adultery. Then he told Risus to ensure that the clerics were literate and had no physical defects. He also told Risus to reject anyone from Africa, since, he alleged, many Africans practiced Manicheanism. Next, Alfanus listed in detail the boundaries of Sarno's diocese. Then he went on to explain the proper time and way to celebrate various ecclesiastical offices and holidays. He listed the days on which it was canonical to ordain new clerics, and then insisted that baptisms be performed exclusively on Easter or Pentecost, unless a person was in danger of

---

[40] Pflugk-Harttung, 2: 82–84, no. 116.

[41] IP, 8: 303 and 377–79; Fonseca, "L'organizzazione," 335; Vitolo, "Vescovi e Diocesi," 126. In the case of Sarno, the bishopric may have already been in place before Alfanus I became archbishop of Salerno. A document dated 1025 found at the abbey of Cava, but not included in the *Codex Diplomaticus Cavensis*, mentions a bishop of Sarno by the name of John. Although there is no further evidence for the cathedral church of Sarno until the 1066 investiture, it may very well be that Alfanus did not establish the See of Sarno at this time, but merely proclaimed its dependence on Salerno. Galante, "La documentazione vescovile," 233–34. As for Acerno, it may have been established as a bishopric after Alfanus I's death. The first reference to it is found in the *Liber Confratrum* of the cathedral church of Salerno, which lists the date of death of a Mirandus bishop of Acerno as either 1091 or 1106. Kehr, IP, 8: 379; Acocella, "La figura e l'opera di Alfano I," 36–37.

[42] Taviani-Carozzi, *La Principauté*, 1017–19. Nonetheless, there is no evidence that these cathedral clerics led a common life regulated by a rule similar to canons in northern Italy. It is interesting to note, however, that Alfanus I received a letter from Peter Damiani in 1062 in which the Roman reformer extolled the virtues of canons living a common life under a rule. Acocella, "La figura e l'opera di Alfano I," 47–50.

[43] Ughelli, 7: 571–72. The document is found in the church of Sarno. For a recent study of the charter, see Galante, "La documentazione vescovile," 234–35.

dying. The new bishop had the right to collect and keep all the dues owed to the church, including tithes and donations ("decimas et oblationes vivorum et mortuorum"), but was required to give one-fourth of them to the clerics of his diocese, one-fourth to the poor and to pilgrims, one-fourth for the restoration of churches, keeping the remaining one-fourth for himself.[44]

Unfortunately no documents provide information on the new archpriests created. We learn of them only in 1169, when the bull issued by Pope Alexander III listed twelve archpriests dependent on the archbishops of Salerno in Campagna, Eboli, Olevano, Montecorvino, Giffoni, Ogliara, San Severino, San Giorgio, Montoro, Forino, Serino, and Nocera.[45] These places, however, became seats of power for the new nobility of the Norman Duchy of Apulia, which means that the archbishops placed their new archpriests in important rural villages that became centers of political authority in the late eleventh and twelfth centuries.[46] Beginning in the mid-twelfth century, moreover, parish churches attached to these archpresbyters began to appear, bringing to light a new level in the cathedral church's hierarchy.[47] (See map 4.)

Emancipation charters issued in the second half of the eleventh century also demonstrate the archbishop's growing influence over religious life in his diocese.[48] Although the archbishop still granted the founders the power to appoint the clergy and rectors, as well as to sell or alienate the church without episcopal permission, in comparison with earlier *chartae libertatis*, he retained more power over the clergy of the religious foundations. In the 1050 *charta libertatis* issued to the church of Santa Lucia, for example, the archbishop required that all the priests and monks come before him, when-

---

[44] A seventeenth-century copy of a 1079 pastoral letter from Archbishop Alfanus, which invested Peter as the new bishop of Policastro, is similar in many ways to this document. However, it is almost certainly a forgery. For an edition and translation of the letter, see Nicola Maria Laudisio, *Sinossi della diocesi di Policastro*, ed. G. Galleazzo Visconti (Rome: Edizioni di Storia e Letteratura, 1976), 13–14, 70–71. For a paleographical analysis of the document, see Galante, "La documentazione vescovile," 235–38.

[45] Paesano, 2: 176–78; Crisci and Campagna, *Salerno Sacra*, 144.

[46] For more on this, see Ruggiero, "Per una storia," 65. Feller has observed the same phenomenon in the Abruzzi, where new parish churches in the eleventh century were founded in or near new settlements, following the lines of *incastellamento*. Feller, *Les Abruzzes*, 790–799. In Apulia, characterized by a proliferation of new bishoprics beginning in the tenth century, the new cathedral churches were also established in new cities. Martin, *La Pouille*, 566–67, 581–82.

[47] Vitolo, "Vescovi e Diocesi," 138.

[48] The archbishops of Salerno issued *chartae libertatis* in 1050 and 1071 to two new religious foundations, Santa Lucia in Balenaria, founded by a *consortium*, and San Nicola in Salerno, built by the viscount Vivus and the abbey of Cava. CDC 7: 147–49, no. 1146 (Cherubini, 181–83, no. 67); CDC 9: 318–22, no. 103.

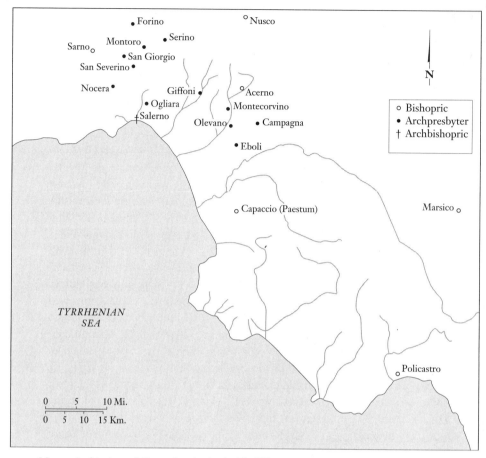

Map 4. Archiepiscopal Dependencies in the Twelfth Century (according to the 1169 Bull of Alexander III)

ever he wished, in order to ascertain if they were acting canonically. In addition, the owners were required to choose the church's clergy from within the diocese and were allowed to install someone from another diocese only with the archbishop's permission.[49] The archbishop also set down certain standards for the church owners and rectors to follow, including the requirement that appointments of priests and clerics follow canon law ("canonum istituta"). In the 1071 emancipation charter issued to the church of San Nicola della Palma in Salerno, the archbishop specifically stated that the owners, Vivus and the abbots of Cava, had to appoint priests, clerics,

[49] CDC 7: 147–49, no. 1146 (Cherubini, 181–83, no. 67). Also see Cava XV, 60.

and monks according to canonical practice and the Rule of St. Benedict. Moreover, he specified that all the church administrators had to behave "according to orthodox tradition" ("catholico more").[50] Thus these two emancipation charters demonstrate one way in which the archbishop was trying to integrate proprietary churches into the new diocesan structure and gain oversight over them.

The archbishop of Salerno also took on important new political functions when he constructed one of the earliest territorial lordships in the region, centered on his *castrum* in Olevano sul Tusciano. Already in the late tenth century, the archbishop owned numerous properties in the region, including mills and forests. By the mid-eleventh century, he exercised economic and judicial power over the local population there, receiving dues and services from them and deciding the disputes that arose among them.[51] In addition, the archbishop had certain rights over all the property in Olevano and its territory, whether it belonged directly to him or was owned by others.

Prince Gisolf II issued a diploma in 1057 that spelled out the duties of the local population in the territory of Olevano toward the archbishop, as well as the limits of archiepiscopal power.[52] The prince granted the inhabitants permission to build and own mills at the mouth of the Tusciano river, keeping the profits for themselves but paying the archbishop rent. They had to let the archbishop use the mills free of charge, but they, in turn, were allowed to collect as much wood as necessary in the archbishop's forests, free from taxation, for constructing the mills. In addition, the prince reconfirmed the archbishop's right to labor services, specifying that the inhabitants had to work for him at sowing and harvest time. However, the prince gave the inhabitants permission to marry off their women as they wished, and he insisted that adulterous women would not be required to go under the archbishop's protection. Instead they would remain under the guardianship of their families, although children born of the illicit relationships were to be placed in the archbishop's care. Thus, the prince did place some limitations on the archbishop's power. Nonetheless, the privilege demonstrates that the archbishop wielded a considerable amount of authority in the territory of Olevano sul Tusciano at the time, having power over the rivers and forests of the region, rights to the labor services and dues owed by the inhabitants, and at least some judicial authority over them. Moreover, it shows

[50] CDC 9: 318–22, no. 103.

[51] An old but useful study of this territorial lordship is found in Carlo Carucci, *Un feudo ecclesiatico nell'Italia meridionale: Olevano sul Tusciano* (Subiaco: Tipografio dei monasteri, 1937). Also see Taviani-Carozzi, *La Principauté*, 963–69.

[52] API XV, vol. 63, no. 23.

that Prince Gisolf II actively promoted the growth of archiepiscopal power in the region.

When Duke Robert Guiscard issued a diploma to Archbishop Alfanus I in 1080, both the territory and authority of the archbishop had expanded.[53] In addition to the *castrum* of Olevano, the archbishop also controlled the *castellum* of Battipaglia located on the Mediterranean Sea at the mouth of the Tusciano river. The churches of San Vittorio of Giffoni, Sant'Angelo near Liciano, San Giorgio near Cosentino, and San Vito on the Sele river were also listed as possessions, as were a number of lands and villages in the region between the Tusciano and Sele rivers. In addition, the archbishop controlled a lake and some forested land, and had right of passage on the Sele river, as well as authority over the ports and fishing nets found along the river. Finally, in his diploma Robert gave to the archbishop the tithe of ducal revenues from the territory of Eboli. At the same time, the duke financed the building of the new cathedral church in Salerno, perhaps the ultimate symbol of enhanced archiepiscopal authority.[54]

Despite the increased power and wealth of the cathedral church of Salerno in the eleventh century, the archbishops never succeeded in implementing the vast privileges and rights granted them by papal bulls. For one, laypeople continued to establish and administer ecclesiastical foundations into the twelfth century and beyond. Charters show lay owners building and donating churches and investing clerics and rectors, without episcopal permission.[55] Some of these religious foundations were quite large, with numerous dependent houses and sizeable staffs of clerics. San Nicola of Capaccio, for example, bought by Gregory son of Pandolfus in 1073, became an extremely powerful foundation in the region, with extensive lands, dependent churches, and territorial powers over the local population.[56] Simi-

---

[53] Ménager, 110–13, no. 35.

[54] For a detailed discussion of the cathedral church of Salerno, see Valentino Pace, "La cattedrale di Salerno," in *Desiderio di Montecassino e l'arte della riforma gregoriana,* ed. Faustino Avagliano, 189–230 (Montecassino: Pubblicazioni cassinesi, 1997).

[55] See, for example, Balducci, 1: 12, no. 28 from 1095; Cava XVIII, 5 from 1106; Cava XX, 96 from 1119; Cava XXI, 50 from 1121; Cava XXI, 70 from 1122; Cava XXII, 16 from 1126; Cava XXII, 54 from 1128; Cava XXIV, 67 from 1138; Cava XXV, 85 from 1144 and Cava XXVI, 112 from 1148.

[56] CDC 10: 59–71, no. 19. See the 1116 and 1118 donations by Gregory and his wife Maria, which included San Matteo in Subarci, Sant'Angelo in Velanzanu, San Felice in Felline, their portions of Sant'Andrea de Lama and San Massimo in Salerno, one-third of the church of San Giovanni outside of Capaccio, one-third of the church of San Bartolomeo in Paczanu, one-third of San Nicola in Orteiano, one-third of the church of San Giovanni in Burgenze, one-third of the church of Santa Maria inside the *castellum* of Corneto, one-third of the church of Santa Marina outside the *castel-*

larly, the abbey of Cava, with its exemption from archiepiscopal authority, controlled numerous ecclesiastical foundations in the region.[57] More importantly, non-episcopal churches continued to exercise religious functions usually reserved for parish churches in other regions. The church of San Nicola della Palma mentioned above received the right to bless wax, sprinkle holy water, place crosses, visit the sick, and bury the dead, despite its proximity to the cathedral church of Salerno.[58] Other non-episcopal churches performed baptisms, administered penance, and celebrated the offices of the Holy Week, and they did not seek episcopal permission before doing so.[59] Although some of these churches were located in isolated rural areas, providing services for villages far away from bishops and archpriests, many were built in towns with episcopal or archpresbyter churches, and some even operated in Salerno, next to the archbishop himself. Thus, not only did numerous ecclesiastical foundations function outside archiepiscopal control, but the archbishops never managed to monopolize specific religious functions in their diocese, such as baptism, penance, or burial.

The metropolitan of Salerno never established rights over a universal tithe or other ecclesiastical tax in his archdiocese. Although the 1066 investiture from Sarno mentioned tithes ("decimas") owed to a bishop in a specific diocese, overall the evidence suggests that whatever revenues the archbishops and their dependencies did collect was not owing to a claim of territorial rights, but the result of specific concessions from lay rulers. Records of papal taxation in 1308–10, found in the Vatican archives, recorded the tithes owed by various churches, monasteries, and clerics in the archdiocese of Salerno and the dioceses of Capaccio, Acerno, Nusco, Sarno, and Policastro.[60] The list is quite long and demonstrates how, even in

---

lum of Corneto, one-third of the church of San Pietro above the *castellum* of Corneto, one-third of the church of San Nicola inside the *castellum* of Asprium(?), their portion of the monastery called "de Gemmato," what pertained to them of the churches of Santa Maria dalle Caselle, San Nicola da lu Murtillitu, San Mauro outside the *castellum* of Trentinara, San Giovanni outside the *castellum* of Trentinara, and Santa Maria inside the *castellum* Trentinara. The donation included all the property, houses, and movable wealth of the foundations, along with the inhabitants which pertained to them. In December of the same year, Gregory and Maria donated lands with their inhabitants in Cilento, in a lu Betrano. Cava C, 34; Cava C, 33.

[57] C, 21 (Guillaume, xx–xxii); D, 26 (Pflugk-Harttung, 2: 169–71, no. 206; Guillaume, xxiii–xxv).

[58] CDC 9: 318–22, no. 103.

[59] Crisci and Campagna, *Salerno Sacra*, 146–52.

[60] *Rationes Decimarum Italiae nei secoli XIII e XIV: Campania*, ed. Mauro Inguanez, Leone Mattei-Cerasoli, and Pietro Sella, vol. 97 of *Studi e Testi* (Vatican City: Biblioteca Apostolica Vaticana, 1942), 383–453 for Salerno, 457–63 for Capaccio, 467 for Acerno, 471–72 for Nusco, 475–76 for Sarno, and 479 for Policastro.

the fourteenth century, religious organization was extremely fragmented and that the archbishop and bishops did not have power over a universal tithe or a well-organized system of parish churches. Two centuries after reform, the archbishop continued to exercise authority over religious houses and ecclesiastical revenues because of specific privileges that the cathedral church had collected piecemeal and not from any kind of territorial jurisdiction. Furthermore, the papal records show that at least some of the bishops in the archdiocese of Salerno had extremely limited resources, suggesting that bishoprics remained a rather weak religious institution well after the eleventh century.

Throughout Norman southern Italy, cathedral churches relied on lay concessions for their revenues, rather than a universal tithe.[61] The tithes received by cathedral churches could sometimes be large, encompassing whole dioceses, and sometimes small, including only a specific city or territory. In Sicily, for example, many bishops were given the tithe on the revenues for the whole of their dioceses, while in Apulia most cathedral churches received tithes connected to extremely limited geographical areas. In many cases, archbishops also received dues paid by the Jewish population.[62] In the case of Salerno, lay rulers were not overly generous. Duke Robert granted the archbishop the tithe on the revenues from the city of Salerno and the territory of Eboli in 1080, while his son Duke Roger Borsa gave the archbishops the tithe of the port of Salerno.[63] Duke William, in turn, gave them the right to collect tithes in Locubia and Felline, two small territories near Salerno. In addition, he granted them the tax paid by the Jewish population of Salerno.[64] This meant that the archbishop controlled very few revenues in his diocese. Moreover, in 1190 the archbishop of Salerno even renounced his rights over two important revenues, the tithe in Salerno and Tusciano (Eboli), granting it to King Tancred in exchange for an annual payment in gold.[65]

Furthermore, the amount of political power exercised by the archbishop

---

[61] Martin, *La Pouille*, 597–600; Kamp "Vescovi e diocesi," 176–79, and "Monarchia ed episcopato nel Regno svevo di Sicilia," in *Potere, società, e popolo nell'età sveva 1210–66: Atti delle seste giornate normanno-sveve, Bari-Castel del Monte-Melfi, 17–20 October 1983* (Bari: Edizioni Dedalo, 1985), 126–28.

[62] Kamp, "Monarchia ed episcopato," 126–28; Martin, *La Pouille*, 600–609.

[63] Ménager, 110–13, no. 35; Balducci, 1: 16, no. 35.

[64] Balducci, 1: 17, no. 41 and 137–38, no. 35.

[65] *Codex Diplomaticus Regni Siciliae*, vol. 2, pt. 1 of *Diplomata regum et principum e gente normannorum: Roger II. regis diplomata latina*, ed. Carlrichard Brühl. (Cologne: Böhlau, 1987), 11. Also see Norbert Kamp, *Kirche und Monarchie im Staufischen Königreich Sizilien* (Munich: Wilhelm Fink, 1973), 1:422–49.

was small in comparison to other lords who rose to power at this time. Although Olevano sul Tusciano was one of the earliest lordships established, it never became very large and was even encroached upon by others carving out lordships in the region in the eleventh century. The counts of the Principate, the lords of Eboli, and the abbey of Cava all built up centers of power in the area, even if the archbishops remained the predominant force in the region.[66] Moreover, Olevano represented the only center of power for the cathedral church, whereas other lords, such as the abbey of Cava and the lords of Sanseverino, possessed lordships in both southern and northern parts of the principality.

Thus, the archbishops never established an ecclesiastical hierarchy encompassing all of the religious houses and clergy in their archdiocese. Not only did a large number of churches, clerics, and ecclesiastical revenues remain outside the effective control of the archbishops, but liturgy and religious practices were never standardized under archiepiscopal oversight. As a result, the archbishop of Salerno did not completely eradicate the fragmented nature of religious life and organization characteristic of the Principality of Salerno in the early medieval period. In addition, the cathedral church of Salerno never grew to be as large or important as the abbey of Cava. As in other regions of southern Italy, the Norman conquest and church reform benefited large Benedictine monasteries more than they did cathedral churches.[67]

Papal Reform and Southern Italy in the Norman Era

At first glance it would appear that the papacy enthusiastically supported the development of a strong, centralized archdiocese in Salerno. Eleventh-century popes established broad jurisdiction for the archbishops over the religious houses and clerics of their archdiocese and helped them to build an ecclesiastical hierarchy by giving them permission to create new bishoprics and archpriests directly dependent on the cathedral church. In addition, the popes actively supported the archbishops by providing protection against soldiers invading ecclesiastical lands and by threatening rulers who interfered in the appointment of bishops, priests, and other clerics in the archdiocese. Yet in reality the relationship between Roman reformers and local

[66] For a more detailed discussion of the various powers operating in the region at the time, see Errico Cuozzo, "'Milites' e 'testes' nelle contea normanna di Principato," *Bullettino dell'Istituto Italiano per il Medio Evo* 88 (1979): 121–63.

[67] Loud, "A Lombard Abbey," 273–75.

ones was far more complex, and the goals of the papacy did not always correspond to the local reform program of the archbishops. For example, the popes, in their attempt to create an efficient ecclesiastical system throughout southern Italy and Sicily administered directly from Rome, subtracted dependencies from Salerno's archdiocese. In addition, the popes granted the abbey of Cava exemption from archiepiscopal authority, which allowed the monks there to develop a separate ecclesiastical hierarchy much more powerful than the cathedral church. Also important was the fact that papal bulls were at times based more on ancient privileges and old papal policies than new political realities, which meant the archbishops had to reform their church taking into account the conflicting demands of the old and the new.[68]

A major example of conflict between old privileges and new exigencies relates to the size of the archdiocese of Salerno. The boundaries of the diocese of Salerno that were drawn up during the Lombard period were based on those of the Principality of Salerno at that time and encompassed bishoprics in regions far from Salerno, including Acerenza in Basilicata, Cosenza in Calabria, Conza in the province of Avellino, and Nola located northeast of Naples. Moreover, the addition in the late tenth century of dependencies in Byzantine territories, such as Bisignano and Malvito, was part of a papal anti-Byzantine policy that no longer held any meaning by the mid-eleventh century, given the Norman conquest of southern Italy. Furthermore, the new ecclesiastical system promoted both by the papacy and local reformers required tighter supervision over ecclesiastical lands and revenues as well as parish clergy on the part of bishops and archbishops. This led to the creation of more compact dioceses and the reassignment of some dependencies to archbishops located in closer proximity. From the point of view of both the papacy and the new Norman rulers, bishoprics were better administered by metropolitans located close enough to exercise real control and supervision, and little by little dependencies located far away were subtracted from Salerno's cathedral church.

Despite the changing political realities, popes in the eleventh century relied on old privileges when they issued new bulls to the archbishops of Salerno. As a result, they reconfirmed the archbishop's power over the seven

---

[68] Throughout southern Italy in the eleventh century cathedral churches had to strike a balance between existing traditions and new exigencies, as well as work out the ancient rivalries which plagued many regions and strike compromises between the goals of local reformers and the ambitions of both the papacy and the new Norman rulers. Kamp, "The Bishops of Southern Italy," 186.

bishoprics of Paestum, Cosenza, Bisignano, Malvito, Acerenza, Conza, and Nola.[69] However, in the mid-eleventh century popes also began to subtract some of these bishoprics from the archbishop's authority, even while continuing to reconfirm their old status as Salernitan suffragans. Conza, Consenza, and Acerenza became metropolitan cities in their own right sometime in the mid-eleventh century.[70] The bishops of Malvito and Bisignano, both in Calabria, while not advancing to the status of metropolitans, became directly dependent on the pope sometime in the twelfth century.[71] Nola became a suffragan of Naples at this time, with the popes finally recognizing a situation that for decades had been a reality.[72] Out of the seven dependencies mentioned in papal bulls from the first half of the eleventh century, the bishopric of Paestum alone remained under the authority of the cathedral church of Salerno by the twelfth century.

Both Archbishop Alfanus I (1058–85) and Archbishop Alfanus II (1086–1121) fought against the losses of their ancient suffragans, asking for new papal privileges confirming the cathedral church's power over them. Certain popes granted their wishes. Between 1061 and 1073, Alexander II confirmed Conza's submission to Salerno's metropolitan, while Gregory VII did the same between 1080–85.[73] In a bull issued by Urban II on 20 July 1098, the archbishop of Salerno received primacy over Conza and Acerenza. Urban, however, clearly recognized their autonomy, and the privilege was little more than ceremonial. According to the bull, the archbishops of these two sees were to be elected in the presence of a papal legate with the advice of the archbishop of Salerno, who afterward would direct the newly elected official to Rome with his letters to be consecrated.[74] Finally, the 1100–1106 privilege from Paschal II gave back the churches of Nola and Malvito to the archbishop of Salerno according to ancient privileges, without specifying what that meant.[75]

Throughout southern Italy and Sicily in the eleventh and early twelfth centuries, confusion and contradictions appear regularly in the documents regarding diocesan boundaries, the status of dependencies, and the exact ju-

---

[69] The bulls do contain some discrepancies, however. For example, Conza is not mentioned in the 994 confirmation, while Nola is missing from the 1012 and 1036 bulls. Ughelli, 7: 376–77; Ughelli, 7: 377; Pflugk-Harttung, 2: 64–65, no. 99.

[70] IP, 8: 9, no. 4; IP, 9: 474, no. 3.

[71] IP, 10: 88, 93.

[72] IP, 8: 297–98.

[73] IP, 8: 352–53, nos. 26 and 28.

[74] IP, 8: 354–55, no. 35; Ughelli, 7: 393–95.

[75] IP, 8: 357, no. 40; Pflugk-Harttung, 2: 172, no. 209.

risdiction of each bishop and archbishop.[76] For example, Bari and Trani had a number of disputes regarding suffragans, while Brindisi and Oria fought over where the archbishop would reside, since unrest in the ninth century had caused the bishop, originally in Brindisi, to relocate to Oria. The bishop of Monopoli fought to free himself of dependency on Brindisi, while the bishop of Montepeloso sought autonomy from Acerenza.[77] The case of Montepeloso is most telling, because it reflects well the confusion inherent in parish organization at the time. At the Synod of Melfi in 1059, the pope deposed the head of the church of Montepeloso for simony, referring to him as a bishop. However, Pope Alexander II in 1068 listed Montepeloso as a dependency of the bishopric of Acerenza. The bull issued by Paschal II to the bishop of Acerenza in 1102, however, did not include Montepeloso as a suffragan. Then in 1123, Pope Calixtus II "restored" the bishopric of Montepeloso. Thus, Montepeloso, between 1060 and 1123, appears both as a bishopric and as a dependency of the cathedral church of Acerenza, which itself was ostensibly a suffragan of Salerno.[78]

The structural problems inherent in the ecclesiastical organization in southern Italy stemmed from a number of different causes. Among them, competition in the eleventh century between the papacy and the Byzantines for control over church organization in southern Italy meant that two cathedral churches were sometimes assigned the same suffragans. In Apulia, double seats were created in the ninth century on account of Muslim attacks that caused cities to be abandoned periodically and their bishops to relocate.[79] In addition, Norman lords at times created new sees for their own purposes, which could infringe upon the rights of other cathedral churches.[80] Contradictions and inconsistencies in the documents make it impossible to draw a precise map of southern Italian dioceses in the eleventh century. Only in the twelfth century does the confusion begin to subside as a coordinated effort on the part of the papacy and the Normans to rationalize the ecclesiastical structures of southern Italy began to show signs of success. Claims found in ancient privileges were finally balanced to meet the new political realities.[81] Thus by the mid-twelfth century, the

---

[76] See Kamp, "Vescovi e diocesi" and "The Bishops of Southern Italy"; Fonseca, "L'organizzazione"; Loud, "Churches and Churchmen" and, in particular, Klewitz, "Studien."

[77] Fonseca, "L'organizzazione," 332–33, 337–38; Kamp, "Vescovi e diocesi," 170–73; Martin, *La Pouille*, 570.

[78] Klewitz, "Studien," 145–47.

[79] Martin, *La Pouille*, 246, 570.

[80] Ibid., 576.

[81] Kamp, "Vescovi e diocesi," 170.

archbishops of Salerno had stopped insisting on their rights over the six churches of Cosenza, Bisignano, Acerenza, Conza, Nola, and Malvito, and papal privileges no longer mentioned them as dependencies of the cathedral church of Salerno. The 1169 bull issued by Alexander III, for example, listed none of the six bishoprics as suffragans.[82] Yet since the archbishops in the eleventh century never exercised any real authority over these six bishoprics, all of which were located outside of the principality, their loss was not very significant.

A graver threat to the power of the cathedral church of Salerno came from the abbey of Cava, whose monks built a large ecclesiastical empire granted exemption from archiepiscopal control by the papacy.[83] The clash between Cava and the cathedral church over control of religious houses first appears in 1089 at the Council of Melfi called by Urban II. During the council, Maraldus the bishop of Paestum complained to the pope that the abbey of Cava posed a threat to the integrity of the cathedral church, since the monks had illegally taken control of a number of religious houses in Cilento.[84] Representatives of Cava claimed that Gregory VII had given the ecclesiastical foundations to them, and after all those present at the council had authenticated Gregory's concession, Pope Urban II reconfirmed Cava's possession. At the same time, however, he conceded to the bishop of Paestum certain privileges over the houses, including the power to consecrate new altars and churches and to collect one-fourth of the tithe on ecclesiastical lands and one-third of the alms paid for the dead. The bishop also received the right to confer the office on clerics serving in the church. Shortly thereafter, in a bull issued from Venosa on 21 September 1089, Urban II reiterated Gregory VII's concession and then placed Cava directly under

---

[82] Paesano, 2: 176–78.

[83] For studies on the dispute between the abbey of Cava and the archbishops, see IP, 8: 311, 317–24; Dieter Girgensohn, "Miscellanea Italiae Pontificiae: Untersuchungen und Urkunden zur Mittelalterlichen Kirchengeschichte Italiens, vornehmlich Kalabriens, Siziliens, und Sardiniens," *Nachrichten der Akademie der Wissenschaften in Göttingen aus dem Jahre 1974. Philologisch-Historische Klasse* (1974): 147–72; and, in particular, Giovanni Vitolo, "La Badia di Cava e gli Arcivescovi di Salerno tra XI e XII secolo," *Rassegna Storica Salernitana*, n.s. 8 (December 1987): 9–16, who shows the dispute to be an exception to the basically harmonious relationship between the abbots and archbishops. Throughout central and southern Italy at this time, conflicts occurred between bishops and abbeys over monastic exemptions. For the Principality of Capua, see Loud, *Church and Society*, 110–23. For the Abruzzi, see Feller, *Les Abruzzes*, 825–40.

[84] Girgensohn, "Miscellanea Italiae pontificiae," 190–91, no. 2. This privilege could be a forgery, although Girgensohn thinks it to be authentic on paleographical grounds. Girgensohn, "Miscellanea Italiae pontificiae," 147–50.

papal authority.[85] He granted the abbey the right to elect its own abbot, whom the pope would consecrate, and permission to build a baptismal church next to the abbey.

Archbishop Alfanus II complained to Urban II about Cava's exemption in 1098, claiming that it harmed the cathedral church.[86] Urban took the archbishop's side and revoked the abbey's exemption a year later in Rome.[87] Soon after, the new pope, Paschal II, confirmed Cava's exemption, although he required the abbots to receive chrism and oil from the archbishops, as well as to have all their altars consecrated and their priests ordained by bishops.[88] This concession, however, gave the archbishops no real authority over Cava and its dependencies, and by 1100, the abbey of Cava controlled a large autonomous ecclesiastical order centered in the archdiocese of Salerno.[89]

Thus, the papacy had an ambivalent relationship with the reform archbishops of Salerno in the eleventh century. On the one hand, popes conceded wide-reaching powers to the archbishops, granting them jurisdiction over the religious foundations, clergy, and ecclesiastical revenues that made up their diocese. On the other hand, they diminished the archbishops' power by subtracting dependencies and granting the abbey of Cava an exemption. The papacy, of course, was interested in the broader issue of how to reform and control church organization throughout southern Italy and Sicily after the Norman conquest. Ancient privileges did not always offer the best solutions to current problems, so the popes reworked them in a way that would allow the papacy to control more directly and more efficiently the religious houses and clergy throughout the region. Sometimes such actions did not benefit local churchmen, such as the archbishops of Salerno. Moreover, the papacy's ambitious program to extend power over the religious organization throughout all of Christendom meant that popes were often overextended. When confronted with problems, reformers in southern Italy could not always depend on papal aid, and instead they had to look locally for help. As a result, lay rulers remained an important source for

---

[85] IP, 8: 318, no. 7.

[86] IP, 8: 323, nos. 15, 16; Pflugk-Harttung, 2: 164–65, no. 198.

[87] IP, 8: 323–34, no. 17.

[88] IP, 8: 324, no. 19.

[89] Vitolo believes that a later privilege of Urban II, meant to clarify the pope's earlier exemption bull, stressed that although the abbey itself was free from archiepiscopal authority, its dependencies were not. Vitolo, "La badia di Cava," 10–11. However, this papal bull only exists in a twelfth-century copy and Vitolo's conclusion, although possible, is also highly speculative. For an edition of the privilege, see Girgensohn, "Miscellanea Italiae pontificiae," 191–93, no. 3.

privileges and protection, and the papacy's desire to rid the ecclesiastical system of lay participation never became a viable option for churchmen in southern Italy.

Throughout Norman southern Italy, bishops and archbishops relied on lay rulers for financial support.[90] Since bishops in early medieval southern Italy as a rule did not have power over a system of parish churches or authority over a unified ecclesiastical tax within their diocese, they had to look to concessions from lay rulers to build their patrimonies and create revenues during the period of ecclesiastical reform in the eleventh century. This enabled the Norman rulers to create a strong bond between the monarchy and the Regno's bishops: dukes and kings assigned revenues, usually in the form of tithes or dues owed by Jewish populations, and these revenues were paid directly by the royal treasury to the cathedral churches. In this way, the Norman rulers made the bishops beneficiaries of Norman income and directly dependent on the fortunes of the Normans. As a result, southern Italian cathedral churches became an integral part of the monarchy at a time when churches in northern Europe were freeing themselves from lay power.[91] Prelates in southern Italy thus never promoted the idea of ecclesiastical liberty. Similarly, other aspects of papal reform were not advanced by local reformers, even if they generally shared the broader ideals of the papal reformers in Rome. Like the popes themselves, local reformers had to balance the conflicting demands of lofty ideals and practical exigencies. At times they also had different ideas regarding the proper way to reform the church. In the end, church reform in southern Italy was a complex process carried out by a variety of individuals negotiating diverse situations and espousing various solutions.

The Career of Archbishop Alfanus I (1058–85)

The career of Archbishop Alfanus I provides an instructive example of how reformers in southern Italy adapted models from Rome and other places to fit local situations. Born to a noble family in Salerno c. 1020, Al-

---

[90] Martin, *La Pouille*, 597–600; Kamp "Vescovi e diocesi," 176–79 and "Monarchia ed episcopato," 126–28.

[91] Kamp "Vescovi e diocesi," 177–78 and "Monarchia ed episcopato," 128. Vitolo and Martin have taken up Kamp's theory in their articles. Vitolo, "Vescovi e Diocesi," 140–41; Martin, "L'ambiente," 219–22. In his study of Apulia, however, Martin has shown that some of the smaller cathedral churches in the region did not receive ducal privileges but rather relied on concessions from local lords for survival. Martin, *La Pouille*, 604–6.

fanus studied a variety of subjects in both Salerno and Avellino in his early years, including Latin, Greek, medicine, and theology.[92] Alfanus left Salerno in c. 1052–54, because of his brothers' involvement in the assassination of Prince Guaimarius IV.[93] At the behest of Desiderius, he traveled to Benevento where he embraced the religious life in the monastery of Santa Sofia. Soon after, the two monks decided to retire to Montecassino, where Alfanus remained for about a year and a half. During this time, Alfanus not only developed a close friendship with Desiderius, but also met and befriended a number of prominent reformers from Rome, including Pope Victor II; Frederick of Lorraine, who later became Pope Stephen IX; Hildebrand, who was elected Pope Gregory VII in 1073; and Peter Damiani. In 1057 he was called back to Salerno by Prince Gisolf II to head the monastery of San Benedetto, and soon after he was named archbishop by the same prince. He was ordained a priest and then consecrated as archbishop in Rome by Pope Stephen IX in March of 1058.

A quick glance at Alfanus' career would lead one to believe that he supported papal reform avidly and fully. Alfanus was not only a friend to many reform popes and their associates in Rome, but he also attended a number of papal councils between 1059 and 1073. He was present at the Lateran Council in 1059, which issued new instructions for papal elections and discussed other issues deemed important to the reformers, such as the utility of the common life for all clerics. In the same year, Alfanus attended papal councils in Melfi and Benevento, and in 1073 he was present at the Lateran Council where Gregory VII was elected pope.[94] During the Berengar controversy, Alfanus supported papal claims, even though he found Berengar's theory on the eucharist to be perfectly orthodox. According to a letter written by a friend or pupil of Berengar to Alfanus shortly after the 1059 Lateran council, Alfanus even went so far as to say that anyone who read and understood Augustine would have no choice but to side with Berengar, but that nonetheless he decided to go along with the majority.[95]

---

[92] Only two sources speak of Alfanus before his appointment as archbishop, the *Chronica Monasterii Casinensis* and Peter the Deacon's *De viris illustribus*, both written at Montecassino. *Chron. Cas.*, 367–69, bk. 3, chaps. 7–8. Peter the Deacon, *De viris illustribus Casinensibus opusculus* in Migne, *PL*, 173: 1030, chap. 19. The information in this paragraph is taken from these sources. For a good summary of Alfanus' early life, see Acocella, "La figura e l'opera di Alfano I," 1–20.

[93] Although Alfanus himself does not appear to have taken part in the palace coup, he fled out of fear that all family members would be held responsible for the event. *Chron. Cas.*, 368, bk. 3, chap. 7; Loud, *The Age of Robert Guiscard*, 122.

[94] Acocella, "La figura e l'opera di Alfano I," 40–44; Paesano, 1: 117–21; 1: 128–29.

[95] Cowdrey, *The Age of Abbot Desiderius*, 91. For an edition of the letter, see R. W. Southern, "Lanfranc of Bec and Berengar of Tours," in *Studies in Medieval History*

Alfanus also received privileges from Pope Stephen IX (1058) and Pope Alexander II (1067), both summarized above, and through these privileges the popes advanced their program to standardize clerical behavior, abolish simony, and place all ecclesiastical lands and houses in the hands of the clergy.[96] The privileges also alluded to another objective of papal reform, namely, the construction of an ecclesiastical hierarchy throughout Christendom controlled and administered by the pope and separate from lay government. To this end, both Stephen and Alexander encouraged Alfanus to centralize church organization and increase the number of bishoprics in his archdiocese.

Other documents suggest even more directly that Alfanus enthusiastically embraced the papal reform program, as outlined above. For example, the investiture charter issued by Alfanus in 1066 to the newly elected bishop, Risus, in the newly established diocese of Sarno, condemned simony, upheld the need to standardize clerical behavior and religious practices, and insisted that all churches, clerics, and ecclesiastical revenues belonged to the bishop alone.[97] A poem written by Alfanus for Hildebrand, while he was still archdeacon, glorified Rome as the center of the world and advocated a renewal of the Roman polity under the leadership of St. Peter and reformers such as Gregory.[98] The construction of the new cathedral church of Salerno, dedicated to the apostle Saint Matthew and consecrated by Gregory VII shortly before his death, also demonstrates the strong ties between the new archbishopric of Salerno and the reform papacy in Rome.

Nonetheless, Alfanus did not promote all aspects of the Roman reform program, nor did other reformers in the area such as the abbots of Cava. For one, they never pushed for an end to clerical marriage, which had been an accepted practice in the region since Christianity was first introduced. Charters found at Cava show that priests and clerics continued to marry up through the twelfth century and beyond in the same way they always had.[99] Even in his investiture of Risus as bishop of Sarno, Alfanus I did not forbid clerical marriage but merely prohibited the new bishop from ordaining priests who engaged in bigamy or adultery.[100] In fact, throughout southern

---

Presented to Frederick Maurice Powicke, ed. R. W. Hunt, W. A. Pantin, and R. W. Southern (Oxford: Clarendon Press, 1948), 48.

[96] Pflugk-Harttung, 2: 82–84, no. 116; Ughelli, 7: 382–83.

[97] Ughelli, 7: 571–72.

[98] Alfanus, *Carmi*, 155–57, no. 22.

[99] See, for example, Cava XIV, 88; Cava XIV, 110; Cava XVI, 41; Cava XVI, 107; Cava XVIII, 76; Cava XVIII, 101; Cava XIX, 3; Cava XX, 30; Cava XXVII, 34; Cava XXVII, 106; Cava XXVII, 107; Cava XXVII, 108; Cava XXVIII, 59; Cava XXVIII, 104; Cava XXVIII, 119; Cava XXIX, 87.

[100] Ughelli, 7: 571–72.

Italy at this time, no concerted effort was ever launched to end the practice of clerical marriage, as was the case in France and even regions in northern and central Italy. Clerical marriage was seen as a valid practice by prelates, as well as the general population, and evidence from the thirteenth century shows that churchmen here continued to resist the push on the part of the papacy to impose celibacy on the clergy.[101]

Reformers in Salerno did not oppose the large variety of religious practices found in the region, and a significant amount of diversity can be found with regards to the liturgy, the language of worship, and the training of clerics in the Norman era and well beyond.[102] Greek foundations, such as the church of San Nicola of Gallocanta, continued to use Greek texts and liturgies and to conduct ceremonies in the Greek language, even after becoming Cava dependencies.[103] In Lombard Lucania, Greek foundations also remained, and evidence for Greek foundations in southern regions exists up through the sixteenth century.[104] Moreover, Greek and Latin clerics continued to serve in the same churches, mixing Greek and Latin liturgy.[105] The only concern vis-à-vis Greek foundations related to integrating them into the new ecclesiastical hierarchies.[106] Even as late as the thirteenth century, the main concern related to Greek prelates was that they accept consecration from and give an oath of allegiance to the pope, not that they perform their offices in Latin according to Roman canon law.[107] Thus, there was no strong push toward religious homogeneity in the province of Salerno, and

---

[101] Loud, *Church and Society*, 235–38.

[102] Kamp, "The Bishops of Southern Italy," 186.

[103] Vitolo, "La Latinizzazione," 84–86. In 1110, the abbot of Cava even invested a Greek priest Bartholomeus to administer the abbey's portion of the church. Cava XIX, 5 (Cherubini, 313–15, no. 127).

[104] In 1572, the bishop of Policastro ordered Greek priests and Greek churches to change to the Latin rite, while in the same era the bishop of Capaccio publicly burned the Greek books and manuscripts belonging to the church of San Nicola of Cuccaro. Cappelli, *Il monachesimo basiliano*, 14; Laudisio, *Sinossi*, 24 and 79–80; Giuseppe Antonini, *La Lucania* (Naples: G. Bisogni, 1798), 339–40.

[105] A letter from Pope Innocent III dated 1210 and addressed to the archbishop of Conza, for example, complained of how Greek and Latin bishops in places such as Auletta, in the Tanagro River Valley, performed services side-by-side. Hubert Houben, "L'espansione del monachesimo latino in Lucania dopo l'avvento dei Normani," in *Mezzogiorno Normanno-Svevo*, 40.

[106] von Falkenhausen, "I monasteri greci," 207–8; Vitolo, "La Latinizzazione," 437.

[107] Peter Herde, "The Papacy and the Greek Church in Southern Italy between the Eleventh and the Thirteenth Century," trans. Carine van Rhijn, Inge Lyse Hansen, G. A. Loud, and A. Metcalfe, in *The Society of Norman Italy*, 240–43.

the liturgical traditions and the education of local prelates continued to diverge from Roman models.

In addition, Alfanus did not object to the practice of lay-owned religious houses and lay-appointed prelates. Before his elevation to archbishop, Alfanus served as custodian (*custos*) of San Benedetto, a private monastery controlled by the Lombard princes. He himself was appointed archbishop by a layman, Prince Gisolf II, as was his successor Alfanus II, appointed by Duke Roger Borsa.[108] During Alfanus' episcopate, members of the princely family continued to administer the church they owned in Salerno, Santa Maria de Domno, and Alfanus even gave some churches to Prince Gisolf in 1062, in exchange for a monastery.[109] In 1071 Alfanus issued an emancipation charter to a newly constructed church built in the city of Salerno itself, and he granted the founder and owner, the viscount Vivus, the right to appoint priests, clerics, and monks, as well as the authority to sell or alienate church property without seeking permission from the archbishop.[110] Clearly Alfanus did not oppose the old tradition of laypeople founding and administering religious houses, and he did not uphold the call by Gregory VII and others to end lay investiture.[111]

Alfanus also welcomed the princes' participation in the religious life and ecclesiastical administration of his diocese, never once hinting that such activity should be interpreted as interference or usurpation.[112] Not only did Alfanus receive financial support from the Lombard princes and Norman dukes, but lay rulers continued to own ecclesiastical foundations, appoint clerics, and control church properties and revenues. They actively participated in episcopal elections and invested important ecclesiastical officials. In the Principality of Salerno, religious life and organization continued to be a joint endeavor directed and controlled by both lay and ecclesiastical leaders. Even Alfanus' poem to Gregory VII can be interpreted as espousing the traditional view of the pope and the Roman church as the spiritual head of

[108] Cowdrey, *The Age of Abbot Desiderius*, 193; Loud, *The Age of Robert Guiscard*, 265.

[109] Cava XXIII, 20.

[110] CDC 9: 318–22, no. 103.

[111] This is true for other regions of southern Italy as well. Martin, *La Pouille*, 617–18; Feller, *Les Abruzzes*, 806.

[112] Only in one instance at the end of the eleventh did an archbishop question a lay ruler's authority in the ecclesiastical realm, when Archbishop Alfanus II successfully challenged Duke Roger's right to dismiss a cleric serving in the church of Santa Maria de Domno. However, this does not mean that the archbishop objected to all lay participation, but rather that he did so only in this one particular case. Cava C, 40; IP, 8: 353–54, nos. 31–32; Pflugk-Harttung, 2: 149–50, no. 184.

Christianity, but not necessarily the administrator of a pan-European ecclesiastical hierarchy.

None of this means that Alfanus disagreed with the overall goals of the papal reformers. The dissimilarities between the reform program promulgated by Alfanus in Salerno and that promoted by reformers in Rome should not be seen as evidence of conflict or discord. Rather, it suggests that church reform in the eleventh century was a complex process that involved individuals who not only held different views on how to achieve the common goal of creating a more Christian society, but also had to adapt reform ideas to local conditions.[113] Religious reform was never a homogenous process, even in Rome itself. Both the precise parameters of the new society, as well as the most effective way to implement change were understood in various ways. For the Principality of Salerno some aspects of reform would have been well-nigh impossible to implement. For example, the lack of a well-organized ecclesiastical hierarchy in the region made imperative the continued participation of the laity in church matters. In former Carolingian regions, in contrast, it was much easier to insist on creating a church organization staffed completely with clerics, for reformers there had a strong episcopal organization to build upon. Similarly, any attempt at standardizing practices and liturgy would have proven difficult in Salerno. Unlike Carolingian regions, no attempt was ever made to promote homogenous religious practices or a unified liturgy in southern Italy before the eleventh century. What is more, for a prelate born and educated in a region as diverse as southern Italy, religious homogeneity would not necessarily seem an important goal. As Saint Nilos announced during his visit to Montecassino in the late tenth century, a mere generation before Alfanus' birth, diverse religious practices could and should be tolerated, as long as they were done with the aim of glorifying and exalting God.[114]

Also the disputes between the archbishop of Salerno and the abbey of Cava should not be seen as proof for a wholly antagonistic relationship. Alfanus himself began his career as a monk, first in the abbey of Santa Sofia and then at Montecassino. In fact, most reform bishops and archbishops in southern Italy in the eleventh century received their education and initiation into religious life in Benedictine abbeys.[115] Moreover, both Alfanus I and Alfanus II remained curiously silent while Cava expanded its power over a vast number of religious houses in the eleventh and early twelfth century,

---

[113] A similar point is made by Cowdrey in his study of eleventh-century Cluny. Cowdrey, *The Cluniacs*, 141–56.

[114] *De S. Nilos Abbate*, 302, chap. 73.

[115] Kamp, "The Bishops of Southern Italy," 191–93.

and most likely this silence represents approval of the monks' undertaking.[116] On account of the size of Salerno's archdiocese, one of the largest in the region, the cathedral church simply did not have the resources to build, restore, and administer the growing number of churches in the archdiocese. The abbey of Cava was thus a welcome source of aid and support in the quest to reform and renew religious life.[117] In many ways the disputes between the two parties for the most part represented a means to define one another's rights and jurisdiction, and neither side seemed interested in completely subjecting the other to its authority. The two parties used dispute resolution as a means of sharing power and responsibilities in a changing political and religious environment.[118]

In the end, reform brought a number of fundamental changes to the cathedral church of Salerno in the eleventh century. For one thing, the archbishops of Salerno developed for the first time ever an ecclesiastical hierarchy that extended the cathedral church's power outside the city of Salerno. They also became more integrated into a larger Latin Christian world on account of intensified contact with ideas and reformers from Rome and further north. Furthermore, they took on a new political role as the cathedral church became one of a number of ecclesiastical powers called upon by the new Norman rulers to help administer their realms. Even if the cathedral church of Salerno did not become the most powerful ecclesiastical institution in the region, nonetheless the archbishops dramatically increased their religious, political, and economic power between 1050 and 1150.

Throughout southern Italy in the eleventh and twelfth centuries, bishops and archbishops expanded their power and wealth and set in place networks of parish churches—with the aid of both the popes and the Normans. Yet in the end, large Benedictine abbeys rather than cathedral churches became the most influential elements in religious organization in most areas of southern Italy. Not only did princes, dukes, and noble families bestow their most generous donations on abbeys, but the monastic communities themselves became the preeminent training grounds for other clerics in the region and often exercised more control over the pastoral life of their territo-

---

[116] Bishops in other areas of southern Italy also supported Cava, either themselves donating to the abbey or encouraging others to do so. See, for example, CDC 7: 34–35, no. 1078; CDC 7: 211–12, no. 1186; Cava B, 35; Cava D, 5; E, 7; Cava E, 15.

[117] Vitolo, "La badia di Cava," 11–12; G. A. Loud, "The Abbey of Cava, Its Property and Benefactors in the Norman Era," *Anglo-Norman Studies* 10 (1986): 152.

[118] A similar point is made by Rosenwein, who argues that a dispute between Fulrad abbot of St. Denis and Angilran bishop of Metz in the eighth century was a means of sharing power among two men with similar purposes. Rosenwein, chap. 6 in *Negotiating Space*.

ries on account of their extensive network of dependent churches. They also were granted exemption by the papacy, which meant that the abbeys effectively operated outside the control of bishops and archbishops. Later on, the office of abbot-bishop would spread throughout the region. In the Principality of Salerno, the abbey of Cava would assume this role, not only establishing itself as the premier religious institution in the region but extending its power to other parts of southern Italy as well.

CHAPTER 5

The Construction of a Monastic Lordship

The Abbey of the Holy Trinity of Cava

The abbey of Cava, founded in c. 1020, became one of the most powerful
and important abbeys in southern Italy under Norman rule. It comprised a
large religious and economic empire based in the province of Salerno and
extending throughout southern Italy and Sicily.[1] The abbey's rise to power
took place in the second half of the eleventh century when the monks
gained control over numerous lands and churches, which they organized
into a centrally administered religious network. Hence the abbey's growth
and consolidation of power occurred in tandem with the Norman conquest
of southern Italy and the early stages of papal reform. By 1100, the abbey of
Cava possessed over fifty dependent houses and was one of the largest landholders in the Principality of Salerno. By 1150, the abbey had over one hundred dependent houses in southern Italy, two territorial lordships in Metiliano and Cilento, and eight sea ports in northern and southern parts of the
province. (See map 5.)

---

[1] Only a few studies have looked into the early history of Cava in any depth: Paul
Guillaume, *Essai historique sur l'abbaye de Cava d'après les documents inédits* (Cava dei
Tirreni: Abbaye des Pères Bénédictins, 1877), Carmine Carlone, *Le origini e la costituzione patrimoniale della Badia di Cava (1025–1124)* (Tesi di laurea: University of
Salerno, 1971–72), and Taviani-Carozzi, *La Principauté*, 1036–86. Also see see Simeone Leone, "La Data di Fondazione della Badia di Cava," *Benedictina* 22 (1975): 335–
46; G. A. Loud, "The Abbey of Cava"; Giovanni Vitolo, "Cava e Cluny," in *L'Italia
nel quadro dell'espansione europea del monachesimo cluniacense: Atti del Convegno internazionale di storia medievale, Pescia, 26–28 November 1981*, ed. Cinzio Violante, 199–
220 (Cesena: Centro storico benedettino italiano, 1985); Leone Mattei-Cerasoli, "Il
ministero parrochiale nei monasteri cavensi," *Benedictina* 3 (1948): 27–34.

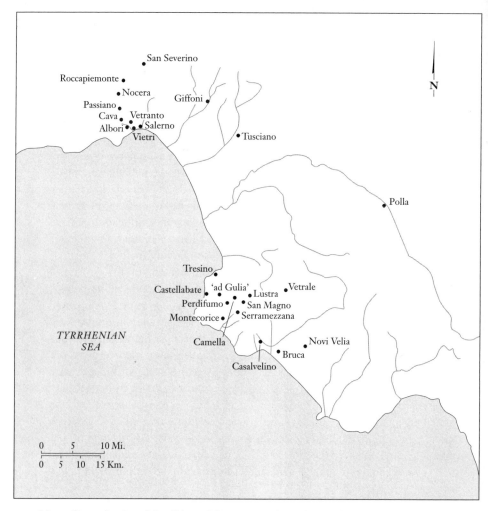

Map 5. Dependencies of the Abbey of Cava, c. 1100 (according to the Bulls of Urban II and Paschal II)

The abbey of Cava was the first large Benedictine monastery to appear in the principality, and it was a preeminent local force for religious reform, with ties to the monastery of Cluny and the reform papacy in Rome. The monks received a donation from Gregory VII, as well as privileges from Urban II and Paschal II confirming their numerous properties and dependent houses.[2] In addition, the abbey of Cluny, where both the founder

---

[2] C, 21 (Guillaume, xx–xxii); D, 26 (Pflugk-Harttung, 2: 169–71, no. 206; Guillaume, xxiii–xxv).

Alferius and the third abbot Peter spent time, exerted a powerful influence, particularly over Peter, who introduced a number of reforms that clearly show Cluny's imprint. He instituted a strictly controlled common life, based on the Benedictine rule. He built up a network of dependent houses and increased the size of the monastic community. He augmented the abbey's landholdings and began to exert both economic and political power over the population living on monastic lands. Finally, he received a papal privilege exempting the abbey from archiepiscopal authority.[3] Thus, by the time of Peter's death, Cava was a powerful and autonomous religious order that resembled Cluny in many ways.

The abbey of Cava also benefited from the Normans' policy of relying on large ecclesiastical foundations to help administer their kingdom. Norman leaders in both southern Italy and Sicily promoted the practice of placing dispersed religious houses under the authority of one large foundation in order to centralize ecclesiastical administration. As a result, abbeys such as Cava, Montecassino, and Venosa received generous donations and became important political forces for the new Norman rulers. The abbey of Cava's rise to power, in fact, was not only due to its formation of a centrally controlled network of dependencies, but was also linked to the development of territorial rights and the construction of two lordships in Metiliano and Cilento. Thus, the abbey of Cava participated in the new political structures that emerged in the principality over the course of the eleventh century, in which a few powerful families and ecclesiastical foundations began to exercise political and economic control over specific territories, replacing kinship groups and consortia as the primary force behind political, social, and religious organization.

In many ways, the ecclesiastical network built up by the monastic community of Cava paralleled the new archdiocese created by the archbishops. The abbots and monks set up a centralized administration to oversee dependencies and expanded their economic power through both agriculture and commerce. In addition, the two lordships they constructed in Metiliano and Cilento were administered in a manner similar to the one developed by the cathedral church in Olevano sul Tusciano. However, unlike the archbishops, who received privileges which they proved unable to put into effect, the abbots of Cava asserted their power first and then sought legitimization afterward through papal and ducal privileges and lay donations. Since the monks had no ancient privileges to fall back on, as the archbishops did, they had to create their rights *de novo*.

---

[3] IP, 8: 324, no. 19; Pflugk-Harttung, 2: 169–71, no. 206; Taviani-Carozzi, *La Principauté*, 1061–64.

Early History

The abbey of Cava was founded c. 1020 by Alferius, a nobleman from Salerno who served in Guaimarius IV's court before becoming a monk.[4] He was one of the prince's most trusted advisors and served as ambassador for Guaimarius in both Germany and Gaul. After receiving his religious calling and abandoning lay life, he went first to the Benedictine monastery of San Michele della Chiusa in Corzie in northern Italy, near the border of France. While there, he met Odilo of Cluny and decided to transfer to the monastery at Cluny, where he remained for some years. Prince Guaimarius, however, called Alferius back to Salerno in order to head the monasteries in his principality. The pious monk accepted the task, but soon grew weary of it, desiring instead to retreat from the world. He settled on top of Mt. Fenestra above modern-day Cava dei Tirreni to build a monastic house on the spot where a monk from Montecassino had formerly lived in seclusion from c. 988–1009.[5] Alferius' fame as a holy and ascetic monk quickly drew disciples to his side.

Princes Guaimarius III and IV issued a privilege to Alferius and his abbey in 1025. According to the document, the princes conceded to Alferius the church and crypt which the abbot had built at his own expense, along with lands nearby. They gave Alferius and his successors permission to amass a congregation of monks, as many as they wished, and granted the religious community the right to choose their new abbots. They also gave the abbey

---

[4] Information on the early history of the abbey of Cava comes almost exclusively from two sources: charters preserved in the Cava archives and the *Vitae Quatuor Priorum Abbatum Cavensium* (*VQPA*), a hagiographical text on the first four abbots of Cava written at the abbey of Venosa a century after Cava's foundation, most likely by Abbot Peter II of Venosa, a monk from Cava who was sent to Venosa in c. 1140 at the request of both Pope Innocent II and Abbot Simon of Cava in order to reform the abbey based on Cava customs. On the authorship of the *VQPA*, see Hubert Houben, "L'autore delle 'Vitae quatuor priorum abbatum Cavensium'," *Studi medievali* 26 (1985): 871–79. In addition to charters and the *VQPA*, there is also the *Annales Cavenses*; however, this source provides only sparse information which rarely goes beyond terse sentences describing political events. MGH, *Scriptores*, 3: 185–97 and CDC 5: Appendix, 1–92. The *Chronicon Cavense*, also edited in the MGH, is actually an eighteenth-century forgery written by F. M. Pratilli. See Nicola Cilento, "Il falsario della storia dei Longobardi meridionali: Francesco Maria Pratilli," in *Italia meridionale longobarda* (Milan/Naples: R. Riccardi, 1971), 24–39. The information on Alferius' life in this paragraph comes from the *VQPA*, 5–7.

[5] For information on the monks who formerly inhabited the site, see *Chron. Cas.*, 221–23, bk. 2, chaps. 30–31. Also see Guillaume, *Essai historique*, 13–14.

permission to collect wood from the mountains throughout the region, as well as power over the waterways on their lands, where the monks could build mills if they wished. In addition, all freemen living on the abbey's property would pertain to the abbey alone and owe no dues or services to either the princes or their representatives. Finally, they granted the monks all the property and possessions of men on monastic lands who died without heirs.[6]

The 1025 privilege granted by Princes Guaimarius III and IV to the abbey of Cava differed from those issued in the ninth and tenth centuries to the princely foundations of San Massimo and Santa Maria de Domno. For one, the abbots and monks had greater autonomy over their community, with the right to elect their own abbots and decide how many monks could enter. In addition, the abbey explicitly received power over the income and inhabitants of their lands, a privilege which the foundation charters for San Massimo and Santa Maria did not contain. Finally the princes granted the abbey jurisdiction over all the properties within its territory, which included the rivers, mills, and forests. The princes, in essence, were giving the abbey the basis for a territorial lordship in and around Metiliano, which would grow in size and wealth over the course of the eleventh and twelfth centuries.[7]

According to the author of the *vita* of Alferius, the abbot had a vision at the end of his life, in which God prophesied that the number of monks at Cava would grow to an innumerable multitude. Before this vision, Alferius had insisted that the monastery include just twelve monks and an abbot, since the monastery barely had the means to provide for thirteen men, but afterward he gave the monks permission to enlarge the monastery, since God obviously meant to provide the means to support a larger monastic community.[8] Well before his death, however, Alferius had begun to increase the abbey's patrimony, receiving donations and making purchases of lands and churches. In 1035, Prince Guaimarius IV donated the church of Sant'Arcangelo in Tusciano.[9] In 1037, Count Alfanus, son of Count Alfanus, donated lands in Tabellaria, Angri, and Nocera, while in 1045 Cava purchased lands in Nocera for 135 gold *solidi*, a high price to pay in that period. Alferius also received control over a church in Bari in 1047, making the abbey of Cava one of the first religious foundations in the region to receive lands and churches outside the principality.[10]

  [6] CDC 5: 93–95, no. 764.

  [7] In 1059, Prince Gisolf II reiterated the privilege of his father and grandfather. CDC 8: 95–97, no. 1284.

  [8] *VQPA*, 8.

  [9] CDC 6: 37–38, no. 895.

  [10] CDC 7: 34–35, no. 1078.

Under Alferius' successor Leo (1050–1079), the monastery's activity increased considerably. During his abbacy the monastery received twenty donations and made ten purchases of lands in Vietri, Cava, Iovi, Roccapiemonte, Nocera, Angri, and Cilento.[11] In addition, the abbey received churches in both Calabria and Bari.[12] Particularly significant was the abbey's expansion into the region of Cilento: Prince Gisolf II donated the churches of Santa Maria de Gulia, Sant'Angelo in Puczillu (near Camella), San Croce in Duliarola (near Castellabate), San Martino, and San Nicola in Serramezzana in 1072, while around the same time, he gave permission to Pope Gregory VII to donate additional churches in Cilento, including Sant'Arcangelo in Perdifumo, Sant'Angelo in Montecorice, San Magno (later San Mango) in Torano, San Zaccaria de Lauro (near Casalvelino), San Fabiano de Casacastra (near Lustra), San Giorgio 'ad duo flumina' (near Casalvelino), San Matteo 'ad duo flumina' (near Casalvelino), San Biagio de Butrano (near Vetrale), San Giovanni in Tresino, and San Salvatore de Nuce (near Camella).[13] In addition, the owners of San Giovanni in Tresino donated and sold their church to Cava between 1071 and 1097.[14] Finally, the abbey founded at least two other churches, San Nicola della Palma in Salerno in c. 1062 and San Leone in Vetranto in c. 1063.[15] Leo himself is recorded as abbot of San Leone from 1071 until his death in 1079, and in c. 1070 the abbot retired to the church, leaving the administration of the abbey in the hands of Peter.[16]

---

[11] Donations: CDC 7: 272–73, no. 1217; CDC 8: 95–97, no. 1284; CDC 8: 136–37, no. 1306; CDC 8: 224–27, no. 1352; CDC 8: 230–32, no. 1355; CDC 9: 114–18, no. 35; CDC 9: 266–68, no. 92; CDC 9: 297–301, no. 97; CDC 9: 308–11, no. 99; CDC 9: 369–72, no. 126; CDC 9: 377–78, no. 129; CDC 9: 379–80, no. 130; CDC 9: 393–95, no. 135; CDC 10: 55–57, no. 17; CDC 10: 140–42, no. 52; CDC 10: 167–69, no. 68; CDC 10: 184–86, no. 75; CDC 10: 187–88, no. 76. Purchases: CDC 8: 137–38, no. 1307; CDC 8: 154–55, no. 1318; CDC 8: 200–201, no. 1340; CDC 8: 316–18, no. 1385; CDC 9: 384–87, no. 132; CDC 10: 149–52, no. 55; CDC 10: 154–57, no. 57; CDC 10: 169–71, no. 69; CDC 10: 174–77, no. 71; CDC 10: 177–80, no. 72.

[12] A group of monks put Sant'Andrea in Calabria under Cava's power in 1053, while the archbishop of Bari donated San Nicola to the abbey in 1053. CDC 7: 193–95, no. 1175; CDC 7: 211–12, no. 1186.

[13] CDC 9: 369–72, no. 126. CDC 9: 372–74, no. 127. On Gregory VII's donation to Cava, see Leone and Vitolo, *Codex Diplomaticus Cavensis* X, xvii–xxiv.

[14] CDC 9: 311–14, no. 100; CDC 10: 3–5, no. 1; CDC 10: 14–16, no. 4; CDC 10: 44–46, no. 13; CDC 10: 106–9, no. 34; Cava XVI, 69.

[15] For San Nicola, see CDC 8: 202–4, no. 1342 and CDC 9: 318–22, no. 103. For San Leone see CDC 8: 224–27, no. 1352, and CDC 9: 316–18, no. 102.

[16] *VQPA*, 17–18.

The Growth of Cava under Abbot Peter (1070–1123)

The real period of Cava's growth occurred under Peter, who served as abbot from 1070 until his death in 1123. Peter revolutionized Cava, both by his reordering of the religious community and his rapid expansion of the abbey's size and economic activities. The *Annales Cavenses*, not incorrectly, referred to him as "the builder and founder" of Cava.[17] During his abbacy, the abbey received over two-hundred and fifty donations and made over one hundred purchases.[18] The number of monks at Cava also grew rapidly, which led Peter to enlarge the abbey, building cloisters, cells, and a refectory for the expanding monastic community, as well as a larger church personally dedicated by Urban II in 1089.[19] Equally as important, Peter established a new lifestyle for the monks at Cava and introduced a new type of monastic order to the region, both based on Cluniac models.

Peter's life, as depicted by the Venosa author, paralleled closely that of Alferius, his uncle.[20] He spent his early years in seclusion, in a cell he built on Mt. Elie, near Amalfi. After he met a monk from Cluny, he decided to travel there, anxious to emulate the religious lifestyle of the Cluniac community. He remained at Cluny for five years, after which he decided to go back home. On his return to southern Italy, he was elected bishop of Policastro.[21] Soon after, in 1070, he became abbot of Cava, when Leo decided to retire to the church of San Leone in Vetranto and named Peter his successor.[22] Thus Peter had a wide variety of religious experiences, which encompassed time as an anchorite, a cenobite, a bishop, and an abbot.

Even more so than Alferius, Peter was heavily influenced by his experience at Cluny, in particular, the abbey's strict adherence to a communal life and written rule. Before the second half of the eleventh century, few monks

[17] *Annales Cavenses*, MGH, *Scriptores*, 3: 191 and CDC 5: Appendix, 41.

[18] On the importance of purchases for the growth of Cava's empire, see G. A. Loud, "The Monastic Economy," 163–70 and "Coinage, Wealth, and Plunder in the Age of Robert Guiscard," *English Historical Review* 14 (September 1999): 815–43.

[19] *VQPA*, 18. Giulio Pane, "La 'crypta cava' e la fabbrica antica," in *La Badia di Cava*, ed. Giuseppe Fienzo and Franco Strazzullo (Cava dei Tirreni: Di Mauro, 1981), 119–52.

[20] *VQPA*, 16–18.

[21] For a summary of the various theories about Peter's early life, including his tenure as bishop of Policastro, see Galante, "La documentazione vescovile," 236–37.

[22] He remained co-abbot with Leo until Leo's death in 1079, and in documents dated 1070–1079, Peter and Leo are alternately referred to as abbot of Cava.

in the Principality of Salerno led a common life or followed a rule.[23] Although monastic rules were not unknown in southern Italy, anchoritic foundations were the predominant form of religious life up through the Norman period. Even Alferius himself, although he spent time in two Benedictine monasteries, built what the author of his *vita* described as a "mansio monachorum," a small mountain-top retreat where Alferius and his few followers lived in isolation in separate caves.[24] The *vita* mentions nothing of a communal life or a rule followed, and in the archives of Cava itself no manuscript of a rule remains from the early period. Moreover, the spot where Alferius built his monastery had a long tradition of anchoritic settlements, and archaeological surveys of the abbey at Cava show that before Peter's abbacy the monastery included only a few walls and some stairs built into the rocks, again suggesting a hermitage rather than a monastery.[25]

Peter, however, transformed the monastic community at Cava by introducing a new type of lifestyle based on his experience at Cluny. This novelty, though, did not meet with approval at first. The author of Peter's *vita* recounts how when Peter attempted to impose the Cluniac rule, after he took over as abbot in c. 1070, the monks resisted his efforts because they disliked the strictness and severity of the Cluniac monastic lifestyle.[26] They even went so far as to complain to the former abbot Leo about Peter's innovation, and as a result, Peter left Cava, not wanting to create problems. He traveled to Cilento, to the monastery of Sant'Arcangelo, where he taught the rule to the monks there.[27] After a while, however, Leo and the monks at Cava repented, calling Peter back to Cava and agreeing to follow the Cluniac rule.[28]

---

[23] Of the numerous churches in the region of Salerno in the early medieval period, evidence of monks under the authority of an abbot can be found for only two foundations. A rule is mentioned in 979 when Aloara is said to live under the rule ("sub regula") of Nicodemus abbot of the monastery of San Lorenzo, and again in 992 for a monk John who lived according to a monastic rule ("statuta regula monachilem vitam") in the monastery of SS Maria and Benedetto. CDC 2: 126–27, no. 309; CDC 2: 331–32, no. 450. After that, the next mention of a monastic rule comes in 1063, when a "regulam monachum" is found in the inventory of the church of SS Michele Arcangelo and Martino in Passiano. CDC 8: 208–12, no. 1345.

[24] *VQPA*, 6.

[25] Guillaume, *Essai Historique*, 14. *VQPA*, 19, note 2. Pane, "La 'crypta cava'," 121–24.

[26] *VQPA*, 18.

[27] Peter is, in fact, documented as abbot of Sant'Arcangelo from August 1067 until June 1072. CDC 9: 96–98, no. 28; CDC 9: 142–45, no. 46; CDC 9: 145–47, no. 47; CDC 9: 257–59, no. 88; CDC 9: 263–65, no. 90; CDC 9: 337–39, no. 109; CDC 9: 354–56, no. 119, with date corrected by Galante, *La Datazione*, 151–55, no. 127; CDC 9: 375–76, no. 128.

[28] *VQPA*, 18.

Although the exact meaning of "Cluniac rule" is unclear, and most likely the abbey of Cava did not adopt Cluniac customs whole cloth, nonetheless Cava became the first large Benedictine abbey in the principality whose monastic community led a strictly controlled common life and engaged in a daily round of offices and prayers, often said in commemoration for donors.[29] At around the same time, another monastic community belonging to the abbey of Cava, San Nicola della Palma in Salerno, also agreed to live "according the rule of St. Benedict" ("secundum beati patris regulam Benedicti").[30] This is the first mention of the Benedictine rule for a religious house in the Principality of Salerno. After this, however, Benedictine-style monasticism spread in the region, suggesting that the abbots of Cava, and, in particular, Abbot Peter, were an important force behind the proliferation of Benedictine abbeys in the province of Salerno.

The introduction of a new monastic lifestyle at Cava was not the only influence exerted by the French abbey. The organization of the Cluniac order also served as a model for Peter, and many parallels can be seen in how the two abbeys were organized and governed.[31] Like Cluny, Cava received an exemption from archiepiscopal authority from the papacy, which allowed the monastery to establish a religious empire independent of episcopal power. In the late fourteenth century, the popes even made the abbey's vast properties and numerous dependent ecclesiastical foundations into an independent diocese.[32] Like Cluny, the abbey of Cava created a network of dependent houses, over which the monks had direct authority. They personally traveled to dependent foundations and sent monks from the abbey

---

[29] Vitolo, "Cava e Cluny," 19–28; Hubert Houben, "Il monachesimo cluniacense e i monasteri normanni dell'Italia meridionale," in *Mezzogiorno Normanno–Svevo*, 7–8. Like the abbey of Farfa, the monastic community at Cava referred to Cluniac customs, but did not necessarily follow them to the letter. Many of the customs at Cava that historians have pinpointed as "Cluniac" are found either in the Benedictine rule or in monasteries which did not follow a Cluniac model. Vitolo, "Cava e Cluny," 23–26; Iogna-Prat, *Order and Exclusion*, 63–64.

[30] CDC 9: 318–22, no. 103. The monastery was founded c. 1062 by Abbot Leo and Viscount Vivus. The mention of the Benedictine rule occurs in the *charta libertatis* issued to the foundation in 1071. For a detailed description of the life and career of Viscount Vivus, see Taviani-Carozzi, *La Principauté*, 784–800.

[31] A point also made by Vitolo, "Cava e Cluny," 29–31, and Houben, "Il monachesimo cluniancense," 23–46. On Cluny see Iogna-Prat, *Order and Exclusion*; Noreen Hunt, *Cluny under Saint Hugh, 1049–1109* (London: Edward Arnold, 1967); Cowdrey, *The Cluniacs and the Gregorian Reform*, and Barbara H. Rosenwein, *Rhinoceros Bound: Cluny in the Tenth Century* (Philadelphia: University of Pennsylvania Press, 1982).

[32] IP, 8: 311, no. 121; Ughelli, 1: 612–14.

to serve as priors. They administered patrimonies centrally, often acting without the permission of individual priors when buying, selling, or leasing their properties. Even dependencies far off in Apulia, Calabria, or Sicily received personal attention from the abbots and monks, who directly participated in their activities.[33] Nonetheless, like Cluny, Cava had a personal rather than a juridical link to its dependencies, meaning that relationships between the mother house and dependent foundations were varied, based on the terms under which the dependency was founded or absorbed by Cava.[34] Finally, the abbey of Cava exercised seigneurial rights on its property, based on a code of customs, similar to the Cluniac monks.[35] Like Cluny, the abbey of Cava established an ecclesiastical lordship in the region, which was a truly novel development: never before had an ecclesiastical foundation created such a large religious order exercising such tight control over a network of dependent houses and the rural population living on its lands.

The abbey of Cava took control of dependencies gradually and at different rates. The date of a donation charter does not always correspond to when the abbey actually began to assert authority; this could take place decades after a donation charter or, in some cases, it could even occur beforehand. The first sign that Cava exercised control over a foundation occurred when abbots and monks began traveling to the house to oversee activities and to give permission to the rectors to issue charters. At the same time, documents generally started to specify that the church or monastery pertained to Cava. In addition, the rector of a dependent house was no longer called "abbot," but rather "prior," "prepositus," or "custos" in recognition of his dependency on Cava. Next, the abbots began to send monks from Cava to serve as priors. Finally, the abbots and monks from Cava personally carried out transactions for dependent houses, without the participation of the priors. By this time, the wealth of the dependency was no

---

[33] San Giovanni in Fabrica, San Giacomo in Lucera, Sant'Egidio in Pantanao, San Pietro in Olivola, and Santa Maria Magdalena in Bari all had priors chosen by the Cava community administering their houses by the mid-twelfth century. Giovanni Vitolo, *Insedimenti cavensi in Puglia* (Lecce: Congedo, 1984), 43–45, 52–55, 73–76, 83, 92–93. Moreover, Abbot Simon was personally present in 1126 and 1131 for two transactions involving San Pietro in Olivola. Loud, "The Monastic Economy," 163.

[34] For more on Cluny's concept of Order and its relationship to dependent houses, see Hunt, *Cluny under Saint Hugh*, 154–84 and Iogna-Prat, *Order and Exclusion*, 54–64.

[35] On Cluny as an ecclesiastical lordship, see Iogna-Prat, *Order and Exclusion*, 27–28.

longer independent, but pertained directly to the abbey of Cava, which administered both the foundation and its patrimony centrally.

The amount of time that elapsed between the first and the last step differed greatly from one ecclesiastical foundation to another, as did the amount of autonomy retained by dependencies. For some foundations, the abbey took control immediately, starting to issue charters and send priors straightaway after the donation charter. Generally, however, the abbey asserted its authority gradually, over a period of two or three decades, and in some cases it took more than fifty years. In a few cases the takeover of a religious house was contested by one or more of the owners, which could then prolong the absorption process for some time. Some houses lost all autonomy, with both their wealth and religious administration directly overseen by the abbey's community. Other ones, in particular, those located far away from Cava, retained more autonomy, continuing to have control over a distinct patrimony and to exercise certain functions without the direct participation of the abbots or monks. Thus, although the abbey administered all its dependencies centrally, it did not administer them homogeneously.

Describing with precision the years of Cava's rapid expansion under Abbot Peter is difficult, despite the numerous charters from the period. In the early years of Cava's growth, the status of dependencies and properties was often ambiguous, and many contradictions appear in the documents, particularly concerning dependent houses. To a large extent the confusion results from the many forgeries found in the archives at Cava, most of which are dated to the eleventh and early twelfth century. Not only do scholars believe more than one-fourth of the privileges issued by the Lombard princes and Norman dukes to be later redactions, but they also consider suspect many other of the abbey's most important donation charters.[36]

The motives behind these forgeries are not homogeneous, and they were written at various times for different reasons. Generally, the abbey created false privileges when it became involved in a dispute and needed to defend its rights over a particular church or certain lands with written evidence. For example, the abbey generated at least two forgeries for the church of SS Maria

---

[36] Many scholars have identified forgeries at Cava, but the two most active scholars in this field are Carmine Carlone and Maria Galante. See, in particular, Carmine Carlone, *Falsificazioni e falsari cavensi e verginiani del secolo XIII* (Altavilla Silentina: Edizioni Studi Storici Meridionali, 1984) and Maria Galante, "Un esempio di diplomatica signorile: i documenti dei Sanseverino," in *Civiltà del Mezzogiorno d'Italia: Libro, Scrittura, Documento in età normanno-sveva: Atti del Convegno dell'Associazione Italiana dei Paleografi e Diplomatisti, Naples-Badia di Cava dei Tirreni, 14–18 October 1991*, ed. Filippo D'Oria, 279–331 (Salerno: Carlone Editore, 1994).

and Nicola in Mercatello during disputes it had with the bishop of Paestum in 1227 and 1362 concerning properties located near the church.[37] The abbey forged a 1043 donation from Prince Guaimarius IV to legitimize its possession of the church of San Martino.[38] Between 1134 and 1136, the abbey produced a set of documents to prove its jurisdiction over the dependent church of San Marciano in Teggiano.[39] A contest between the abbey of Cava and the monastery of Santa Maria de Vanze over the church of Sant'Andrea in Lecce led to the creation of a number of forgeries by both religious foundations.[40] Forgeries for Eboli, Auletta, and Pertosa were prepared between 1258 and 1259 to defend the abbey's rights in these areas against the count of the Principate, Galvano Lancia.[41] A false 1082 donation of the church of Santa Maria in Giuncarico most likely was crafted around 1270 when the lords of Rocchetta and Lacedonia began to fight with the abbey over their rights in the region.[42] Two donations of lands in Sisinbrio to Sant'Arcangelo in Perdifumo, dated 1093 and 1102, were probably written in the late twelfth century when disputes over property in the region arose.[43]

Carmine Carlone has shown that most of the forged diplomas attributed to Roger Borsa granted to the abbey "feudal privileges" that only became commonplace from 1150 on.[44] These privileges included the administration

---

[37] The forgeries are Cava A, 31 (CDC 6: 232–33, no. 1020) and Cava XII, 106 (CDC 9: 387–92, no. 133). Based on paleographical evidence, most scholars who have examined the documents place their origin in 1362, during the second dispute with the bishop of Paestum. Giuseppe Bergamo, *Chiese e monasteri di Eboli tra il Mille e il Mille trecento*, Tesi de laurea, University of Salerno, 1976; Galante, *La Datazione*, 126–28; Leone and Vitolo, CDC 9: 387–91.

[38] Cava A, 28 (CDC 6: 249–50, no. 1030). API XV, vol. 63, no. 22. In addition to the writing style, dating inaccuracies have also proved the document to be a forgery.

[39] Cava II, 8 (CDC 1: 172–73, no. 134); Cava II, 31 (CDC 1: 201–2, no. 157); Cava II, 45 (CDC 1: 222–23, no. 172); and Cava VIII, 80 (CDC 6: 121–22, no. 954). See Carmine Carlone, "I principi Guaimario e i monaci cavensi nel vallo di Diano," *Archivi e cultura* 10 (1976): 47–60.

[40] Cava B, 26. See Giovanni Antonucci, "Falsificazioni bantine e cavensi," *Archivio Storico per la Calabria e la Lucania* 13 (1943–44): 1–15.

[41] Carlone, *Falsificazioni*, 41.

[42] Cava B, 25. Vitolo, *Insedimenti Cavensi*, 69–70.

[43] Cava XV, 83; Cava XVII, 28. See Galante, *La Datazione*, 152–54, note 1.

[44] Cava C, 19 (Heinemann, 13–14, no. 6); Cava C, 25 (Heinemann, 14–16, no. 7); Cava C, 35 (Heinemann, 171–18, no. 8); Cava D, 33. Carlone has shown that these charters all exhibit similar physical characteristics, suggesting that they were written at the same time. He has identified another group of documents that similarly exhibit common traits, dating them, however, to a slightly earlier period. Carlone has designated the period between 1231 and 1290 as the era of "grande falsificazione." Carlone, *Falsificazioni*, 37–42.

of justice on monastic lands, the authority to free condemned prisoners, the ability to name judges and public notaries, the power to decide disputes between the monastery and their vassals, exemption from certain dues and the rights to others, and the capacity to make vassals of the abbey perform homage to the abbots. Carlone has proposed that many of these charters were written in the late thirteenth century when the monks at Cava needed to provide the Sicilian king with written proof of their rights. In 1285 Pope Honorius IV issued a bull to the king of Sicily, instructing him to respect the rights of all the ecclesiastical foundations in the kingdom. The king agreed, requiring, however, that all of the foundations prove their privileges and properties through written documentation. According to Carlone, the monks at Cava spent a busy year creating charters to verify their claims. He also believes that the forgery program led to the deposition of Abbot Rainaldus in 1300, an event that historians have been hard pressed to explain.[45]

The forgeries found at Cava do not necessarily represent a deceitful grab for power on the part of the monks in a later period. In some cases the forgeries represent later copies of authentic documents or replacements for ones that were lost or damaged.[46] In other cases the forgeries served to legitimize authority over lands or religious houses that the abbey had been exercising for years without any written documentation. During the early period of the abbey's expansion, written proof of power and privileges was not as important as it later came to be. In fact, the twelfth century represents a turning point in the history of literacy in all areas of Europe, and written proof of ownership and rights became fundamental at this time when disputes and law cases arose.[47] Although in southern Italy there was a long history of written documentation, seen in the rich archives of the abbey of Cava itself, even there not all transactions, customs, and legal agreements were written down. With the rise of new forms of royal justice and new requirements for written proof in the late twelfth and thirteenth century, powerful entities such as those at the abbey of Cava found themselves in the difficult position of having to provide written evidence for rights long exercised but never formally recorded in writing.

Yet forgeries alone do not explain the confusion and ambiguity in the archives, which, above all, reflect the long process of absorbing and organizing vast numbers and varied types of religious houses with complex owner-

---

[45] Carlone, *Falsificazioni*, 45–52.

[46] Galante, "Un esempio di diplomatica signorile," 292.

[47] See, in particular, M. T. Clanchy, *From Memory to Written Record: England, 1066–1307* (Cambridge: Harvard University Press, 1979) and Brian Stock, *The Implications of Literacy: Written Language and Models of Interpretation in the Eleventh and Twelfth Centuries* (Princeton: Princeton University Press, 1983).

ship patterns. Unlike the archbishop of Salerno, who had many ancient privileges to fall back on—privileges that gave him broad authority over the clergy and religious houses of his diocese—the abbots of Cava had to build up their power *de novo* by allying themselves with the leading laypeople in the region, including the Lombard princes, the Norman dukes, and other prominent lay families. The monks at Cava created their religious empire slowly and piecemeal, and at any given point in the late eleventh and early twelfth century, the archives depict a work in progress.[48] As in the case with lay lords, the abbey of Cava developed its relationship with dependencies gradually and by various means. Donations could encompass two or more generations, and during this time, people could forget certain information or reevaluate the situation. Moreover, as more precise ideas about the correct way to administer and supervise dependencies crystallized, later documents reflecting the new ideas do not always correspond to earlier ones. Finally, documents could provide conflicting information depending on their origins. The papacy or the Norman rulers could see the situation quite differently than the families and communities who controlled and administered religious houses.

Despite the ambiguity of charter information, it is clear that Peter formed relationships with all the important lay powers in the Principality of Salerno and surrounding areas. Not only did he receive generous donations and privileges from Lombard princes and Norman dukes, summarized above, but he also received gifts of lands and religious houses from all the powerful families who were carving out lordships in the region. The relationship between the lay powers and the abbey of Cava was generally one of mutual aid and benefit. Lay lords seeking to form an alliance with the abbey, for both spiritual and worldly reasons, gave the abbey properties or religious foundations. For example, Gaitelgrima, countess of Sarno, and her son Richard both gave numerous lands in and around Sarno.[49] Richard Seneschal, son of Count Drogo, who became lord of Mottola, was a generous donor of lands in both Campania and Apulia.[50] Similarly, Jordan, lord of Corneto; Malfredus, count of Fasanella; Rao, rector of Atena; Richard, lord of Lauro; and William, lord of Novi, all donated churches and lands to the abbey located in their lordships.[51] These donors were not in competition for power with Cava, and generally they gave nothing of great value. In some cases the gifts

---

[48] Loud has similarly stressed the piecemeal process of the creation of Cava's lordship. Loud, "The Monastic Economy," 161–62.

[49] Cava B, 17; Cava B, 24; Cava C, 27; Cava E, 31.

[50] Cava C, 22; Cava D, 21 and 22.

[51] Cava C, 10; Cava B, 38; Cava D, 25; Cava C, 11; Cava D, 47.

merely represented the redistribution of ecclesiastical property, as when Prince Jordan I of Capua donated to Cava some lands in Nocera that had formerly belonged to the princely foundation of San Massimo.[52]

Sometimes donors received money or privileges in exchange for donations. For example, a number of donors gave lands and religious foundations when they became monks in the abbey or in exchange for burial in the abbey or its dependencies and prayers after their death.[53] In some cases, the abbey of Cava gave money "causa benedictionis," making the transactions seem more like sales than donations.[54] Generally, the amounts were small, equal to less than one hundred *tarì*, but in some cases the abbey gave quite large sums of money. In 1104, for example, Mansus, son of Guido, donated lands in Salerno to Cava, which he would continue to possess during his lifetime. After his death, the abbey would receive them upon payment of two hundred *tarì*.[55] In 1113, Ursus, son of John, gave the abbey men whom Duke William had given to him in 1111, along with all the dues and services owed by them. The abbey paid him five hundred *tarì* and the donation was not made "pro anima."[56] In 1110, the abbey gave Guaimarius of Giffoni grandson of Duke Guido eighteen hundred *solidi* for a donation of lands in Lucania.[57]

Other times, the abbey offered money in exchange for confirmation of holdings. In 1098, Alferada, daughter of Count John, received eighty *solidi* in exchange for a confirmation of the abbey's possession of property donated by her mother in Tresino, Metiliano, and Passiano.[58] Jordan, son of Prince Jordan of Capua, confirmed the abbey's possession of lands in 1111 for a payment of one hundred *solidi* "causa benedictionis."[59] In 1113, Ermilina, the widow of Gloriosus, who had donated Monte Licosa to the abbey, confirmed her husband's donation in exchange for two hundred *tarì*.[60] Roger lord of Sanseverino confirmed the abbey's possession of monasteries and lands in Cilento in 1116 in exchange for six hundred *tarì* "causa benedictionis."[61] In 1126 the abbey gave Ugo Mansella, a *camerarius* of the duke, one

---

[52] Cava B, 14. Loud, "The Monastic Economy," 149.

[53] See Cava XIV, 98; Cava XIV, 100; Cava C, 16; Cava XV, 30; Cava C, 29; Cava D, 3; Cava XVI, 51; Cava XVI, 56; Cava XVI, 68; Cava XVI, 87; Cava XVIII, 48; Cava XVIII, 102; Cava XVIII, 104; Cava XX, 45.

[54] Cava XV, 47; Cava XVI, 34; Cava XVI, 87; Cava XVIII, 50; Cava XVIII, 119; Cava XIX, 13; Cava XIX, 118; Cava XX, 22; Cava F, 3; Cava XX, 80.

[55] Cava XVII, 101.

[56] Cava E, 25. Also see Cava XVIII, 63; Cava XIX, 56; Cava F, 29.

[57] Cava E, 13.

[58] Cava XVI, 85.

[59] Cava E, 21.

[60] Cava XIX, 89.

[61] Cava F, 1; Cava XX, 91.

thousand one hundred and fifty *solidi* for his recognition of the abbey's possessions in Cilento.[62] Even Duke William received fifteen hundred *solidi*
from the abbey in 1117 when he reconfirmed donations and privileges previously bestowed on the monks.[63] In these cases, the money paid bought
recognition and legitimization of what the abbey already possessed.

Some donations and confirmations represented the end to a dispute over
lands. In 1109, for example, Cava accused Gloriosus, son of Count Pandolfus, of illegally possessing lands and churches in Cilento, which belonged to
the abbey.[64] Gloriosus denied the charge, showing a charter that proved his
ownership. Afterward, Gloriosus and the abbey of Cava reached a compromise by which Gloriosus confirmed the property on the abbey in exchange
for three hundred *tarì* "causa benedictionis." In 1115, Prince Jordan of Capua
donated and reconfirmed lands on San Massimo which had been disputed
for a time.[65] In addition, the abbey received confirmations from the counts
of the Principate and the lords of Sanseverino in areas where the abbey's
power overlapped with that of the counts and lords.[66]

In addition to donations, powerful lords at times swore oaths to the abbey
of Cava, promising to protect the monastic community and defend monastic
property. In 1111, for example, Jordan lord of Nocera issued a confirmation
of Cava's property, including the *castellum* of Sant'Adiutore, and then swore
on the Gospels to protect both monastic lands as well as the abbot himself.[67]
William, Count of the Principate, made a similar pledge in 1116, not only
confirming Cava's possession of lands and men but also promising that neither himself nor any of his men would seek to take or violate monastic property.[68] Both oaths were performed in front of a large group of important
personages and the ceremonies themselves appear to have been solemn occasions. They were in no way oaths of vassalage, but rather pledges to protect and defend Cava's patrimony, both made in the period immediately
after Roger Borsa's death, which was a time of political upheaval throughout
the Norman Duchy of Apulia.[69] Like donations, the oaths represented alliances between powerful lay lords and the abbey of Cava.

---

[62] Cava F, 34.

[63] Cava F, 2 (Heinemann, 27–28, no. 15). For other examples, see Cava XVIII, 22;
Cava XXI, 49; Cava XXII, 109; Cava XXII, 120; Cava XXVI, 66.

[64] Cava XVIII, 105.

[65] Cava E, 45.

[66] For the counts of the Principate, see E, 47 (Loud, "The Abbey of Cava," 176–
77); Cava F, 45. For the Sanseverinos, see Cava E, 34; Cava F, 1; Cava F, 36.

[67] Cava E, 21.

[68] Cava E, 47 (Loud, "The Abbey of Cava," 176–77). His son and heir Nicholas
made a similar pledge in 1128. Cava F, 45.

[69] Loud, "The Abbey of Cava," 165–67.

Families that competed for power with the abbey of Cava often have apocryphal documents attributed to them. For example, numerous forgeries exist in the archives from early members of the Sanseverino family, who established a large and important lordship in Cilento at the same time the abbey of Cava did.[70] The Sanseverinos represented the largest rival to the abbey's power in Cilento. Although the family eventually became an ally of the abbey, charters and other documents from the early twelfth century clearly demonstrate that the road to friendship was a difficult and rocky one. In the *Vitae Quatuor Priorum Abbatum Cavensium*, Roger, son of Turgisius, appears first as an enemy to the monks, and then as a convert and monk himself. According to the monastic author, Roger was in the habit of abusing the abbey's peasants in Cilento, and no amount of pleas or threats could deter him. One day Abbot Peter, while visiting the region, reacted angrily to some of Roger's activities. He asked for help from the archangel Michael, who rushed to Peter's aid and killed Roger's infant by causing a roof to fall on top of him. This miracle evidently was not enough for Roger, who continued to harass monastic property. He forcibly ejected monastic peasants from some lands and then appeared the next day to confront the abbot with a group of armed followers. Peter, however, appeared not with soldiers but with unarmed monks chanting the Psalms. This action, according to the author, softened Roger's heart so much that he underwent a sudden conversion and prostrated himself in front of Peter. Soon after he took the monastic habit and died a monk at Cava.[71]

Documents at Cava aid little in reconstructing the actual events. An 1114 document of dubious origin mentions Roger stealing pigs and other possessions from the abbey's lands in Metiliano and Sant'Adiutore.[72] Clearly, conflicts occurred regularly between the abbey and Roger at this time, and given that both parties were building up local power bases side-by-side, such friction is not surprising. In Cilento, disputes continued between the monks and the Sanseverino family up through the end of the twelfth century, when three charters dated 1183–87 defined the boundaries of their lands.[73] How-

---

[70] Maria Galante believes Cava XX, 73 and E, 34 to be false, while she has raised suspicions about the authenticity of the following Sanseverino documents, based on paleographic analysis: Cava B, 18; Cava B, 20; Cava XIII, 114; Cava B, 23; Cava B, 29; Cava C, 14; Cava D, 12; Cava XVII, 55; Cava XVII, 70; Cava D, 38; Cava D, 45; Cava E, 26; Cava E, 41; Cava F, 6; Cava XXI, 1. Other scholars consider the following Sanseverino documents suspect: Cava B, 19; Cava XIX, 82; Cava XX, 37; Cava XX, 72; Cava XX, 118; Cava F, 12; Cava F, 18; Cava XXI, 20; Cava XXI, 28. Galante, "Un esempio di diplomatica signorile."

[71] *VQPA*, 21–22. Also see the discussion by Loud, "The Abbey of Cava," 165–66.

[72] Cava E, 33. Carlone, *Falsificazioni*, 20–21.

[73] Cava I, 41; Cava L, 18; Cava L, 21.

ever, the relationship between Cava and the Sanseverinos should not be seen as wholly antagonistic. Despite the conflicts, the two parties also formed a friendship, and Roger did, in fact, die a monk at Cava. In reality, the relationship between the abbey and the Sanseverinos reflects the volatile cycles of alliance and hostility found among all the rulers and lords in Norman southern Italy, including the Norman dukes and counts themselves. Ties of friendship between two parties could turn quickly into conflict and dispute, depending on the circumstances, as each individual player attempted to position himself for reaping the greatest personal gains possible. Thus, the forged Sanseverino charters make up part of the negotiation process between the abbey of Cava and the Sanseverino family, reflecting the numerous oral and written compromises worked out between the two parties over the course of a century. The alliance between the two continued to be negotiated and re-negotiated well beyond the medieval period. The forgeries from the later period reflect the re-evaluation of this complex relationship that encompassed generations of monks and family members.[74]

Thus, as in other areas of Europe, gifts to saints and religious houses had a variety of meanings, religious and otherwise, and brought a range of benefits to both the donors and recipients. In its most basic form, the donors made gifts in the hope that the saints would help them and their kin in the afterlife, while the abbeys accepted them in order to garner the material support necessary for their survival and well-being. Often the donor and his family also received tangible services from the monastic community, such as burial rights, anniversary masses, and other commemorative rituals. In addition, donations were used as a means to establish social links between the donors and the abbeys, with the goal of increasing the power and prestige of both parties involved.[75] Finally, in the Principality of Salerno they were the means by which the lay nobility shared out power with the abbey of Cava in the new political landscape ushered in by the Norman conquest of the region. Since property ownership meant power over both the land and the people living on it, donations to Cava not only increased the economic base of the abbey, but also gave the monks important political roles. As a result, gifts to saints were associated with a larger political process through which

---

[74] For a good study on similar relationships between monks and lay families in medieval France, see Barbara H. Rosenwein, Thomas Head, and Sharon Farmer, "Monks and Their Enemies: A Comparative Approach," *Speculum* 66 (October 1991): 764–96.

[75] Detailed studies of this phenomenon in other regions of medieval Europe can be found in Rosenwein, *To Be the Neighbor*; White, *Custom, Kinship and Gifts to Saints*; and Chris Wickham, *The Mountains and the City: The Tuscan Appenines in the Early Middle Ages* (Oxford: Clarendon Press, 1988).

both lay lords and monks struggled for hegemony in a changing political world.[76]

The Creation of Monastic Lordships in Metiliano and Cilento

The abbey of Cava's rise to power was intricately linked to the new political and economic structures which developed in the region in the eleventh and early twelfth centuries. The establishment of territorial lordships became the key to power in the Norman period, and the abbey of Cava grew into a preeminent religious and political power in the period due not only to its development of a large, centrally controlled network of dependencies but also to the construction of territorial power on its property. The monastic community of Cava, moreover, became important political and religious administrators for the new Norman rulers, who both encouraged and supported Peter and the monks at Cava as they built up an ecclesiastical hierarchy and established two important monastic lordships in Metiliano and Cilento.

The area surrounding the abbey, stretching along the Via Popilia from Passiano to Metiliano to Vietri and the Mediterranean Sea, became the logical center for Cava's new religious empire. The Cava community quickly built up a network of dependent houses here, building new ecclesiastical foundations and gaining control over other ones through donations. The bulls of Urban II and Paschal II, issued in 1089 and 1100, listed eight dependencies, while charters give evidence for an additional four.[77] Three of the churches, Santa Maria, Sant'Elie, and Santa Maria in Vetranto, were founded by abbots Leo and Peter at the end of the eleventh century. The other nine were donated to the abbey, and since most of the foundations had multiple owners, the donations came from numerous people and often stretched over a long period of time. The church of San Giovanni in Vietri, for example, was given piecemeal to the abbey between 1080 and 1107. Similarly, the church of San Nicola of Gallocanta was donated by various family members

---

[76] White, *Custom, Kinship and Gifts to Saints*, 31.

[77] The eight churches mentioned in the papal bulls include Sant'Elie, Santa Maria, San Leone in Vetranto, San Giovanni in Vietri, San Martino de Forma in Passiano, Santa Maria in Transboneia (Dragonea), Sant'Andrea in Albori, and Santa Maria in Vetranto. Cava C, 21 (Guillaume, xx–xxii) and Cava D, 26 (Pflugk-Harttung, 2: 169–71, no. 206; Guillaume, xxiii–xxv). In addition, Cava received donations of portions of Santa Maria in Staffilo, San Nicola of Gallocanta, Sant'Arcangelo in Passiano, and San Salvatore in Passiano in the late eleventh and early twelfth centuries.

between 1087 and 1118. In some cases we have no information on how the
abbey actually absorbed a religious foundation. The house is either listed as a
Cava dependency in a papal bull or the abbey shows up in a charter exercising authority over the foundation. Sant'Andrea of Albori, for example, appears in the bulls of Paschal II and Eugene III, although no charter evidence
provides any clue to how the abbey took control of it.

The monks of Cava established direct control over the religious foundations located near the abbey. Unlike churches and monasteries in other regions, the foundations here lost almost all autonomy. The abbey absorbed
their lands and dependencies, administering both centrally without an abbot
or prior as an intermediary. Whereas other dependent foundations continued to issue charters and receive donations, the foundations here virtually
disappear from the archives after the abbey took control. In some cases, the
monks even appeared to be exercising authority before the foundations were
fully donated to the abbey. Thus the monks acted both quickly and decisively in order to establish a tightly controlled network of religious houses
in the region surrounding their monastery.

The church of San Giovanni in Vietri provides a useful example of Cava's
quick and aggressive absorption of religious foundations in the region. The
church, a proprietary house founded by a certain Iohannacius, son of Ursus
Atrianese, at the beginning of the eleventh century, was donated piecemeal
to Cava by numerous owners between 1080 and 1107.[78] However, as early as
1089, after only three donations, Urban II's bull listed it as a Cava dependency.[79] In 1093, after four additional donations of portions of the church,
documents claimed that the church pertained to Cava, and from this time
on Cava directly administered the church. A monk from Cava rather than an
abbot oversaw transactions.[80] In an 1106 document, a *custos* appeared as the
church head.[81] After 1107, when the final donation appears in the Cava
archives, the church all but disappears from the documents, its property
having been absorbed into the Cava patrimony.

The church of San Nicola of Gallocanta also was donated piecemeal to
Cava in the late eleventh and early twelfth centuries, and evidence suggests

---

[78] See CDC 6: 40–42, no. 898 for its foundation. For donations of the house to
Cava, see CDC 10: 341–44, no. 142; CDC 10: 344–46, no. 144; Cava XIV, 58; Cava
XIV, 80; Cava XV, 9; Cava XV, 21; Cava XV, 37; Cava XVIII, 9; Cava XVIII, 67. In
general, the documents do not specify what portion of the church each donor possessed. This church is not to be confused with San Giovanni di Staffilo, donated between 1090 and 1117 to Cava.

[79] Cava C, 21 (Guillaume, xx–xxii).

[80] Cava XV, 97.

[81] Cava XVIII, 40.

that conflict occurred as the abbey sought to take over the foundation. San Nicola was a proprietary house bought by Count Adelbertus in 996.[82] By the mid-eleventh century, the church pertained to two sons of Adelbertus, Count Landoarius and Count Lambertus, along with their children. In 1070, a document attributed one-half of the church to the one surviving grandson of Count Landoarius, Landoarius son of Adelbertus, and the other half to the three surviving sons of Count Lambertus, Peter, Adelbertus, and Landoarius, each of whom possessed one-sixth.[83] After the death of these four, the church then passed into the possession of their heirs, who included the five sons of Adelbertus (Lambertus, Costantinus, Richard, Ebolus, and Landolfus), and the widow and four sons of Landoarius (Gemma, John, Peter, Pandolfus, and Lambertus.)

The descendants of Count Lambertus formed close ties with Cava, which eventually led to the absorption of their half of the church by the abbey. Landoarius son of Lambertus became a monk at Cava in 1087, donating his one-sixth of the church when he did so.[84] Years later, his nephew Richard, son of Adelbertus, also entered the monastic community at Cava.[85] Finally, between 1113 and 1116, portions of the church belonging to other grandsons of Lambertus were donated to Cava: in 1113, Aloara, widow of Ebolus, donated her one-quarter Morgengabe of Ebolus' portion of the church to the abbey of Cava, while in 1114 Landolfus donated his portion and in 1116 his brother Costantinus with his sister-in-law Sichelgaita, widow of another brother Lambertus, donated their portion.[86]

Count Landoarius, to the contrary, seemed less enthusiastic about allying himself with Cava. Sometime before 1092, he, his mother Gaitelgrima, and his wife Ermelina made a pact not to sell, donate, or alienate the church to another party and to seek the monks' approval before appointing a new abbot. After the death of his mother and wife, Landoarius issued a charter to Theophilus, San Nicola's abbot, confirming the privilege and requiring his heirs to uphold it as well.[87] Clearly Landoarius wanted the church to retain its autonomy, and the charters he issued in the 1090s could very well have been in direct response to Lambertus' donation of his one-sixth of the church in 1087. It is interesting to note, too, that the period of Count Landoarius' charters coincide with the period of instability following the death

[82] CDC 3: 54–50, no. 494 (Cherubini, 126–29, no. 30).

[83] CDC 9: 271–90, no. 94 (Cherubini, 241–45, no. 96).

[84] Cava XIV, 78 (Cherubini, 264–65, no. 104).

[85] Cava XX, 34 (Cherubini, 323–24, no. 133).

[86] Cava XIX, 90 (Cherubini, 319–20, no. 130); Cava E, 37 (Cherubini, 321–22, no. 132); Cava XX, 34 (Cherubini, 323–24, no. 133).

[87] Cava XV, 48 (Cherubini, 286–87, no. 114).

of Robert Guiscard. Other small religious houses in southern Italy were also absorbed by larger foundations, most likely because of their ability to provide protection.[88]

Landoarius' attempt to stave off Cava's ambitions ultimately failed. After his death sometime between 1097 and 1109, his second wife Gemma, as well as his sons from his first wife, began alienating the church. In 1112 Gemma gave one-twelfth minus one-eighth ("una uncia minus octaba parte unius uncie") of the church to Peter, a judge, son of Buccone, who soon afterward donated part of this to the abbey of Cava.[89] In January 1118, John, Peter, and Pandolfus, sons of Landoarius and Ermelina, all donated their portions of the church to Cava, and at the end of the charter it was claimed that the abbey now owned the whole of the church.[90] It is unknown why Landoarius' descendants had a change of heart, but clearly their donations went against their father's wishes, suggesting that Cava's takeover of at least one-half of the church was more forced than voluntary. In the 1140s, in fact, the abbey received charters confirming the donations of Landoarius' sons, a phenomenon not recorded for other houses.[91] This may have very well been a result of the contested nature of Cava's absorption of the church.

The abbey of Cava began exercising at least partial control over San Nicola in 1110, after only a small portion (one-sixth) pertained to them. In that year, eight months after Gemma and John had invested Bartolomeus as abbot of the church, Cava re-invested the same Bartolomeus as abbot.[92] In a diploma from 1111, San Nicola is specified as a Cava dependency, although this charter is probably a forgery.[93] After this, the church all but disappears from the documents, aside from the donation charters dated between 1112 and 1118. It is listed in Eugene III's 1149 bull as a Cava dependency, and then in 1151 a monk from Cava named Omfridus twice leased out lands pertaining to the church in Bosanola.[94] In the lease, the church was specified as pertaining to Cava, and the monk was referred to as prior of the church, and he carried out the transactions with the permission of the abbot of Cava.

The examples of San Giovanni in Vietri and San Nicola of Gallocanta

[88] Loud, "Churches and Churchmen," 50–51.

[89] Cava XIX, 31 (Cherubini, 315–17, no. 128) and Cava XIX, 52 (Cherubini, 317–18, no. 129).

[90] Cava XX, 59 (Cherubini, 326–28, no. 135).

[91] Cava XXV, 109 (Cherubini, 328–29, no. 136); Cava XXVII, 7 (Cherubini, 330–33, no. 137).

[92] Cava XIX, 5 (Cherubini, 313–15, no. 127).

[93] Cava E, 19 (Heinemann, 21–23, no. 12).

[94] Cava H, 7; Cava XXVIII, 2 (Cherubini, 331–33, no. 138); Cava XXVIII, 3 (Cherubini, 333–35, no. 139).

demonstrate well how aggressive the monastic community at Cava was at extending its power over religious houses in the area around Cava. Although no conflict appears in the evidence for the absorption of San Giovanni, the abbey began to exercise control over the foundation even before it had collected donations from all the owners. In the case of San Nicola, the church became part of the Cava order against the wishes of at least some of the owners.[95] Although at first glance the charter evidence found in the abbey of Cava paints a relatively problem-free picture of the growth of Cava's religious empire, when read carefully, hints of conflict emerge as the abbey vigorously absorbed the nearby religious houses into the quickly expanding Cava order.

In addition to absorbing religious houses, the abbots of Cava also established political authority in Metiliano and Vietri almost immediately after the abbey's foundation. Privileges issued in 1025 and 1059 by the Lombard princes granted the monks the authority to tax and judge the population and exempted them from paying dues to or providing services for the palace.[96] They also gave the abbey control over rivers and forests. By the end of the eleventh century, charters show that dues and services owed by the local population had become customary.[97] In a 1090 sharecropping agreement, for example, the tenant was required to cultivate the land and pay dues "in the same way as other *coloni* of the monastery living in Metiliano do" ("sicut alii coloni ipsius monasterii de ipso loco Metiliano adimpleverint").[98] In 1113, some sharecroppers in Transboneia had to "perform [services] and pay [revenues] to the monastery just as other *coloni* of the monastery who live in that place do" ("faciant et dent parti ipsius monasterii sicut alii coloni ipsius loci eiusdem monasterii fecerint et dederint ad partem monasterii").[99] In an 1146 lease on lands in Balnearia and an 1148 one in Passiano, tenants had to pay dues and provide services "according to the custom of the place and the men of the abbey of Cava" ("secundum consuetudinem loci et hominum monasterii Cavensis").[100] Moreover, the number of sharecropping contracts issued by Cava in this region decreased at the beginning of the twelfth cen-

---

[95] Feller has noticed a similar phenomenon in the Abruzzi, where members of *consortia* at times opposed one another regarding the donation of their religious houses to large monasteries in the region. Feller, *Les Abruzzes*, 824.

[96] CDC 5: 93–95, no. 764; CDC 8: 95–97, no. 1284.

[97] A point also made by Loud, who believes this trend was not necessarily detrimental to tenants since it placed limitations on seigneurial power. "The Monastic Economy," 157–58.

[98] Cava XV, 24.

[99] Cava XIX, 81.

[100] Cava XXVI, 36 and Cava XXVI, 120.

tury as the abbey's rights became established and the abbots automatically collected dues and services on lands there.

In addition to receiving dues and services from the local population, the abbots and monks also began to treat the inhabitants as personal property. In a 1080 document from Robert, the duke asserted that "all men pertaining to the abbey, both inside and outside our city, will forever be under the authority of the abbot, his successors, and the monastery" ("omnibus hominibus eidem monasterio foris ac nostra civitate et deintus pertinentibus . . . in potestate sint se(m)per prefati domni abbati et successorum eius et partium ipsius monasterii").[101] The men, moreover, could move off the abbey's lands only with the abbot's permission. In 1110, Duke Roger conferred on Cava all the *servi* who lived on the abbey's property in Metiliano, Vietri, Passiano, Priato, Sepi, Transboneia, Albori, Fuenti, Cetara, Nocera, and Salerno, claiming that the men were under the protection ("defensio") of Cava.[102] They would pay dues to the abbey alone, and the abbots and monks were to decide disputes that arose among them.

Beginning at this time, the inhabitants of Metiliano, Vietri, and Salerno were sold or donated along with the property they lived on. Donations and sales of *villanos* or *censiles homines* specifically stated that their wives, children, and all their properties were alienated along with them.[103] In addition, small property-holders had limited authority over their lands, and the local inhabitants had to seek permission before selling or donating their property. In 1108, for example, a woman named Roka, daughter of John, received lands in Metiliano from a certain John, son of Sellictus. In the document, which Abbot Peter witnessed, Roka was obliged to ask permission from the abbey of Cava before she alienated the lands. Moreover, if she wished to sell the property, she had to offer it first to the abbey of Cava for the "just price." According to the document, the woman was required to do this "according to the custom of the other faithful of the above-mentioned monastery who have alienated their properties" ("secundum consuetudinum aliorum fidelium suprascripti monasterii qui res suas stabiles alienaverint").[104]

Duke Roger gave the monastery of Cava the port of Vietri sul Mare in 1086, with the right to navigate, fish, and tax commercial activity.[105] This is the beginning of Cava's commercial interests, which led the monks to travel throughout the Mediterranean on commercial voyages, in particular, to

---

[101] CDC 10: 331–33, no. 138.
[102] Cava E, 14 (Heinemann, 18–19, no. 9).
[103] See, for example, Cava XVI, 107 and Cava XIX, 56.
[104] Cava XVIII, 78.
[105] Cava B, 39 (Ménager, 178–80, no. 51; Guillaume, xii–xiii).

North Africa and the Crusader States. Although information on the abbey's commercial voyages in the early period is scarce, in the *Vitae Quatuor Priorum Abbatum Cavensium*, monks from Cava show up a number of times in Mediterranean ports, sometimes specifically engaged in commercial activity. Peter and some other monks, for example, sailed from Calabria to Cilento.[106] Shortly after Peter's death, c. 1125–27, monks from Cava showed up twice in North Africa. The first incident involved John, who sailed from Sicily to Africa. In the second episode, a monk from Cava, returning from a North African city with merchandise he had purchased for the monastery, was stranded because of the war there between Roger II of Sicily and the Muslim ruler. The ruler had refused to allow Christians to leave during Roger's naval attack on the city.[107] More importantly, the abbots and monks engaged in local commerce, sending boats and taxing merchandise on the rivers running through their lands. A recent study, in fact, has demonstrated that the monks' involvement in local commerce was a decisive factor in the creation of Cava's monastic economy.[108] By selling the produce they received from tenants, the monks acquired vast amounts of coinage that they used to buy not only more lands, but also grazing rights, *castella*, ports, market privileges, woods, and even people. It could very well be the case that purchases rather than donations were the main impetus behind Cava's rapid economic growth.

In the 1080s, the monks of Cava began to limit access to the waterways and forests on their lands. Starting at this time, rights to water and forest use were spelled out in sharecropping agreements and land alienations. In two 1108 sharecropping agreements in Albori, for example, the tenants were explicitly allowed to use the water of the Albori river and had the right to cut down trees nearby as well.[109] In an 1116 donation, the donor specifically reserved the right to continue using the roads and water on the lands he gave to the abbey.[110] Cava also began to tax fishing in the rivers and sea on or adjoining their properties. In an 1154 lease, for example, Cava gave a portion of the Irno river to a group of men in exchange for eight *solidi* and one-tenth of the fish they caught.[111]

Sometime at the beginning of the twelfth century, the abbey of Cava

[106] *VQPA*, 23.

[107] *VQPA*, 31–33 For more details on Cava's commercial activities, see Paul Guillaume, *Le navi cavensi nel Mediterraneo durante il medio evo, ovvero vita di S. Costabile di Lucania fondatore di Castellabate* (Cava dei Tirreni: Badia della SS Trinità, 1876).

[108] Loud, "Coinage, Wealth, and Plunder."

[109] Cava XVIII, 56; Cava XVIII, 57.

[110] Cava XIV, 72; Cava XVIII, 56; Cava XVIII, 57; Cava XX, 19.

[111] Cava XXVIII, 112. Also see Cava F, 15; Cava XXV, 29.

took possession of the fortress ("*castellum*") of Sant'Adiutore, which lay strategically on the road between Cava and Salerno. The origins of this for-tified center, as well as how the abbey came to control it, are unknown, and the documents contain much contradictory information. The first mention of the fortress occurs in 1093, when a certain Rainaldus "de castello sancti adiutoris" leased lands in Metiliano from the church of Santa Croce.[112] In 1104, it is mentioned as pertaining to Robert and William, sons of Angerius, from Britanny.[113] The *Annales Cavenses* claimed that the abbey purchased the fortress in 1110 for 1500 *sclifati*.[114] However, the abbey itself contains a number of forgeries concerning the *castellum*. In two of these forgeries, a certain Salpertus donated the fortress, along with lands in Albori, to the abbey.[115] In another, Duke Roger donated the fortress, after which his wife and son then confirmed the gift.[116] From 1113 on, documents stated that the fortress pertained to the abbey, and thus sometime before this date the monks clearly took possession.[117]

In a forged document attributed to Duke Roger and dated 1089, the abbey of Cava received territorial rights over all the men living on the *teni-mento* which Gisolf II had supposedly given to the abbey, which stretched from Metiliano and the *castrum* of Sant'Adiutore to Passiano, Transboneia, Fuenti, and Cetara.[118] According to the apocryphal document, all the inhab-itants of these places would pay the various dues they owed (including, "tributa," "pensiones," "angarias," and "perangarias") to the monks and no one else. Similarly all the inhabitants of the "*pheudum*" of Metiliano, do-nated to the abbey by a certain Salpertus, would pay dues to and perform services for the abbey alone. In addition, the monks had the ability to decide disputes which arose between them and their vassals living on these lands. They could freely receive homage and oaths of fidelity ("juramentum et homagium fidelitatis") from the inhabitants. The abbey also had rights over

[112] Cava XV, 89.

[113] Cava XVII, 114. Angerius was the brother of Turgisius, the first lord of San-severino.

[114] *Annales Cavenses*, CDC 5: Appendix, 39. *Sclifatus* or *schifatus* was a term used in Italian documents for the old type of Byzantine *solidus* after the introduction of a lighter *solidus* in imitation of the Arab dinar at the end of the tenth century. Travaini, *La Monetazione*, 10.

[115] CDC 8: 77–81, no. 1275; Cava C, 12 (Ménager, 203–12, no. 59; Heinemann, 5–11, no. 4).

[116] Cava E, 17 (Heinemann, 19–20, no. 10); Cava E, 16 (Heinemann, 20–21, no. 11). Also see Cava E, 19 (Heinemann, 21–23, no. 12).

[117] Cava XIX, 85; Cava XIX, 67; Cava XX, 20. The abbey also received a *castellum* in Apulia from Duke Roger at around this time. Cava D, 2; Cava E, 4.

[118] Cava C, 17 (Heinemann, 11–12, no. 5).

all the property and waterways within these territories, and property-holders had to seek permission before selling or bequeathing lands. The document described the precise boundaries of the territories, and, at the end of the document, it was stated that the abbey would have "full authority" over the territory, exercising power "in the same manner as we (Duke Roger) do over our *pheuda*" ("auctoritatem plenariam . . . sicut nos tenentes pheuda nostra") Although this document is a forgery, the rights described in it would be exercised by the abbey in a later period, from the mid-twelfth century on.[119]

Cilento became the other center of Cava's power in the region, and the abbey's interest here began during Peter's abbacy. Peter himself forged links early on with the southern part of the principality. After coming back from Cluny, he was named bishop of Policastro and then became abbot of the monastery of Sant'Arcangelo in Perdifumo for five years. When he became co-abbot of Cava in 1070, he immediately began to expand the abbey's holdings in the region. The abbey of Cava quickly took control of all the important ecclesiastical foundations before 1100, and used the houses to administer its vast landed holdings in the region. Although the foundations in the region retained some autonomy, buying and exchanging lands, receiving donations, and transacting leases and sharecropping agreements on their own, the abbots and monks from Cava participated in the foundations' activity, often showing up during transactions. The priors were directly answerable to Cava, and some were even chosen from the Cava community.

The majority of the ecclesiastical foundations in Cilento in the pre-1050 period were administered autonomously by their religious communities, without a specific connection to a local family or *consortium*. They had a special relationship with the Lombard princes, who served as protectors or guardians for at least some of the foundations. They also had some sort of connection to the papacy, although the exact nature of the relationship is unclear. In the mid-eleventh century, as a number of new lay lords settled in the region and established territorial lordships, they, too, claimed authority over some of the religious houses in the area. Thus, unlike northern regions where the abbots of Cava had to deal with large numbers of individuals and families when absorbing religious houses, for the vast majority of ecclesiastical foundations in Cilento the abbots needed only papal or princely permission, with the recognition of local lords in some cases. As a result, the abbey of Cava formed its network of religious houses in Cilento more quickly and more easily.

---

[119] For other forgeries which similarly describe rights exercised by Cava in a later period, see Carlone, *Falsificazioni*, 37–39.

The first donations in the region came from Prince Gisolf II, who gave Cava lands and four churches in 1072, including Sant'Angelo in Puczillu, San Croce in Duliarola, San Martino, and San Nicola in Serramezzana.[120] An undated charter from Pope Gregory VII found in the Cava archives gave the abbey power over eight other religious foundations: Sant'Arcangelo in Perdifumo, San Magno in Torano, San Fabiano de Casacastra, San Giorgio 'ad duo flumina', San Zaccaria de Lauro, Sant'Angelo in Montecorice, Santa Maria de Gulia, and Santa Lucia. Although this charter has been shown to be a forgery, documents from a later period demonstrate that the donation most likely did take place, and the bulls of both Urban II and Paschal II specifically attributed the eight dependent houses found in the forgery to Gregory.[121] San Giovanni in Tresino, a family-owned foundation, went under the authority of Cava between 1071 and 1097, through both donation and purchase.[122] San Matteo 'ad duo flumina' was given to Cava by Guaimarius lord of Giffoni grandson of Duke Guido in 1096.[123] Santa Marina in Novi, San Biagio in Butrano, and San Salvatore de Nuce were also Cava dependencies according to the bulls of Urban II and Paschal II, although it is unclear how the abbey came to possess them. Duke William reconfirmed the abbey's rights over portions of San Giorgio 'ad duo flumina' and San Zaccaria de Lauro in 1116, while Roger, lord of Sanseverino, reconfirmed Cava's portion of one-fourth of the same church of San Giorgio in the same year.[124]

Despite the donations and confirmations of at least eight houses in Cilento in the 1070s and 1080s, the foundations did not immediately go under the authority of Cava. The abbots of Cava did not participate in the house's activities or transactions, and the foundations themselves continued to be administered by abbots, rather than priors.[125] Beginning in c. 1090,

---

[120] CDC 9: 369–72, no. 126; CDC 9: 372–74, no. 127.

[121] For example, Robert Gusicard's 1080 privilege confirmed the abbey's possession of Sant'Arcangelo and San Magno. CDC 10: 331–33, no. 138. A 1083 dispute between the abbey and a ducal vicecount Bosus attributed Sant'Arcangelo, Sant'Angelo, San Zaccaria, Santa Maria de Gulia, San Magno, San Fabiano, San Nicola in Serramezzana, and San Giovanni in Tresino to the abbey. Cava B, 33 (Ménager, 136–41, no. 43). For the fullest discussion on the forged papal privilege and Gregory VII's donations to Cava, see the introduction to Leone and Vitolo, *Codex Diplomaticus Cavensis* X, xvii–xxiv. Also see IP, 8: 316–17. For an edition of the forgery, see Guillaume, *Histoire*, Appendix, vi–vii.

[122] CDC 9: 311–14, no. 100; CDC 10: 3–5, no. 1; CDC 10: 14–16, no. 4; CDC 10: 44–46, no. 13; CDC 10: 106–09, no. 34; Cava XVI, 69.

[123] Cava D, 9; Cava D, 13.

[124] Cava E, 50 (Heinemann, 25–27, no. 14); Cava XX, 91; Cava F, 1.

[125] For Sant'Arcangelo, see charters dated 1072–1085: CDC 9: 354–56, no. 119, with date corrected by Galante, *La Datazione*, 151–55, no. 127; CDC 9: 375–76, no.

however, the abbey of Cava began to exercise direct control over the foundations purportedly donated by Gregory VII in the 1070s.

Sant'Arcangelo in Perdifumo, which became one of the most important of Cava's dependencies in the region, was the first to go under direct Cava administration. Beginning in 1092, Sant'Arcangelo's head, Desideus, was no longer called "abbot," but rather "prior."[126] Peter began to travel regularly to the abbey at this time in order to help defend its rights. In both 1092 and 1093, the abbot was present during land disputes initiated by the monastery.[127] Again in 1110, Peter was at the abbey when he witnessed a land donation.[128] Moreover, even when Peter was not present, the priors of Sant'Arcangelo often sought his permission before issuing charters. In 1107, for example, a document was written at the request ("per commanditia") of Peter.[129] Beginning in 1114, the documents began to state specifically that the foundation pertained to the abbey of Cava.[130]

In a dispute between the abbey of Cava and the bishop of Paestum in 1100, priors from six ecclesiastical foundations in Cilento showed up as witnesses for Cava: Sant'Arcangelo in Perdifumo, San Magno in Torano, San Giovanni in Tresino, Sant'Angelo in Montecorice, Santa Maria de Gulia, and San Nicola in Serramezzana.[131] Already in 1074, a prior had been documented for San Giovanni in Tresino.[132] For San Fabiano, after the 1100 dispute, a document from 1103 referred to the monastery's head as "prepositus" and specifically mentioned that San Fabiano pertained to the abbey of Cava.[133] Similarly, an 1109 document for San Giovanni in Tresino called the head a "prepositus" and stated that it belonged to Cava.[134]

128; Cava XIII, 119; Cava XIV, 8; Cava XIV, 32; Cava XIV, 33; Cava XIV, 34. For San Nicola in Serramezzana, see CDC 10: 37–40, no. 11. For San Magno, see CDC 10: 298–300, no. 125; CDC 10: 318–20, no. 135; Cava XIV, 5. For San Fabiano, see CDC 10: 310–12, no. 131 and Cava XIII, 110. For San Giorgio, see Cava XIV, 38.

[126] Cava XV, 54; Cava XV, 55; Cava XV, 70; Cava XV, 82; Cava XVIII, 64. In a 1091 document, Desideus had been called "abbas." Cava XV, 40.

[127] Cava XV, 55; Cava XV, 70.

[128] Cava XIX, 4.

[129] Cava XVIII, 64.

[130] The first document that mentions the monastery of Sant'Arcangelo as a dependency is dated October 1114. According to the charter, "the church with all its purtenances belongs to the monastery of the Holy Trinity" ("ipse ecclesie cum omnibus suis pertinentiis pertinet in monasterio sancte et individue trinitatis"). Cava XX, 12.

[131] Cava D, 27.

[132] CDC 10: 106–9, no. 34.

[133] Cava XVII, 74.

[134] The church's head is called Amatus monk, priest, and "prepositus." Cava XVIII, 103. Shortly thereafter a new prior named John appeared as the church's head. Cava XIX, 76.

In addition to the appearance of priors, representatives from the Cava community began to personally participate in the activities of their dependencies in Cilento, traveling to the area to witness and approve activities or simply giving their permission to the priors to issue charters. As mentioned above, Abbot Peter traveled to Sant'Arcangelo at least three times, in 1092, 1093, and 1110.[135] In the 1100 dispute in Agropoli involving lands belonging to foundations in Cilento, a monk named John presented the charters and oversaw the defense.[136] In 1121 Peter sent a monk, Rossemannus, to Tresino to defend San Giovanni's rights in the area.[137]

In addition to taking over religious houses in the region, the monks established broad political and economic authority over the local population in the same way they did in the areas of Cava and Vietri. Religious houses in the region, in fact, had already established far-reaching rights over tenants in the mid-eleventh century, when a series of charters, dated between 1053 and 1085, document the practice of landholders in the region donating properties to monasteries and then taking them back again for an annual rent and labor services.[138] The donors and their families at the same time placed themselves "under the authority and jurisdiction of the abbot and monastery"("sub dominio et iudicium de ipsum abbas de ipso monasterio"). As a result, when the monks of Cava took over the ecclesiastical foundations in Cilento at the end of the eleventh century, they found themselves in the position of powerful landlords with the right to collect dues and services from tenants, as well as the authority to decide disputes which arose among them.[139] Documents from the late eleventh century listed the rural inhabi-

---

[135] Cava XV, 55; Cava XV, 70; Cava XIX, 4.

[136] Cava D, 27.

[137] Cava XXI, 53.

[138] CDC 7: 197–98, no. 1177, with date corrected by Galante, *La Datazione*, 144, no. 116; CDC 9: 354–56, no. 119, with date corrected by Galante, *La Datazione*, 151–55; CDC 9: 375–76, no. 128; Cava XIII, 119; Cava XIV, 8; Cava XIV, 33; Cava XIV, 34.

[139] Lay lords in the region also had extensive power over the inhabitants of their lands. In 1091, for example, Duke Roger gave lands on the Sele river to two brothers, Peter and John. The two brothers received not only the property, but all the inhabitants who lived on the lands, along with their wives, children, and property. Peter and John and their heirs had the right to collect dues and demand services from them, as well as the authority to decide disputes which arose among them. Cava XVII, 13. Other examples include a document from 1109 which speaks of men in Tresino who had formerly pertained to Count Mansus; documents from the Sanseverino family, who controlled numerous "villanos" and "homines" in Cilento; and documents for Guaimarius of Giffoni, who gave the abbey of Cava many lands and men in the region. Cava XVIII, 105. Cava E, 28; Cava E, 27; Cava E, 32; Cava E, 34; Cava F, 1. Cava C, 32; Cava D, 13; Cava E, 13.

tants who pertained to the abbey in the region, along with their wives, children, and property.

The abbey's expansion into Mediterranean commerce also had its roots in this region. Along with Vietri, ports in Cilento constituted the center of the abbey's commercial empire. The abbey, in fact, gained power over eight ports through donations and purchases. In 1113, Turgisius, son of Turgisius Sanseverino, along with others, donated the marina of Cilento to the abbey of Cava, which included six ports.[140] In 1124 the abbey bought another port at the foot of their *castrum* from Count Landolfus for fifteen *tarì*.[141] In 1137 the monks purchased a port on the Sele river for one hundred gold *solidi* and one-twelfth of another port on the same river for sixty Salernitan *tarì*.[142]

The use of water and access to forests and pastures became restricted in Cilento in the late eleventh century, just as it did in Metiliano and Vietri. Again the evidence comes from charters that begin to specify rights over lands formerly considered common use. For example, when a husband and wife sold lands in Persiceto to San Magno in 1079, they reserved the right to use the forests and pastures free of charge.[143] In two donations to Cava in 1086, one from Malfredus count of Fasanella and the other from Jordan lord of Corneto, the donors gave explicit permission to the abbey to collect wood in their forests and to pasture animals on their lands.[144] In a 1097 donation, Guaimarius, lord of Giffoni, gave sea rights to the abbey of Cava along with the lands he donated in Lucania.[145] In 1114, Robert of Eboli gave Cava the right of free passage on the Sele river which ran through his lands.[146] Similarly, sharecropping agreements specified whether a tenant could use water or cut down trees in forests, and sales and donations mentioned whether waterways were included.[147]

In 1123, Duke William gave Abbot Constable permission to build a fortified center in Cilento to protect the monastery's vast holdings in the region.[148] The *castrum* of Castellabate, located on the Mediterranean near the monastery of Santa Maria de Gulia, had a dual role: to protect monastic

[140] Cava E, 27.
[141] Cava XXI, 113.
[142] Cava XXIV, 24; Cava XXIV, 27.
[143] CDC 10: 272–74, no. 113.
[144] Cava B, 38; Cava C, 10; Cava D, 13; Cava E, 35.
[145] Cava D, 13.
[146] Cava D, 13; Cava E, 35.
[147] Cava XIV, 16; Cava XV, 64; Cava B, 38; Cava C, 10; Cava D, 13; Cava D, 36; Cava E, 35.
[148] Cava F, 24 (Guillaume, xxvii–xxviii; Ventimiglia, *Notizie storiche*, appendix 7; Heinemann, 29–30, no. 17).

lands and commercial interests and to control the countryside. In the privilege granting the abbey permission to build the *castrum* in Cilento, the duke specifically conceded to the monks at Cava full authority over the *castrum* and its territory. The abbey could send men there to build the *castrum* and could place *censiles* and other "men of the monastery" inside the center to live. These men, moreover, would pertain to the abbey alone, free from ducal taxation or interference and under the monks' judicial authority.

In 1138, the abbey of Cava granted a privilege to the inhabitants and landholders of Castellabate.[149] The charter was addressed to two categories of people: those under the jurisdiction and power of the abbey and those outside its jurisdiction but living within the *castrum*'s territory. Both groups had to seek the abbey's permission before building houses or planting vines, olive trees, chestnut trees, or orchards. Similarly, inhabitants who wanted to sell their property had to offer it first to the abbey, at a price that was four *tarì* less than its value. If the abbey did not want to buy it, the property owners had to sell it to residents who were under the jurisdiction of the abbey, at any price they wanted. In addition, uncultivated lands were to be given only to those residents under the jurisdiction of the abbey.

All inhabitants had to give to the abbey one-tenth of their wine production, as well as one animal for every thirty owned and one hog for every twenty. In addition, each family unit had to provide labor services to the abbey at sowing and harvest time. Landholders living outside the abbey's jurisdiction had to bring an unspecified tribute ("salus") at Easter and Christmas to the abbot.[150]

Thus, the creation of the powerful Cava order included not only the establishment of a large religious empire administered from the top, but also the construction of two important lordships, one in the region stretching from Metiliano to Vietri and the other in the southern part of the province in Cilento. By the mid-twelfth century, the abbey was the most powerful force in the economic, religious, and social life of these two areas. The monks collected dues and services from the local inhabitants and controlled a variety of economic activities, including agriculture, commerce, fishing, and pasturing. They served as judges for the local inhabitants, who became personally tied to the abbey, required to seek the monks' permission before they sold their lands or moved to a new place. Finally, the abbey built forti-

---

[149] Cava XXIV, 61.

[150] Graham Loud has suggested that this privilege actually reduced the obligations and dues owed, which very well may be true given that that a payment of one-tenth on the wine production is extremely low for the region, where tenants generally paid one-third or one-fourth. Loud, "The Monastic Economy," 157–58.

fied centers to protect and control the regions. As a result, the abbey of Cava did not only control churches and religious organization, but became a true territorial lordship, exercising political, judicial, and economic power over the inhabitants of their properties. By the mid-twelfth century, moreover, the abbey's rights had become an established norm, and the documents often abbreviated dues and services owed to the abbey by saying that tenants had to pay "as was customary" or, in at least one example, "according to the custom of the place and the men of the abbey" ("secundum consuetudinem loci et hominum monasterii").[151] The abbey of Cava, in imitation of Cluny, became the first monastic lordship in the Principality of Salerno over the course of the eleventh century, and its power would continue to be felt throughout the Middle Ages and indeed well beyond.

Throughout southern Italy, religious reform was mainly carried out by large Benedictine monasteries interested in creating monastic empires based on hierarchical networks of dependent foundations, political and economic lordships, and mother houses that served as centers for clerical training and religious culture. Montecassino is, of course, the premier example of this, but smaller monasteries, such as the abbey of Santa Sofia in Benevento, also took over numerous lands, religious houses, and *castella* in the Norman era, creating religious empires similar to that of Montecassino and Cava, albeit on a smaller scale. By the early fourteenth century, Santa Sofia had four times the wealth of the cathedral church of Benevento.[152] The Norman foundation of Venosa also grew into an important political and economic force in Apulia, serving as a training ground for prelates as well.[153] In the Abruzzi, monasteries such as Casauria gained independence in the tenth century, after which they, too, constructed networks of dependent churches and established lordships. In the eleventh century, monasteries rather than bishoprics represented the most important element in ecclesiastical reorganization.[154] Even in Apulia, where most monasteries were small

---

[151] Cava XIV, 44; Cava XV, 24; Cava XV, 75; Cava XVIII, 109; Cava XIX, 81; Cava XIX, 83; Cava XIX, 112; Cava XXII, 52; Cava XXIII, 119; Cava XXIV, 103; Cava XXVI, 36; Cava XXVI, 58; Cava XXVI, 72; Cava XXVI, 91; Cava XXVI, 98; Cava XXVI, 120; Cava XXVII, 37; Cava XXVII, 102; Cava XXVIII, 6.

[152] On Montecassino, see Cowdrey, *The Age of Desiderius*, 1. For Santa Sofia, see Loud, "A Lombard Abbey," 278–86.

[153] Hubert Houben, "Melfi e Venosa: Due città sotto il dominio normanno-svevo," in *Mezzogiorno Normanno-Svevo*, 327–28. Martin believes that the abbey of Venosa actually had little spiritual influence in Apulia, representing more a political and economic force due to its large landholdings and close relationship to Norman dukes. Martin, *La Pouille*, 674–76.

[154] Feller, *Les Abruzzes*, 839–40, 850.

in comparison to their counterparts in Campania, they nonetheless played a premier role in religious reform and in providing pastoral care for the population in the Norman period and beyond.[155] The eleventh century thus represents a period in which southern Italy became dotted with large Benedictine monasteries, such as Cava, exercising religious, political, and economic power simultaneously, similar to Cluny and other abbeys further north.

Church reform in the Principality of Salerno was not as controversial or as difficult as in other regions of Latin Christendom. While the investiture controversy and conflict between papal and imperial power disrupted life in many parts of Germany and northern Italy, bishops and abbots in southern Italy did not as a rule object to the new papacy that emerged in Rome over the course of the eleventh and twelfth centuries. Partly this is due to the fact that when churchmen in places such as Salerno did not choose to aggressively implement all aspects of papal reform, popes in general did not push the issue. Yet more important was the fact that prelates in Salerno did not possess the type of prestige and power that their counterparts in the empire did. As a result, papal reform served to increase their authority, instead of infringing on it as occurred in northern Italy and Germany. Since papal reform supported and promoted the growth of the cathedral church of Salerno and the creation of a powerful new monastic empire based on the abbey of Cava, prelates in Salerno in turn backed up the reform papacy.

[155] Martin, *La Pouille*, 659–60, 690–91.

Epilogue

Changes and Continuities

Before the eleventh century, religious life and church organization in Salerno and its province bore little resemblance to Carolingian regions. Episcopal authority was weak and no system of parish churches developed. Many rituals reserved for bishops alone in northern Italy, such as baptism, were performed by a variety of clerics administering religious houses not directly under episcopal authority. Anchoritic monasticism predominated, and few regular clerics followed a monastic rule, such as the one attributed to St. Benedict. Categories of religious life overlapped, and even the difference between the clergy and the laity was often blurred. Religious practices were marked by a striking degree of variation, and there was no push to standardize. Religious foundations tended to be small and ephemeral, and they were generally built and maintained by a family or *consortium*. They followed local custom and catered to the neighboring population.

Since Salerno was not part of the Carolingian empire, it makes sense that it did not participate in the transformations characteristic of Frankish territories. Instead, Salerno and southern Italy remained firmly enmeshed in a Mediterranean culture up through the Norman conquest. Political and religious organization was based on cities, and Roman law continued to hold force alongside Lombard law. Greek was commonly used as a liturgical language, and practices generally identified as "Eastern" were widespread. Ecclesiastical hierarchies were a rarity, and most Christians worshiped in small churches and monasteries built by families and village communities. The anchoritic rather than cenobitic tradition prevailed, and holy men and women who traveled tended to visit Mediterranean areas rather than territories to the north. The region of Salerno, in fact, exhibited much continuity with its

Roman past. This is not to deny the far-reaching transformations brought to the region by the Lombard conquest, nor the fact that the population of southern Italy remained in contact with its northern neighbors throughout the early medieval period. Nonetheless, Salerno and its province exhibited a noticeable Mediterranean flavor and remained in closer contact with other Mediterranean regions, both Christian and Muslim. Although historians often speak of southern Italy as a frontier region in the early Middle Ages, in many ways it was well integrated into the Mediterranean world of which it was a part.

The eleventh century marks a moment in time that many medieval historians have described as the birth of Europe. Traditionally, historians connected this new society to the rise of centralized states and the growth of feudal monarchies, generally tracing the experience of one specific country. More recently, historians have tried to discern changes that encompassed all of the areas that eventually became known as Europe. Robert Bartlett, for example, has shown how the emergence of a new elite led to the development of an identifiable European culture, arising out of a group of societies that formerly had been highly distinct units. This new aristocracy included lay families supported by rents as well as clerics sustained by tithes.[1] Similarly, R. I. Moore has traced how a warrior elite who supported themselves mainly off of wartime booty was replaced by a new educated elite who based their income on rents, tithes, or salaries.[2] For both historians, the new political system was characterized by monarchs employing salaried officials, lordships based on castles and serfs, and a parish church system supported by tithes.

In many ways the Norman conquest of southern Italy and the eleventh-century program of church reform resulted in the integration of the Principality of Salerno into the new Europe being created at the time. First of all, it saw the creation of a new political landscape characterized by fortified centers and seigneurial rights. Consortial communities based on inheritance or the possession of common goods, characteristic of Salerno in the early Middle Ages, were replaced by territorial communities based on collective concessions where inhabitants in a particular territory lived according to specific customs and privileges conceded to them by the local lord.[3] The Normans themselves established a monarchy with salaried officials, similar

---

[1] Robert Bartlett, *The Making of Europe: Conquest, Colonization, and Cultural Change, 950–1350* (Princeton: Princeton University Press, 1993).

[2] R. I. Moore, *The First European Revolution, c. 970–1215* (Oxford: Blackwell, 2000).

[3] Taviani-Carozzi, *La Principauté*, 917–18.

to England and France. In Salerno, the papacy along with local prelates advocating religious reform brought the area into the sphere of the new Catholic Church based on Rome. The archbishop of Salerno and the abbey of Cava both created ecclesiastical hierarchies directly under papal power, and they both espoused many aspects of the papal reform program emanating from Rome. Moreover, the new vocabulary that appears in charters announces a change in mentality: terms such as *dominus* and *senior*, *villanus* and *colonos*, *prior* and *parocchia* are used for the first time in the region.

Yet beneath the language and rhetoric of the documents, much continued as before.[4] The religious program of both Cava and the cathedral church focused almost exclusively on administrative reforms, and many practices unique to the area continued into the twelfth century and beyond. Clerical marriage remained common throughout former Lombard areas, and proprietary houses independent of both monastic and episcopal oversight not only survived but represented an important element of ecclesiastical organization in Salerno, as well as in Apulia and the Abruzzi. Greek foundations and Eastern traditions also did not disappear, and certain liturgical usages distinctive of the region, and contrary to Roman practice, persisted well beyond the medieval era. Church organization remained fragmented in many areas and jurisdictional overlaps continued to be common. Moreover, the new lords who established political power in the eleventh century all upheld local customs and law, and communities continued to exhibit a large deal of diversity in their political, religious, and economic structures.

In addition, rulers in southern Italy continued to be part of a Mediterranean world distinct from that of northern Europe. Not only did the literature and art of southern Italy remain part of a larger environment that included both Byzantine and Muslim territories, but the rulers of the Norman Duchy of Apulia and the Kingdom of Sicily had a noticeably different relationship to rulers in other areas of the Mediterranean in comparison to their counterparts in northern Europe. For example, during the first crusade, Robert Guiscard's son, Bohemund, was much more interested in continuing his father's expansion into Byzantine territories than he was in capturing Jerusalem. Similarly, during the second crusade, Roger II was focused on fighting the Byzantine emperor Manuel and showed little desire to travel to the Holy Land. Moreover, unlike King Louis VII and other monarchs from

---

[4] Similarly, Barthélemy has cautioned against equating change in vocabulary with a change in practice. Dominique Barthélemy, "The Year 1000 without Abrupt or Radical Transformation," in *Debating the Middle Ages: Issues and Readings*, ed. Lester K. Little and Barbara H. Rosenwein (Oxford: Blackwell, 1998), 134–47.

northern Europe, Roger II's relations with Muslim rulers were not formulated based on crusading ideas but on the political realities of the Mediterranean where Christian and Muslim kingdoms existed side by side.[5] Almost a century later, Frederick II, who is famous for his close ties to Muslim artists and intellectuals, was able to negotiate with Muslim rulers a bloodless takeover of Jerusalem. In many ways, one could even argue that the eleventh century marks the moment in which southern Italy became a frontier region, on the edge of a new European civilization that was just beginning to define itself, and an older Mediterranean culture based on the borders of ancient Rome.

[5] Matthew, *The Norman Kingdom of Sicily*, 56–59.

Works Cited

Primary Sources

Acocella, Nicola. *La Traslazione di San Matteo: Documenti e testimonianze*. Salerno: Grafica di Giacomo, 1954.

Acta sanctorum quotquot toto orbe coluntur. Edited by Joannus Bollandus, et al. Venice/Paris, 1643–1940.

Alfanus I. *I Carmi di Alfano I*. Edited by Anselmo Lentini and Faustino Avagliano. Miscellanea Cassinese, vol. 38. Montecassino: M. Pisani, 1974.

Amatus of Montecassino. "Ystoire de li Normani." In *Storia dei Normanni di Amato di Montecassino*. Edited by Vincenzo de Bartholomaeis. Fonti per la Storia d'Italia, vol. 76. Rome: Tipografia del Senato, 1935.

Amatus of Montecassino. *The History of the Normans by Amatus of Montecassino*. Translated by Prescott N. Dunbar. Woodbridge: Boydell & Brewer, 2004.

Amatus of Montecassino. *Storia dei Normanni*. Edited and translated by Giuseppe Sperduti. Cassino: Francesco Ciolfi, 1999.

Amelli, A., ed. "Acta Synodi Ecclesiae." In *Spicilegium Casinense* 1:388–93. Montecassino, 1888.

Amelli, A., ed. "Synodus Orietana." In *Spicilegium Casinense* 1: 377–81. Montecassino, 1888.

Annales Cavenses. Edited by George H. Pertz. *Monumenta Germaniae Historica. Scriptores*, 3: 185–97. Hanover, 1839.

Annales Cavenses. Edited by M. Morcaldi, M. Schiani, and S. De Stefano. *Codex Diplomaticus Cavensis* 5, Appendix, 14–72.

Balducci, Antonio. *L'Archivio Diocesano di Salerno: Cenni sull'Archivio del Capitolo Metropolitano*. Salerno: Camera di Commercio, Industria e Agricoltura, 1959.

Battelli, Giulio, Guglielmo Cavallo, Armando Petrucci, Alessandro Pratesi, ed.

Archivio Paleografico Italiano XV. Vols. 62, 63, 67. Rome, 1956. Reprint, Turin: Molfese & Figli, 1968–82.

Βίος καὶ πολῖτεία ὅς Πάτρος ἡμῶν Νείλος τοῦ νεοῦ Edited by Germano Giovanelli. Grottaferrata: Badia di Grottaferrata, 1972.

Catalogus Baronum. Edited by Evelyn Jamison. Fonti per la Storia d'Italia, vol. 101. Rome: Istituto Storico per il Medio Evo, 1972.

Carlone, Carmine. *Documenti per la Storia di Eboli (799–1264).* Salerno: Carlone Editore, 1998.

Cherubini, Paolo, ed. *Le Pergamene di S. Nicola di Gallucanta (secc. IX–XII).* Salerno: Edizioni Studi Storici Meridionali, 1990.

Chronica Monasterii Casinensis. Edited by Hartmut Hoffmann. In *Monumenta Germaniae Historica. Scriptores,* vol. 34. Hannover, 1980.

Chronicon Salernitanum. Edited by Ulla Westerbergh. Studia Latina Stockholmiensia, vol. 3. Stockholm: Almovist and Wiksell, 1956.

Chronicon Salernitanum. Translated by Arturo Carucci. Salerno: Editrice Salernum, 1988.

Chronicon Vultunense del monaco Giovanni. Edited by Vincenzo Federici. Fonti per la Storia d'Italia, vol. 58. Rome: Istituto Storico Italiano per il Medio Evo, 1925.

Codex Diplomaticus Cavensis. Vols. 1–8. Edited by M. Morcaldi, M. Schiani, and S. De Stefano. Naples: P. Piazza/H. Hoepli, 1873–1893.

Codex Diplomaticus Cavensis. Vols. 9–10. Edited by Simeone Leone and Giovanni Vitolo. Cava dei Tirreni: Badia di Cava, 1984–1990.

Codex Diplomaticus Regni Siciliae. Vol. 2, pt. 1 of *Diplomata regum et principum e gente normannorum: Roger II. regis diplomata latina.* Edited by Carlrichard Brühl. Cologne: Böhlau, 1987.

Di Meo, Alessandro. *Annali critico-diplomatici del Regno di Napoli della mezzana età.* Naples: Simoniana, 1795–1819.

Garufi, C. A. *Necrologio del Liber Confratrum di S. Matteo di Salerno.* Fonti per la storia d'Italia, vol. 56. Rome: Istituto Storico Italiano per il Medio Evo, 1922.

Girgensohn, Dieter, ed. "Miscellanea Italiae pontificiae. Untersuchungen und Urkunden zur mittelalterlichen Kirchengeschichte Italiens, vornehmlich Kalabriens, Siziliens, und Sardiniens." *Nachrichten der Akademie der Wissenschaften in Göttingen. Philologisch-historische Klasse* (1974): 129–96.

Héfèle, Charles Joseph. *Histoire des Conciles d'après les documents originaux.* Translated by H. Leclercq. Paris: Letouzey et Ané, 1910.

Heinemann, Lothar von. *Normannische Herzogs- und Königsurkunden aus Unteritalien und Sicilien.* Tübingen: Druck von H. Laupp Jr., 1899.

Hoffmann, Hartmut. "Die Alteren Abstlistern von Montecassino." *Quellen und Forschungen aus Italienischen Archiven und Bibliotheken* 47 (1967): 224–354.

Ibn Hawqal. *Configuration de la Terre.* Translated by J. H. Kraemers and G. Wiet. Paris: G.-P. Maisonneuve, 1964.

Kehr, Paul Fridolin, ed. *Italia Pontificia.* Vols. 1–10. Berlin: Weidmann, 1905–74.

Leges Langobardorum. Edited by F. Bluhme. In *Monumenta Germaniae Historica. Leges,* vol. 4. Hanover, 1869.

The Lombard Laws. Translated by Katherine Fischer Drew. Philadelphia: University of Pennsylvania Press, 1973.

Liber Censuum de l'église romaine. Vols. 1–3. Edited by Louis Duchesne and Paul Fabre. Paris: A. Fontemoing, 1889–1952.

Malaterra, Geoffrey. *De Rebus Gestis Rogerii Calabriae et Siciliae Comitis et Roberti Guiscardi Ducis fratris eius*. Edited by Ernesto Pontieri. Rerum Italicarum Scriptores, vol. 5, pt. 1. Bologna: Nicola Zanichelli, 1928.

Martin, Jean-Marie, Errico Cuozzo, Stefano Gasparri, and Matteo Villani, eds. *Regesti dei Documenti dell'Italia Meridionale, 570–899*. Rome: Ecole Française de Rome, 2002.

Ménager, Léon-Robert. *Recueil des actes des ducs normands d'Italie (1046–1127). I. Les premiers ducs (1048–87)*. Società di Storia Patria per la Puglia. Documenti e monografie, vol. 45. Bari: Società di Storia Patria per la Puglia, 1981.

Morin, D. Germain, ed. "Un concile inédit tenu dans l'Italie méridionale à la fin du IXe siècle." *Révue Benedictine* 17 (1900): 143–51.

Muratori, Ludovico Antonio. *Antiquitates Italicae Medii Aevi*. Milan: Barbiellini, 1738–1742.

Paesano, Giuseppe. *Memorie per servire alla storia della chiesa salernitana. Vols. 1–3*. Naples: V. Manfredi, 1846–57.

Patrologia cursus completus. Series Latina. Edited Jacques-Paul Migne. 244 vols. Paris: Garnier, 1841–1902.

Peter the Deacon. *De Viris Illustribus Casinensibus*. Edited and translated by Giuseppe Sperduti. Cassino: Francesco Ciolfi Editore, 1995.

Pflugk-Harttung, Julius von. *Acta Pontificium Romanorum Inedita*. Vols. 1–3. Stuttgart: W. Kohlhammer, 1881–86.

Rationes Decimarum Italiae nei secoli XIII e XIV: Campania. Edited by Mauro Inguanez, Leone Mattei Cerasoli, and Pietro Sella. Studi e Testi, vol. 97. Vatican City: Biblioteca Apostolica Vaticana, 1942.

Regii Neapolitani Archivi Monumenta. 6 vols. Edited by Bartholomaei Capasso. Naples: Francisci Giannini, 1845–61.

Talamo-Atenolfi, Giuseppe. *I testi medioevali degli atti di S. Matteo l'Evangelista*. Rome: C. Bestetti, 1958.

Ughelli, Ferdinando. *Italia Sacra*. Vols. 1–10. Venice: S. Coleti, 1717–22.

La Vita di San Fantino il Giovane: Introduzione, Testo Greco, Traduzione, Commentario e Indici. Edited and translated by Enrica Follieri. Brussels: Société des Bollandistes, 1993.

Vita di Sant'Elia il Giovane. Edited and translated by Giuseppe Rossi Taibbi. Palermo: Istituto siciliano di studi bizantini e neoellenici, 1962.

Vita di S. Nilo. Translated by Germano Giovanelli. Grottaferrata: Badia di Grottaferrata, 1966.

Vita et Conversatio Sancti Patris Nostri Sabae Iunioris. Edited and translated by Giuseppe Cozza-Luzi. *Studi e Documenti di Storia e Diritto*, vol. 12 (Rome: Tipografia poliglotta, 1891), 37–56, 135–68, 311–23.

Vita et Conversatio Sanctorum Patrum Nostrorum Christophori et Macarii. Edited and

translated by Giuseppe Cozza-Luzi. *Studi e Documenti di Storia e Diritto,* vol. 13
(Rome: Tipografia poliglotta, 1892), 375–400

Vitae Quatuor Priorum Abbatum Cavensium. Edited by Leone Mattei Cerasoli.
Rerum Italicarum Scriptores, vol. 6, pt. 5, 4–35. Bologna: Nicola Zanichelli, 1941.

William of Apulia. *La Geste de Robert Guiscard.* Edited and translated by Marguerite
Mathieu. Palermo: Tipografia Pio X, 1961.

Secondary Sources

Acocella, Nicola. "Il Cilento dai Longobardi ai Normanni (secoli X e XI): Struttura
amministrativa e agricola." *Rassegna Storica Salernitana* 22 (1961): 35–82; 23 (1962):
45–132.

———. "La figura e l'opera di Alfano I di Salerno." *Rassegna Storica Salernitana* 19
(1958): 1–74.

Amann, Emile. *L'époque carolingienne.* Vol. 6. *Histoire de l'Eglise depuis les origines
jusqu'à nos jours.* Paris: Bloud and Gay, 1937.

Amann, Emile and Auguste Dumas. *L'Eglise au pouvoir des laïques (888–1057).* Vol. 7.
Histoire de l'Eglise depuis les origines jusqu'à nos jours. Paris: Bloud and Gay, 1942.

Anastos, M. V. "The Transfer of Illyricum, Calabria, and Sicily." *Studi Bizantini e
Neoellenici* 9 (1954): 14–31.

Antonini, Giuseppe. *La Lucania.* Naples: F. Tomberli, 1795. Reprint, Naples: G.
Bisogni, 1798.

Antonucci, Giovanni. "Falsificazioni bantine e cavensi." *Archivio Storico per la Calabria e la Lucania* 13 (1943-44): 1–15.

Arnaldi, Girolamo. "Profilo di storia della Chiesa e del papato fra tarda antichità e
alto medioevo." *La Cultura* 35/1 (1997): 5–31.

Avagliano, Giovanni. "Impianto urbano e testimonianze archeologiche." In *Guida
alla storia di Salerno e della sua provincia,* edited by Alfonso Leone and Giovanni Vitolo, 33–51. Salerno: P. Laveglia, 1982.

Avril, François, and Jean-René Gaborit. "L'Itinerarium Bernardi monachi et les
pélégrinages d'Italie du Sud pendant le Haut-Moyen-Age." *Mélanges d'archéologie
et d'histoire* 79 (1967): 269–98.

Azzara, Claudio. "Ecclesiastical Institutions." In *Italy in the Early Middle Ages, 476–
1000,* edited by Cristina La Rocca, 85–101. Oxford: Oxford University Press, 2002.

———. "The Papacy." In *Italy in the Early Middle Ages, 476–1000,* edited by Cristina
La Rocca, 102–17. Oxford: Oxford University Press, 2002.

Barthélemy, Dominique. "The Year 1000 Without Abrupt or Radical Transformation." In *Debating the Middle Ages: Issues and Readings,* edited by Lester K. Little
and Barbara H. Rosenwein, 134–47. Oxford: Blackwell, 1998.

Bartlett, Robert. *The Making of Europe: Conquest, Colonization, and Cultural Change,
950–1350.* Princeton: Princeton University Press, 1993.

Batiffol, Pierre. *L'abbaye di Rossano. Contribution à l'Histoire de la Vaticane.* Paris: A. Picard, 1891.

Bergamo, Giuseppe. *Chiese e monasteri di Eboli tra il Mille e il Mille trecento.* Tesi di laurea, University of Salerno, 1976.

Blumenthal, Uta-Renate. *The Investiture Controversy: Church and Monarchy from the Ninth to the Twelfth Century.* Philadelphia: University of Pennsylvania Press, 1988.

Bognetti, Gian Piero. "La continuità delle sedi episcopali e l'azione di Roma nel regno longobardo." In *Le Chiese nei regni dell'Europa occidentale e i loro rapporti con Roma sino all'800: Settimana di studio del centro italiano di studi sull'alto medioevo, 7–13 April 1959,* 7: 415–54. Spoleto: Centro Italiano di Studi sull'Alto Medioevo, 1960.

——. "Tradizione longobarda e politica bizantina nelle origini del ducato di Spoleto." In *L'età longobarda,* 3:441–57. Milan: Giuffrè, 1967.

Borsari, Silvano. *Il monachesimo bizantino nella Sicilia e nell'Italia meridionale prenormanne.* Naples: Istituto italiano per gli studi storici, 1963.

Bougard, François. "Public Power and Authority." In *Italy in the Early Middle Ages, 476–1000,* edited by Cristina La Rocca, 34–58. Oxford: Oxford University Press, 2002.

Boyd, Catherine E. *Tithes and Parishes in Medieval Italy: The Historical Roots of a Modern Problem.* Ithaca: Cornell University Press, 1952.

Bracco, Vittorio. *Salerno Romana.* Salerno: Palladio Editrice, 1979.

Brogiolo, Gian Pietro and Sauro Gelichi. *La città nell'alto medioevo italiano: Archeologia e storia.* Rome/Bari: Laterza, 1998.

Brooke, C. N. L. "The Church in Towns, 1000–1250." In *The Mission of the Church and the Propagation of the Faith, Studies in Church History,* edited by G. J. Cuming, 6:59–83. Cambridge: Cambridge University Press, 1970.

Brown, Peter. *The Rise of Western Christendom: Triumph and Diversity* A.D. 200–1000. Oxford: Blackwell, 1996.

Bünemann, Richard. *Robert Guiskard 1015–1085. Eine Normanner erobert Süditalien.* Cologne: Böhlau, 1997.

Calvino, Raffaele. *Diocesi scomparse in Campania.* Naples: F. Fiorentino, 1969.

Camodeca, Giuseppe. "L'età romana." In *Storia del Mezzogiorno,* edited by Giuseppe Galasso, 1.2:7–79. Naples: Edizione del Sole, 1986.

Campbell, James. "The Church in Anglo-Saxon Towns." In *The Church in Town and Countryside, Studies in Church History,* edited by Derek Baker, 16: 119–35. Oxford: Blackwell, 1979.

Cappelli, Biagio. *Il monaschesimo basiliano ai confini calabro-lucani.* Naples: F. Fiorentino, 1963.

Caput Aquis Medievale. Vols. 1–2. Salerno: P. Laveglia, 1976.

Carlone, Carmine. *Falsificazioni e falsari cavensi e verginiani del secolo XIII.* Altavilla Silentina: Edizioni studi storici meridionali, 1984.

——. "I principi Guaimario e i monaci cavensi nel vallo di Diano." *Archivi e cultura* 10 (1976): 47–60.

——. *Le origini e la costituzione patrimoniale della Badia di Cava (1025–1124).* Tesi di laurea, University of Salerno, 1971–72.

Carucci, Carlo. *Un feudo ecclesiastico nell'Italia meridionale: Olevano sul Tusciano.* Subiaco: Tipografio dei monasteri, 1937.

——. *La provincia di Salerno dai tempi più remoti al tramonto della fortuna normanna: Economia e vita sociale.* Salerno: Il Tipografio Salernitano, 1922.

Caspar, Erich. *Roger II (1101–1154) und die Gründung der normannisch-sizilischen Monarchie.* Innsbruck: Wagner, 1904.

Chalandon, Ferdinand. *Histoire de la domination normande en Italie méridionale et en Sicile.* Paris: A. Picard, 1907.

Charanis, Peter. "On the Question of the Hellenization of Sicily and Southern Italy during the Middle Ages." *American Historical Review* 52 (1946): 74–86.

La Chiesa Greca in Italia dall'VIII al XVI secolo. Atti del Convegno storico interecclesiale, Bari, 30 April–4 May 1969. Padua: Editrice Antenore, 1973.

Christie, Neil. *The Lombards: the Ancient Longobards.* Oxford: Blackwell, 1995.

Cilento, Nicola. "Centri urbani antichi, scomparsi e nuovi nella campagna medievale." In *Atti del Colloquio internazionale di archeologia medievale, Palermo-Erice, 20–22 September 1974,* 155–63. Rome: S. Sciascia, 1976.

——. *Civiltà napoletana del medioevo nei secoli VI–XIII.* Naples: Edizioni Scientifiche Italiane, 1969.

——. "Il falsario della storia dei Longobardi meridionali: Francesco Maria Pratilli." In *Italia meridionale longobarda,* 24–39. Milan/Naples: R. Riccardi, 1971.

——. *Italia meridionale longobarda.* Milan/Naples: R. Ricciardi, 1971.

——. *Le origini della signoria capuana nella Longobardia minore.* Istituto Storico per il Medio Evo Studi Storici, vols. 69–70. Rome: Istituto Storico per il Medio Evo, 1966.

——. "La politica 'meridionale' di Gregorio VII nel contesto della riforma della Chiesa." *Rassegna Storica Salernitana,* n.s. 3 (June 1985): 123–136.

Clanchy, M. T. *From Memory to Written Record: England, 1066–1307.* Cambridge: Harvard University Press, 1979.

Cosimato, Donato and Pasquale Natella. *Il Territorio del Sarno: Storia, società, arte.* Cava dei Tirreni: Di Mauro, 1981.

Cowdrey, H. E. J. *The Age of Abbot Desiderius: Montecassino, the Papacy, and the Normans in the Eleventh and Twelfth Centuries.* Oxford: Clarendon Press, 1983.

——. *The Cluniacs and the Gregorian Reform.* Oxford: Clarendon Press, 1970.

——. *Pope Gregory VII, 1073–1085.* Oxford: Clarendon Press, 1998.

Crisci, Generoso. *Il cammino della Chiesa salernitana nell'opera dei suoi vescovi.* Naples/Rome: Libreria Editrice Redenzione, 1976–80.

Crisci, Generoso and Angelo Campagna. *Salerno sacra: Ricerche storiche.* Salerno: Edizioni della Cura arcivescovile, 1962.

Cuozzo, Errico. " 'Milites' e 'testes' nella contea normanna di Principato." *Bullettino dell'Istituto Storico Italiano per il Medio Evo* 88 (1979): 121–63.

——. "L'unificazione normanna e il regno normanno-svevo." In *Storia del Mezzogiorno,* edited by Giuseppe Galasso, 2.2: 593–825. Naples: Edizione del Sole, 1986.

Da Costa-Louillet, G. "Saints de Sicile et d'Italie méridionale aux VIIIe, IXe e Xe siècles." *Byzantion* 29–30 (1959–60): 89–173.

Davies, Wendy. *Small Worlds: The Village Community in Early Medieval Brittany.* Berkeley: University of California Press, 1988.

Delogu, Paolo. *Mito di una città meridionale (Salerno, secoli VIII–IX)*. Naples: Liguori, 1977.

——. "Storia del Sito." In *Caput Aquis Medievale*, 1:23–32. Salerno: P. Laveglia, 1976.

Del Treppo, Mario. *Amalfi: Una città del Mezzogiorno nei secoli IX–XIV*. Naples: Giannini, 1977.

——. "La vita economica e sociale in una grande abbazia del Mezzogiorno: S. Vincenzo al Volturno nell'alto Medioevo." *Archivio storico per le province napoletane 35* (1956): 3–82.

Dereine, Charles. "Chanoines." In *Dictionnaire d'Histoire et de Géographie Ecclésiastique*, 12:353–406.

——. "Vie commune, règle de Saint Augustin et chanoines réguliers au XIe siècle." *Revue d'histoire ecclésiastique* 41 (1946): 365–406.

Drell, Joanna. *Kinship and Conquest: Family Strategies in the Principality of Salerno during the Norman Period, 1077–1194*. Ithaca: Cornell University Press, 2002.

Duby, Georges. *La société aux XIe et XIIe siècles dans la région mâconnaise*. Paris: A. Colin, 1953.

Dyson, Stephen L. *The Roman Villas of Buccino: The Wesleyan University Excavation of Buccino, Italy, 1969–72*. Oxford: B. A. R., 1983.

Ebner, Pietro. *Economia e società nel Cilento medievale*. Rome: Edizioni di Storia e Letteratura, 1979.

——. "I monasteri bizantini nel Cilento: I Monasteri di S. Barbara, S. Mauro e S. Marina." *Rassegna Storica Salernitana* 28 (1967): 77–142.

Everett, Nicholas. *Literacy in Lombard Italy, c. 568–774*. Cambridge: Cambridge University Press, 2003.

Falkenhausen, Vera von. "I Longobardi meridionali." In *Storia d'Italia: Il Mezzogiorno dai Bizantini a Federico II*, edited by André Guillou et al., 3: 251–364. Turin: UTET, 1983.

——. "Il Monachesimo italo-greco e i suoi rapporti con il monachesimo benedettino." In *L'Esperienza monastica benedettina e la Puglia: Atti del Convegno, Bari-Noci-Lecce-Picciano, 6–10 October 1980*, 119–35. Galatina: Congedo, 1983.

——. "I monasteri greci dell'Italia meridionale e della Sicilia dopo l'avvento dei Normanni: continuità e mutamenti." In *Il passaggio dal dominio bizantino allo stato normanno nell'Italia meridionale: Atti del II Convegno internazionale di studi sulla civiltà rupestre medioevale nel Mezzogiorno d'Italia, Taranto-Mottola, 31 October–4 November 1973*, 197–229. Taranto: Amministrazione Provinciale, 1977.

——. "Patrimonio e politica patrimoniale dei monasteri greci nella Sicilia normanno-sveva." In *Basilio di Cesarea: la sua età e il Basilianesimo in Sicilia: Atti del congresso internazionale, Messina, 3–6 December 1979*, 777–90. Messina: Centro di Studi Umanistici, 1983.

——. *Untersuchungen über die byzantinische Herrschaft in Süditalien vom 9. bis ins 11. Jahrhundert*. Wiesbaden: O. Harrassowitz, 1967. Italian edition, *La dominazione bizantina nell'Italia meridionale dal IX all'XI secolo*. Bari: Ecumenica Editrice, 1978.

Fanning, Steven C. "Lombard Arianism Reconsidered." *Speculum* 56 (April 1981): 24–58.

Feine, H. E. "Studien zum langobardisch-italischen Eigenkirchenrecht." *Zeitschrift der Savigny-Stiftung für Rechtsgeschichte* 30 (1941): 1–95; 31 (1942): 1–105.

——. "Ursprung, Wesen, und Bedeutung des Eigenkirchentums." *Mitteilungen des Instituts für österreichische Geschichtsforschung* 58 (1950): 195–208.

Feller, Laurent. *Les Abruzzes médiévales: territoire, économie, et société en Italie centrale du IXe au XIIe siècle.* Rome: Ecole Française de Rome, 1998.

Figliuolo, Bruno. "Gli Amalfitani a Cetara: vicende patrimoniali e attività economiche (secc. X-XI)." *Annali dell'Istituto Italiano per gli Studi Storici* 6 (1979/80): 30–82.

——. "Longobardi e Normanni." In *Storia e civiltà della Campania: il medioevo,* edited by Giovanni Pugliese Carratelli, 37–86. Naples: Electa Napoli, 1992.

——. "Morfologia dell'insediamento nell'Italia meridionale in età normanna." *Studi Storici* 32 (1991): 25–68.

Fliche, Augustin. *La réforme grégorienne et la reconquête chrétienne (1057–1125).* Vol. 8. *Histoire de l'Eglise.* Paris: Bloud and Gay, 1940.

Follieri, Enrica. "Il culto dei santi nell'Italia greca." In *La Chiesa Greca in Italia dall'VIII al XVI secolo. Atti del Convegno storico interecclesiale, Bari, 30 April–4 May 1969,* 553–77. Padua: Edictrice Antenore, 1973.

Fonseca, Cosimo Damiano. "Aspetti istituzionali dell'organizzazione ecclesiastica meridionale dal VI al IX secolo." In *Dalla prima alla seconda distruzione. Momenti e aspetti della storia cassinese (secc. VI–IX): Convegno internazionale di studio sul Medioevo meridionale, Cassino-Montecassino, 27–31 May 1984.* Montecassino: Pubblicazioni Cassinensi, 1987. Reprinted in *Particolarismo istituzionale e organizzazione ecclesiastica del Mezzogiorno medievale,* 3–20. Galatina: Congedo Editore, 1987.

——. "L'organizzazione ecclesiastica dell'Italia normanna tra l'XI e il XII secolo: i nuovi assetti istituzionali." In *Le Istituzioni ecclesiastiche della 'societas christiana' dei secoli XI–XII: diocesi, pievi, e parrocchie: Atti della Sesta Settimana della Mendola, Milan, 1–7 September 1974,* 2:327–52. Milan: Vita e Pensiero, 1977.

——. "Particolarismo istituzionale e organizzazione ecclesiastica delle campagne nell'Alto Medioevo nell'Italia meridionale." In *Cristianizzazione ed organizzazione ecclesiastica delle campagne nell'Alto Medioevo: espansione e resistenze: Settimana di studio del centro italiano di studi sull'alto medioevo,* 28:1163–1203. Spoleto: Centro Italiano di Studi sull'Alto Medioevo, 1982. Reprinted in *Particolarismo istituzionale e organizzazione ecclesiastica del Mezzogiorno medievale,* 21–49. Galatina: Congedo Editore, 1987.

Forchielli, Giuseppe. *La pieve rurale. Ricerche sulla storia della costituzione della Chiesa in Italia e particolarmente nel Veronese.* Rome: G. Bardi, 1931.

Francovich, Riccardo. "Changing Structures of Settlements." In *Italy in the Early Middle Ages, 476–1000,* edited by Cristina La Rocca, 144–67. Oxford: Oxford University Press, 2002.

Frank, Thomas. *Studien zu italienischen Memorialzeugnissen des XI. und XII. Jahrhunderts.* Berlin/New York: de Gruyter, 1991.

Fraschetti, Augusto. "Le vicende storiche." In *Storia del Vallo di Diano,* edited by Nicola Cilento, 201–15. Salerno: P. Laveglia, 1982.

Fumagalli, Vito. *Terra e società nell'Italia padana.* Turin: Einaudi, 1976.

Gabrieli, Francesco. "Ibn Hawqal e gli Arabi di Sicilia." *Rivista degli Studi Orientali* 36 (1961): 245–53.

Galante, Maria. *La datazione dei documenti del Codex Diplomaticus Cavensis.* Salerno: Grafiche Moriniello, 1980.

———. "La documentazione vescovile Salernitana: aspetti e problemi." In *Scrittura e produzione documentaria nel Mezzogiorno longobardo: Atti del Convegno internazionale di studio, Badia di Cava, 3–5 October 1990,* edited by Giovanni Vitolo and Francesco Mottola, 223–56. Salerno: Edizioni 10/17, 1991.

———. "Un esempio di diplomatica signorile: i documenti dei Sanseverino." In *Civiltà del Mezzogiorno d'Italia: Libro, Scrittura, Documento in età normanno-sveva: Atti del Convegno dell'Associazione Italiana dei Paleografi e Diplomatisti, Naples-Badia di Cava dei Tirreni, 14–18 October 1991,* edited by Filippo D'Oria, 279–331. Salerno: Carlone Editore, 1994.

Gamber, Klaus. "La liturgia delle diocesi dell'Italia centro-meridionale dal IX al XI secolo." In *Vescovi e Diocesi in Italia nel Medioevo (sec. IX–XIII). Atti del II Convegno di storia della chiesa in Italia, Rome, 5–9 September 1961,* 145–56. Padua: Antenore, 1964.

Gasparri, Stefano. "The Aristocracy." In *Italy in the Early Middle Ages, 476–1000,* edited by Cristina La Rocca, 59–84. Oxford: Oxford University Press, 2002.

———. *I Duchi Longobardi.* Studi Storici dell'Istituto Storico Italiano per il Medio Evo, vol. 102. Rome: Istituto Storico Italiano per il Medio Evo, 1978.

Gay, Jules. *L'Italie méridionale et l'Empire Byzantin depuis l'avènement de Basile Ier jusqu'à la prise de Bari par les Normands (867–1071).* Paris: A. Fontemoing, 1904.

Giardina, Andrea. "Allevamento ed economia della selva in Italia meridionale: Trasformazioni e continuità." In *Società romana e produzione schiavistica,* edited by Andrea Giardina and Aldo Schiavone, 87–113. Bari: Laterza, 1981.

Gilchrist, John. "Was there a Gregorian Reform Movement in the Eleventh Century?" *The Canadian Catholic Historical Association, Study Sessions* 37 (1970): 1–10.

Girgensohn, Dieter. "Miscellanea Italiae Pontificiae: Untersuchungen und Urkunden zur Mittelalterlichen Kirchengeschichte Italiens, vornehmlich Kalabriens, Siziliens, und Sardiniens." *Nachrichten der Akademie der Wissenschaften in Göttingen aus dem Jahre 1974. Philologisch-Historische Klasse* (1974): 129–96.

Gleijeses, Vittorio. *Castelli in Campania.* Naples: Società Editrice Napoletana, 1973.

Greco Pontrandolfo, Angela and Emanuele Greco. "L'Agro picentino e la Lucania occidentale." In *Società romana e produzione schiavistica,* edited by Andrea Giardina and Aldo Schiavone, 1: 137–151. Bari: Laterza, 1981.

Grossi, Paolo. *Il dominio e le cose. Percezioni medievali e moderne dei diritti reali.* Milan: Giuffrè, 1992.

Guillaume, Paul. *Essai historique sur l'abbaye de Cava d'après les documents inédits.* Cava dei Tirreni: Abbaye des Pères Bénédictins, 1877.

———. *Le navi cavensi nel Mediterraneo durante il medio evo, ovvero vita di S. Costabile di Lucania fondatore di Castellabate.* Cava dei Tirreni: Badia della SS Trinità, 1876.

Guillou, André. "La Lucanie byzantine: Etude de géographie historique." *Byzantion* 35 (1965): 119–49.

———. "Il monachesimo greco in Italia meridionale e in Sicilia nel medioevo." In

L'eremitismo in Occidente nei secoli XI e XII: Atti della seconda Settimana internazionale di studio, Mendola, 30 August–6 September 1962, 354–79. Milan: Società Editrice Vita e Pensiero, 1965.

———. *Studies on Byzantine Italy*. London: Variorum Reprints, 1970.

Hartmann, Wilfried. *Die Synoden der Karolingerzeit im Frankenreich und in Italien*. Paderborn: Ferdinand Schöningh, 1989.

Hen, Yitzhak. *The Royal Patronage of Liturgy in Frankish Gaul To the Death of Charles the Bald (877)*. Woodbridge: Boydell & Brewer, 2001.

Herde, Peter. "Il papato e la Chiesa greca nell'Italia meridionale dall'XI al XIII secolo." In *La Chiesa Greca in Italia dall'VIII al XVI secolo: Atti del Convegno storico interecclesiale, Bari, 30 April–4 May 1969*, 1:213–55. Padua: Editrice Antenore, 1972–73. English translation: "The Papacy and the Greek Church in Southern Italy between the Eleventh and Thirteenth Century." Translated by Carine van Rhijn, Inge Lyse Hansen, G. A. Loud, and A. Metcalfe. In *The Society of Norman Italy*, edited by G. A. Loud and A. Metcalfe, 213–51. Leiden: Brill, 2002.

Hildebrandt, M. M. *The External School in Carolingian Society*. Leiden: Brill, 1992.

Hodges, Richard. *Light in the Dark Ages: The Rise and Fall of San Vincenzo al Volturno*. Ithaca: Cornell University Press, 1997.

Houben, Hubert. "L'autore delle 'Vitae quatuor priorum abbatum Cavensium'," *Studi medievali* 26 (1985): 871–79.

———. "Confraternite e religiosità dei laici nel Mezzogiorno medievale (sec. XII–XV)." In *Mezzogiorno Normanno-Svevo: Monasteri e castelli, ebrei e musulmani*, 355–77. Naples: Liguori, 1996.

———. "I castelli del Mezzogiorno normanno-svevo nelle fonti scritte." In *Mezzogiorno Normanno-Svevo: Monasteri e castelli, ebrei e musulmani*, 159–76. Naples: Liguori, 1996.

———. "Melfi e Venosa: Due città sotto il dominio normanno-svevo." In *Mezzogiorno Normanno-Svevo: Monasteri e castelli, ebrei e musulmani*, 319–36. Naples: Liguori, 1996.

———. "Il monachesimo cluniacense e i monasteri normanni dell'Italia meridionale." In *Mezzogiorno Normanno-Svevo: Monasteri e castelli, ebrei e musulmani*, 7–22. Naples: Liguori, 1996.

———. "Urbano II e i Normanni (con un'appendice sull'itinerario del papa nel Sud)." In *Mezzogiorno Normanno-Svevo: Monasteri e castelli, ebrei e musulmani*, 115–43. Naples: Liguori, 1996.

Howe, John. *Church Reform and Social Change in Eleventh-Century Italy: Dominic of Sora and His Patrons*. Philadelphia: University of Pennsylvania Press, 1997.

Hunt, Noreen. *Cluny under Saint Hugh, 1049–1109*. London: Edward Arnold, 1967.

Iogna-Prat, Dominique. *Order and Exclusion: Cluny and Christendom Face Heresy, Judaism, and Islam (1000–1150)*. Translated by Graham Robert Edwards. Ithaca: Cornell University Press, 2003.

Jenal, Georg. *Italia ascetica atque monastica: das Asketen- und Mönchtum in Italien von den Anfängen bis zur Zeit der Langobarden (ca. 150/250–604)*. Stuttgart: Hiersemann, 1995.

Johannowsky, Werner. "Caratteri e fasi delle culture pre-istoriche e classiche." In *Guida alla storia di Salerno e della sua provincia*, edited by Alfonso Leone and Giovanni Vitolo, 415–31. Salerno: P. Laveglia, 1982.

Kalby, Gino. "Gli Insediamenti rupestri della Campania." In *La civiltà rupestre medioevale nel Mezzogiorno d'Italia. Ricerche e Problemi: Atti del primo convegno internazionale di studi, Mottola-Casalrotta, 29 September-3 October, 1971*, edited by Cosimo Damiano Fonseca, 153–72. Genova: Edizioni dell'Istituto Grafico S. Basile, 1975.

Kamp, Norbert. *Kirche und Monarchie im Staufischen Königreich Sizilien*. Vols. 1–3. Munich: Wilhelm Fink, 1973.

——. "Monarchia ed episcopato nel Regno svevo di Sicilia." In *Potere, società, e popolo nell'età sveva 1210–66: Atti delle seste giornate normanno-sveve, Bari-Castel del Monte-Melfi, 17–20 October 1983*, 123–49. Bari: Dedalo, 1985.

——. "Soziale Herkunft und Geistlicher Bildungsweg der Unteritalienischen Bischoefe Normannisch-Staufische Zeit." In *Le Istituzioni ecclesiastiche della 'societas christiana' dei secoli XI–XII: diocesi, pievi, e parrocchie: Atti della sesta settimana internazionale di studio, Mendola-Milan, 1–7 September 1974*, 89–116. Milan: Vita e Pensiero, 1977. English translation, with modification and updates: "The Bishops of Southern Italy in the Norman and Staufen Periods." Translated by G. A. Loud and Diane Milburn. In *The Society of Norman Italy*, edited by G. A. Loud and A. Metcalfe, 185–209. Leiden: Brill, 2002.

——. "Vescovi e diocesi nell'Italia meridionale nel passaggio dalla dominazione bizantina allo stato normanno." In *Il passaggio dal dominio bizantino allo stato normanno nell'Italia meridionale: Atti del II Convegno internazionale di studi sulla civiltà rupestre medioevale nel Mezzogiorno d'Italia, Taranto-Mottola, 31 October-4 November 1973*, 165–195. Taranto: Amministrazione provinciale, 1977.

Klewitz, Hans-Walter. "Studien über die Wiederherstellung der Römishen Kirche in Süditalien durch das Reformpapsttum." *Quellen und Forschungen aus italienischen Archiven und Bibliotheken* 25 (1934/35): 105–87. Reprinted in *Reformpapsttum und Kardinalkolleg*, 137–205. Darmstadt: Wissenschaftliche Buchgesellschaft, 1957.

——. "Zur Geschichte der Bistumsorganisation Campaniens und Apuliens im 10. und 11. Jahrhundert." *Quellen und Forschungen aus italienischen Archiven und Bibliotheken* 24 (1932–33): 1–61.

Lake, Kirsopp. "The Greek Monasteries in South Italy." *Journal of Theological Studies* 4 (1903): 345–68, 517–542; 5 (1904): 22–41.

La Rocca, Cristina. "Cristianesimi." In *Storia Medievale*, 113–39. Rome: Conzelli, 1998.

Laudisio, Nicola Maria. *Sinossi della diocesi di Policastro, ed. G. Galeazzo Visconti*. Naples: Tipografia de Dominicis, 1831. Reprint, Rome: Edizioni di Storia e Letteratura, 1976.

Lenormant, François. *La Grande-Grèce. Paysage et histoire*. Paris: A. Levy, 1883.

Leone, Alfonso and Giovanni Vitolo, ed. *Guida alla Storia di Salerno e della sua provincia*. Salerno: P. Laveglia, 1982.

Leone, Simeone. "La Data di Fondazione della Badia di Cava." *Benedictina* 22 (1975): 335–46.

Leone, Simeone, and Giovanni Vitolo, eds. *Minima Cavensis. Studi in margine al IX volume del Codex Diplomaticus Cavensis.* Salerno: P. Laveglia, 1983.

Licinio, Raffaele. *Castelli medievali: Puglia e Basilicata dai Normanni a Federico II e Carlo I d'Angio.* Bari: Dedalo, 1994.

Lizier, Augusto. *L'Ecomonia rurale dell'età prenormanna nell'Italia meridionale: Studi su documenti editi dai secoli IX-XI.* Palermo: Reber, 1907.

Llewellyn, Peter. *Rome in the Dark Ages.* London: Faber, 1971.

Lomas, Kathryn. *Rome and the Western Greeks 350 BC–AD 200: Conquest and Acculturation in Southern Italy.* London/New York: Routledge, 1993.

Loud, G. A. "The Abbey of Cava, its Property and Benefactors in the Norman Era." *Anglo-Norman Studies* 10 (1986): 143–77. Reprinted in *Conquerors and Churchmen in Norman Italy.* Aldershot: Ashgate, 1999.

——. *The Age of Robert Guiscard: Southern Italy and the Norman Conquest.* Harlow: Pearson, 2000.

——. *Church and Society in the Norman Principality of Capua.* Oxford: Clarendon Press, 1984.

——. "Churches and Churchmen in an Age of Conquest: Southern Italy, 1030–1130." *Haskins Society Journal* 4 (1992): 37–53. Reprinted in *Conquerors and Churchmen in Norman Italy.* Aldershot: Ashgate, 1999.

——. "Coinage, Wealth, and Plunder in the Age of Robert Guiscard." *English Historical Review* 114 (September 1999): 815–43.

——. *Conquerors and Churchmen in Norman Italy.* Aldershot: Ashgate, 1999.

——. "Continuity and Change in Norman Italy: The Campania during the Eleventh and Twelfth Centuries." *Journal of Medieval History* 22 (1996): 313–43. Reprinted in *Conquerors and Churchmen in Norman Italy.* Aldershot: Ashgate, 1999.

——. "A Lombard Abbey in a Norman World: St Sophia, Benevento, 1050–1200." *Anglo-Norman Studies* 19 (1996): 273–306. Reprinted in *Montecassino and Benevento in the Middle Ages.* Aldershot: Ashgate, 2000.

——. "The Monastic Economy of the Principality of Salerno during the Eleventh and Twelfth Centuries." *Papers of the British School at Rome* 71 (2003): 141–79.

——. *Montecassino and Benevento in the Middle Ages.* Aldershot: Ashgate, 2000.

Loud, G. A., and A. Metcalfe, ed. *The Society of Norman Italy.* Leiden: Brill, 2002.

——. "Southern Italy in the Tenth Century." In *The New Cambridge Medieval History*, edited by Timothy Reuter, 3:624–45. Cambridge: Cambridge University Press, 1999.

Manselli, Raoul. "Roberto il Guiscardo e il Papato." In *Roberto il Guiscardo e il suo tempo: Atti delle prime giornate normanno-sveve, Bari, 28–29 May 1973*, 169–88. Rome: Dedalo, 1975; reprint, Bari: Dedalo, 1991.

Markus, R. A. *Gregory the Great and His World.* Cambridge: Cambridge University Press, 1997.

Martin, Jean-Marie. "L'ambiente longobardo, greco, islamico, e normanno." In *Storia dell'Italia Religiosa*, edited by Gabriele De Rosa, Tullio Grogy, and André Vauchez, 1:193–242. Rome/Bari: Laterza, 1993.

——. "Cennamus episcopus. Aux avant-postes de l'Hellénisme sud-italien vers l'an mil." *Rivista di studi bizantini e neoellenici* 27 (1964): 89–99.

——. "Città e Campagna: Economia e società (sec. VII–XIII)." In *Storia del Mezzogiorno*, edited by Giuseppe Galasso, 3: 257–382. Naples: Edizione del Sole, 1990.

——. *Italies normandes XIe–XIIe siècles*. Paris: Hachette, 1994.

——. *La Pouille du VIe au XIIe siècle*. Rome: Ecole Française de Rome, 1993.

——. "Le régime domanial dans l'Italie méridionale Lombarde. Origines, caractères originaux et extinction." In *Du Latifondium au Latifondo: un heritage de Rome, une création médiévale ou moderne? Actes de la Table ronde internationale du CNRS organisée à l'Université Michel de Montaigne-Bordeaux III, 17–19 December 1992*, 289–95. Paris: Diffusion de Boccard, 1995.

——. "Settlement and the Agrarian Economy." In *The Society of Norman Italy*, edited by G. A. Loud and A. Metcalfe, 17–45. Leiden: Brill, 2002.

Mattei-Cerasoli, Leone. "Il ministero parrochiale nei monasteri cavensi." *Benedictina* 3 (1948): 27–34.

Matthew, Donald. *The Norman Kingdom of Sicily*. Cambridge: Cambridge University Press, 1992.

McCormick, Michael. *Eternal Victory. Triumphal Rulership in Late Antiquity, Byzantium and the Early Medieval West*. Cambridge: Cambridge University Press, 1986.

——. *Origins of the European Economy: Communications and Commerce, A.D. 300–900*. Cambridge: Cambridge University Press, 2001.

Ménager, Léon-Robert. "La 'byzantinisation' religieuse de l'Italie méridionale (IXe-XIIe siècles) et la politique monastique des Normands d'Italie." *Revue d'Histoire Ecclésiastique* 53 (1958): 747–74.

——. "Les fondations monastiques de Robert Guiscard." *Quellen und Forschungen aus italienischen Archiven und Bibliotheken* 39 (1959): 1–116.

Miller, Maureen C. *The Formation of a Medieval Church: Ecclesiastical Change in Verona, 950–1150*. Ithaca: Cornell University Press, 1993.

Montanari, Massimo. *L'Alimentazione contadina nell'alto medioevo*. Naples: Liguori Editore, 1979.

Moore, R. I. *The First European Revolution, c. 970–1215*. Oxford: Blackwell, 2000.

Morini, Enrico. "Eremo e cenobio nel monachesimo greco dell'Italia meridionale nei secoli IX e X." *Rivista di storia della Chiesa in Italia* 31 (1977): 1–39, 354–90.

Morris, Colin. *The Papal Monarchy: The Western Church from 1050 to 1250*. Oxford: Clarendon, 1989.

Musca, Giosuè. *L'Emirato di Bari, 847–71*. 2nd ed. Bari: Dedalo, 1967.

Natella, Pasquale and Paolo Peduto. *Il castello di Mercato S. Severino*. Naples: Hermes, 1965.

Noble, Thomas F. X. *The Republic of St. Peter: The Birth of the Papal State, 680–825*. Philadelphia: University of Pennsylvania Press, 1984.

Noyé, Ghislaine. "Villes, économie et société dans la province de Bruttium-Lucanie du IVe au VIIe siècle." In *La Storia dell'Alto Medioevo Italiano (VI–X secolo) alla Luce dell'Archeologia. Convegno internazionale, Siena, 2–6 December 1992*, edited by Riccardo Francovich and Ghislaine Noyé, 693–733. Florence: Edizioni all'Insegno del Giglio, 1994.

Pace, Valentino. "La cattedrale di Salerno." In *Desiderio di Montecassino e l'arte della riforma gregoriana*, edited by Faustino Avagliano, 189–230. Montecassino: Pubblicazioni cassinesi, 1997.

Paesano, Giuseppe. *Memorie per servire alla storia della chiesa salernitana*. Vols. 1–3. Naples: V. Manfredi, 1846–57.

Palmieri, Stefano. "Duchi, principi, e vescovi nella Longobardia meridionale." In *Longobardia e longobardi nell'Italia meridionale: Le istituzioni ecclesiastiche. Atti del 2° Convegno internazionale di studi promosso dal Centro di cultura dell'Università cattolica del Sacro Cuore, Benevento, 29–31 May 1992*, edited by Giancarlo Andenna and Giorgio Picasso, 43–99. Milan: Vita e Pensiero, 1996.

Pane, Giulio. "La 'crypta cava' e la fabbrica antica." In *La Badia di Cava*, edited by Giuseppe Fienzo and Franco Strazzullo, 119–52. Cava dei Tirreni: Di Mauro, 1985.

Peduto, Paolo. "Insediamenti altomedievali e ricerca archeologica." In *Guida alla storia di Salerno e della sua provincia*, edited by Alfonso Leone and Giovanni Vitolo, 441–73. Salerno: P. Laveglia, 1982.

Pertusi, Agostino. "Aspetti organizzativi e culturali dell'ambiente monacale greco dell'Italia meridionale." In *L'eremitismo in Occidente nei secoli XI e XII: Atti della seconda Settimana internazionale di studio, Mendola, 30 August–6 September 1962*, 382–426. Milan: Società Editrice Vita e Pensiero, 1965.

Pontieri, Ernesto. *I normanni nell'Italia meridionale*. Naples: Libreria Scientifica Editrice, 1948.

Poupardin, René. *Les institutions politiques et administratives des principautés lombardes*. Paris: H. Champion, 1907.

Ramseyer, Valerie. "Territorial Lordships in the Principality of Salerno, 1050–1150." *Haskins Society Journal* 9 (2001): 79–94.

Richards, Jeffrey. *The Popes and the Papacy in the Early Middle Ages, 476–752*. London: Routledge and Kegan Paul, 1979.

Rigon, Antonio. "Le Istituizioni ecclesiastiche della Cristianità." In *La società medievale*, edited by Silvana Collodo and Giuliano Pinto, 217–53. Bologna: Monduzzi, 1999.

Rosenwein, Barbara H., Thomas Head, and Sharon Farmer. "Monks and Their Enemies: A Comparative Approach." *Speculum* 66 (October 1991): 764–96.

Rosenwein, Barbara H. *Negotiating Space: Power, Restraint, and Privileges of Immunity in Early Medieval Europe*. Ithaca: Cornell University Press, 1999.

——. *Rhinoceros Bound: Cluny in the Tenth Century*. Philadelphia: University of Pennsylvania Press, 1982.

——. *To Be the Neighbor of Saint Peter: The Social Meaning of Cluny's Property, 909–1049*. Ithaca: Cornell University Press, 1989.

Rousseau, Olivier. "La Visite de Nil di Rossano au Mont-Cassin." In *La Chiesa Greca in Italia dall'VIII al XVI secolo. Atti del Convegno storico interecclesiale, Bari, 30 April–4 May 1969*, 1111–37. Padua: Edictrice Antenore, 1973.

Ruggiero, Bruno. " 'Parrochia' e 'Plebs' in alcune fonti del Mezzogiorno longobardo e normanno." *Campania Sacra* 5 (1974): 5–11. Reprinted in *Potere, istituzioni, chiese locali: Aspetti e motivi del Mezzogiorno medioevale dai Longobardi agli Angioini.*

Bologna: Centro salentino di studi medioevali Nardò, 1977, 175–81; reprint, Spoleto: Centro Studi sull'Alto Medioevo, 1991.

———. "Per una storia della pieve rurale nel Mezzogiorno medievale." *Studi medievali* 3rd. series, 16 (1975): 583–626. Reprinted in *Potere, istituzioni, chiese locali: Aspetti e motivi del Mezzogiorno medioevale dai Longobardi agli Angioini.* Bologna: Centro Salentino di Studi Medioevali Nardò, 1977, 59–87; reprint, Spoleto: Centro Studi sull'Alto Medioevo, 1991.

———. *Principi, nobiltà e chiesa nel Mezzogiorno longobardo: l'esempio di S. Massimo di Salerno.* Naples: Università di Napoli, 1973.

Russo Mailler, Carmela. *Il Medioevo a Napoli nell'età ducale (sec. VI-1140).* Salerno: Università degli Studi di Salerno, 1988.

Sansterre, Jean-Marie. "Saint Nil de Rossano et le monachisme latin." *Bollettino della Badia greca di Grottaferrata* 45 (1991): 339–86.

Santoro, Lucio. "Le difese di Salerno nel territorio." In *Guida alla storia di Salerno e della sua provincia*, edited by Alfonso Leone and Giovanni Vitolo, 2: 481–540. Salerno: P. Laveglia, 1982.

Scaduto, Mario. *Il Monachesimo basliano nella Sicilia medievale: rinascita e decadenza, sec. XI–XIV.* Rome: Edizioni di storia e letteratura, 1947; reprint, 1982.

Schipa, Michelangelo. *Storia del Principato Longobardo di Salerno.* In *La Longobardia meridionale (570–1077)*, edited by Nicola Acocella, 87–278. Rome: Edizioni di storia e letteratura, 1968.

Schmiedt, Giulio. "Le fortificazioni altomedievali in Italia viste dall'aereo." In *Ordinamenti militari in occidente nell'alto medioevo: Settimana di studi del centro italiano di studi sull'alto medioevo, 30 March–5 April 1967*, 15: 859–627. Spoleto: Centro Italiano di Studi sull'Alto Medioevo, 1968.

Skinner, Patricia. *Women in Medieval Italian Society, 500–1200.* Harlow: Pearson, 2001.

———. *Family Power in Southern Italy: The Duchy of Gaeta and Its Neighbours, 850–1139.* Cambridge: Cambridge University Press, 1995.

Southern, R. W. "Lanfranc of Bec and Berengar of Tours." In *Studies in Medieval History Presented to Frederick Maurice Powicke*, edited by R. W. Hunt, W. A. Pantin, and R. W. Southern, 27–48. Oxford: Clarendon Press, 1948.

———. *Western Society and the Church in the Middle Ages.* Harmdonsworth: Penguin Books, 1970.

Sparano, Antonella. "Agricoltura, industria e commercia in Salerno." *Annali della facoltà di lettere e filosofia, Università di Napoli* 10 (1962–63): 181–217.

Spinelli, Giovanni. "Il papato e la riorganizzazione ecclesiastica della Longobardia meridionale." In *Longobardia e longobardi nell'Italia meridionale: Le istituzioni ecclesiastiche. Atti del 2° convegno internazionale di studi promosso dal Centro di cultura dell'Università cattolica del Sacro Cuore, Benevento, 29–31 May 1992*, edited by Giancarlo Andenna and Giorgio Picasso, 19–42. Milan: Vita e Pensiero, 1996.

Starace, Francesco. "L'Ambiente ed il paessaggio dai Latini a Ruggerio d'Altavilla." In *Storia del Mezzogiorno*, edited by Giuseppe Galasso and Rosario Romeo, 1.2: 209–76. Naples: Edizione del Sole, 1986.

Stock, Brian. *The Implications of Literacy: Written Language and Models of Interpretation in the Eleventh and Twelfth Centuries.* Princeton: Princeton University Press, 1983.

Stutz, Ulrich. *Geschichte des kirchlichen Benefizialwesens.* Berlin: Müller, 1895; reprint, Aalen: Scientia, 1965.

Taviani-Carozzi, Huguette. *La Principauté lombarde de Salerne (IXe–XIe): Pouvoir et société en Italie lombarde méridionale.* Rome: Ecole Française de Rome, 1991.

——. *La Terreur du monde. Robert Guiscard et la conquête normande en Italie.* Paris: Fayard, 1996.

Tellenbach, Gerd. *The Church in Western Europe from the Tenth to the Early Twelfth Century.* Translated by Timothy Reuter. Cambridge: Cambridge University Press, 1993.

Thomas, John Philip. *Private Religious Foundations in the Byzantine Empire.* Washington, D. C.: Dumbarton Oaks, 1987.

Toubert, Pierre. *Les Structures du Latium médiéval: Le Latium méridional et la Sabine du IXe siècle à la fin du XIIe siècle.* Rome: Ecole française de Rome, 1973.

——. "La vie commune des clercs aux XI–XIIe siècles: un questionnaire." *Revue Historique* 231 (1964): 11–26.

Tramontana, Salvatore. *Mezzogiorno normanno e svevo.* Messina: Peloritana Editore, 1972.

——. "La monarchia normanna e sveva." In *Storia d'Italia: Il Mezzogiorno dai Bizantini a Federico II,* edited by André Guillou, 3:437–810. Turin: UTET, 1983.

Travaini, Lucia. *La Monetazione nell'Italia Normanna.* Rome: Istituto storico italiano per il Medio Evo, 1995.

Ullmann, Walter. *The Growth of Papal Government in the Middle Ages.* 2nd ed. London: Methuen, 1962.

——. *A Short History of the Papacy in the Middle Ages,* 2nd ed. London/New York: Routledge, 2003.

Vaccari, Alberto. *La Grecía nell'Italia meridionale: Studi letterari e bibliografici.* Orientalia Christiana, vol. 13. Rome: Pontificio istituto orientale, 1925.

Ventimiglia, Domenico. *Notizie storiche del Castello dell'Abbate e de' suoi casali nella Lucania.* Naples: Reale, 1827.

Vitolo, Giovanni. "Da Apudmontem a Roccapiemonte. Il castrum come elemento di organizzazione territoriale." *Rassegna Storica Salernitana,* n.s. 6 (December 1986): 129–42.

——. "L'Archivio della Badia della SS. Trinità di Cava." In *Guida alla storia di Salerno e della sua provincia,* edited by Alfonso Leone and Giovanni Vitolo, 894–99. Salerno: P. Laveglia, 1982.

——. "La Badia di Cava e gli Arcivescovi di Salerno tra XI e XII secolo." *Rassegna Storica Salernitana,* n.s. 8 (December 1987): 9–16.

——. *Caratteri del monachesimo nel Mezzogiorno altomedievale (secc. VI–IX).* Salerno: P. Laveglia, 1984.

——. "Il castagno nell'economia della Campania medievale." *Rassegna Storica Salernitana,* n.s. 11 (June 1989): 21–34.

——. "Cava e Cluny." In *L'Italia nel quadro dell'espansione europea del monachesimo clu-*

niacense: Atti del Convegno internazionale di storia medievale, Pescia, 26–28 November, 1981, edited by Cinzio Violante et al., 199–220. Cesena: Centro storico benedettino italiano, 1985.

——. "La conquista normanna nel contesto economico del Mezzogiorno." *Rassegna Storica Salernitana*, n.s. 9 (June 1988): 7–22.

——. *Insediamenti cavensi in Puglia*. Lecce: Congedo, 1984.

——. "Istituzioni ecclesiastiche e pietà dei laici nella Campania medievale: la confraternità di S. Maria di Montefusco (secc. X–XV)." *Campania Sacra* 8/9 (1977/78).

——. "La Latinizzazione dei monasteri Italo-Greci del Mezzogiorno medievale. L'Esempio di S. Nicola di Gallocanta presso Salerno." *Benedictina* 19 (1982): 437–60. Reprinted in *Studi in margine al IX volume del Codex Diplomaticus Cavensis*, 75–90. Salerno: P. Laveglia, 1983.

——. "Organizzazione dello spazio e vicende del popolamento." In *Storia del Vallo di Diano*, edited by Nicola Cilento, 43–77. Salerno: P. Laveglia, 1982.

——. "Produzione e commercio del vino nel Mezzogiorno medievale." *Rassegna Storica Salernitana*, n.s. 10 (December 1988): 65–76.

——. "Vescovi e Diocesi." In *Storia del Mezzogiorno*, edited by Giuseppe Galasso, 3:73–151. Naples: Edizione del Sole, 1990.

Vuolo, Antonio. "Agriografia beneventana." In *Longobardia e longobardi nell'Italia meridionale: Le istituzioni ecclesiastiche. Atti del 2° Convegno internazionale di studi promosso dal Centro di Cultura dell'Università del Sacro Cuore, Benevento, 29–31 May 1992*, edited by Giancarlo Andenna and Giorgio Picasso, 199–237. Milan: Vita e Pensiero, 1996.

Wallace-Hadrill, J. M. *The Frankish Church*. Oxford: Clarendon Press, 1983.

White, Stephen D. *Custom, Kinship, and Gifts to Saints: The Laudatio Parentum in Western France, 1050–1150*. Chapel Hill: University of North Carolina Press, 1988.

Whittow, Mark. *The Making of Byzantium, 600–1025*. Berkeley and Los Angeles: University of California Press, 1996.

Wickham, Chris. *Early Medieval Italy: Central Power and Local Society, 400–1000*. Ann Arbor: University of Michigan Press, 1981.

——. "European Forests in the Early Middle Ages: Landscape and Land Clearance." In *L'ambiente vegetale nell'alto medioevo: Settimana di studio del centro italiano di studi sull'alto medioevo, 30 March–5 April 1989*, 37.2: 479–548. Spoleto: Centro Italiano di Studi sull'Alto Medioevo, 1990.

——. *The Mountains and the City: The Tuscan Appenines in the Early Middle Ages*. Oxford: Clarendon Press, 1988.

Index

VOLUMES IN THE SERIES

**CONJUNCTIONS OF RELIGION AND POWER
IN THE MEDIEVAL PAST**

Edited by Barbara H. Rosenwein